Eight great champions g
back with a comment ab

Players often indulge in a bit of ban̶t̶e̶r̶ ̶w̶i̶t̶h̶ ̶e̶a̶c̶h̶ ̶o̶t̶h̶e̶r̶ ̶ in locker rooms, player lounges or airports around the world. It's give and take and so I accept it when it comes my way! Some of the following I had the privilege of sharing a court with. The younger ones I could only admire from outside the lines. I thank them all for their 'kind' contributions and for entering into the spirit of this book!

'His serve wasn't as great as his love of heavy metal music.'
   – Pat Cash

*'I'm glad I never had to watch **him** play.'*
   – Novak Djokovic

'I think he's that guy I see at the coin toss at my Wimbledon finals.'
   – Roger Federer

'If he'd worked as hard as me when he played I still wouldn't have lost to him!'
   – Ivan Lendl

'If he'd only had a bit more of my talent he might have made an average player.'
   – John McEnroe

'He's one of those I see around the tour from time to time but I'm not entirely sure what he actually does.'
   – Andy Murray

'His Spanish is terrible.'
   – Rafa Nadal

But perhaps the final quote has to go to my old friend:

'I've heard all these stories and more from him over the years. It's a pity he didn't include the better stuff as well!'
   – Dennis Archer

The Wimbledon Foundation

A portion of any profit will be donated to the Wimbledon Foundation to support its work. Established in 2013, the Wimbledon Foundation is the charity of The All England Lawn Tennis Club and The Championships and uses the collective strength of Wimbledon to make a positive difference to people's lives.

Each year, the Foundation works with more than 100 charities to champion opportunity for all. In the London boroughs of Merton and Wandsworth, projects funded by the Foundation provide vital support to people facing a wide range of challenges, including homelessness, mental health and employability. Nationally, its youth leadership programme, Set for Success, uses the power of sport combined with mentoring by world class athletes to improve the wellbeing and future opportunities of young people across the UK. Internationally, its partnership with WaterAid supports their mission to ensure everyone has access to clean water, decent toilets and good hygiene.

CHAMPIONSHIP POINTS

ANDREW JARRETT

ISBN 978-1-7392799-0-5 (paperback)
ISBN 978-1-7392799-1-2 (ebook)

Copy editing: petegentryeditorial.com
Cover design: Theo Ambrose Press
Cover photo: Sally Grace Photography
Typesetting: preparetopublish.com

The Order of Play

Foreword
Tim Henman

Millions of people around the world love tennis, and that includes the many within the sport who make it all happen. Though it's players on court who usually make the headlines, they can't have their stage without the backroom support staff working behind the scenes. Coaches, officials, trainers, agents, ground staff, plus many others including office personnel, catering, security, IT, construction and transportation staff, are all vital to the operation of this incredible world. It's mostly unseen by those on the outside.

As a player, coach and official in international tennis for more than 40 years, Andrew saw the sport from many different perspectives. Few others can claim such variety, and each was to Grand Slam level. As The Championships Referee at Wimbledon for 14 years, he ran the tennis side of the event, and it was the culmination of his own long journey through the sport. We worked closely together there and shared the same passion and determination to achieve the highest possible standards for the finest tennis event in the world.

Andrew's book is filled with amusing insights into his life on the tennis tour which was demanding, frustrating and filled with characters and countless opportunities to laugh, cry, go crazy and yet still make dreams come true. His observations, his honesty, his knowledge of the sport and his love of the bizarre are all recounted with his self-deprecating humour, as he narrates tales from his playing, coaching and officiating days.

It's very much Andrew's own take on the tennis world and it makes for a very enjoyable, fascinating and entertaining read.

7

Introduction

Hi, I'm Andrew. I'm a bloke that's been rattling around the world of tennis for a long time. My friends say I've never had a proper job and that's probably true but life takes some odd directions and in my case it was strange enough for me to become The Championships Referee at the greatest event in the world, Wimbledon. Now that wasn't in the original plan at all!

As a ten-year-old boy, in my garden at home in Derby, I had the worthy ambitions of winning the FA Cup for Derby County, playing at Wembley for England, scoring a hundred as a Test batsman for England against the Australians at Lord's, kicking the winning points for England against France at Twickenham and sinking a ten-foot putt to win The Open Championship at St Andrews. Oh yes, I also wanted to win Wimbledon as well. I was in a hurry to get on with it. And if all went to plan all of this might be achieved before my tea was ready!

Now that's quite a wish list and there are still plenty of these left to achieve. But over the years since leaving school in 1975, back deep in a previous century, I've been a tennis player, a captain, a coach, a private tennis club manager, a journalist, a PR man, a TV commentator and, more recently, a referee. Perhaps in that great decline the next step is to die, so before that happens I'll write this in case I forget it all! My mum had dementia before she died so I know that's not nice and my mates say it would be a shame for the tales that follow not to get at least one airing before the inevitable.

My journey in tennis has been spread over six decades and in that time attitudes to life have changed. It's also true of me and those around me. The young boy I used to be back in the 1960s saw the world very differently to the old bloke in his 60s that I've become. The life experiences of the past decades were from a different era. Now in the early 2020s the pace of change is as great as ever. A Covid-19 pandemic, world economy upheavals, social justice campaigns and the threat of war are causing a reset in how everyone views the world. But this look-back over past years details a sporting life lived through different and less turbulent times. Meanwhile, tennis has to cope with the new realities of life. Whether it's the Grand Slams, the Tour events or the fledgling professional events in the foothills of the international circuit they have no choice but to evolve and adapt. But as pro tennis is forced to change I hope it retains the laughter and fun along the way.

As the Referee at Wimbledon for 14 years I headed up the officiating for The Championships and it was certainly the highlight of that particular part of my career in tennis. But at all events I worked in Britain or overseas there were decisions to be made. There were others to take care of the off-court details but the referee is at the heart of everything connected to the matches and the play. Having been both a player and a coach previously I understood how many of them felt about officialdom. Out of touch with reality, disconnected from anything like hard work and best of all a member of the 'boring old farts' club, so naturally they should be treated with more than a bit of suspicion, right? The best response was to play up to it – so bring it on!

I love sport and all of those who 'get it'. Those who dedicate hours, days, months, years, lifetimes to playing, watching and supporting sport in all its marvellous forms. Many might see sport as being a frivolous distraction from all the ills of the world and they may be right; it's very good fun, though! I try not to take myself too seriously and have a healthy disregard for those who do. Far better to promise little and deliver a lot than to tell me how good you are and then turn out to be full of sh★t. There's enough of those people around. Oh I say, did I just nearly swear?! I guess the 'man in grey suit' image doesn't really fit me. It's tough enough for me to wear long trousers let alone a suit and tie. When I had to do it to play my role then I did. The rest of the time I'm someone else. I'm me, I'm Andrew.

Of the many different roles I've had in tennis, which is the best? Without doubt it's being a player. The moments before the walk on and then the nervous entrance to any court, let alone a big one, are ones to be savoured. The matches themselves are a physical and mental trial where you find out a lot about yourself. Self-belief and trust in yourself and your own abilities are prerequisites. Not every day will go your way, but you have to believe that tomorrow will be better than today and then strain every sinew to make sure it is. You control your own destiny. You win or lose based on your own efforts and ability and you can't blame anyone else.

I've been lucky to have different careers through the wonderful and very varied world of tennis. When I sat in the Referees' Office at Wimbledon and looked back over the many parts of that tennis life it seemed incredible. There's no doubt that you need to be able to take advantage of opportunities that come your way. It's true in life generally. You don't choose where you're born but you do make decisions regarding your education, your business and even your love life. You may not get too many chances so take them when you can in case you don't get a second opportunity.

The chance to go to London and train to be a professional tennis player was a major one. It was fortunate that my age group was at the start of a new initiative that meant the Lawn Tennis Association (LTA) would part-fund some of the considerable cost. My years as a full-time player were never less than eventful with plenty of ups and downs along the way – all good training for life. Then came the decision to move into coaching followed later by the opportunity to work with Britain's best players at the time. Still comparatively young in my late 20s it meant I had a head start in this career since I'd had the experience of playing on some big stages and could use this to help others as they did the same. The times changed, though, with the birth of my daughter and my desire to be more home-based. A few years in the quiet backwater of a private club environment at Hurlingham in London followed. It was another learning experience where my past tennis history was useful but could only help me a little as I took on the challenges of management and of working with club members and their committees.

I couldn't have foreseen my next move within the sport, into officiating. It certainly wasn't planned out in advance. Like most players I'd never given chair umpires, line umpires or referees much thought as long as they didn't make decisions that adversely affected me. So the telephone call from Wimbledon that brought me into this part of the tennis world really did come out of the blue. I considered it all very carefully knowing that this was a world where there was to be little credit, a fair bit of potential downside and not much financial reward. But the draw of The Championships and of Wimbledon was too great. I decided to go for it. Many years later when I was appointed Championships Referee the time and effort put into achieving the goal were rewarded. So much could have derailed the project. The many smaller events all contain every opportunity to screw up big time. The officiating world can be cruel and mistakes are quickly passed around with relish and used against the perpetrators if it suits those in charge. But somehow I managed to survive and eventually thrive.

Dealing with all the leading players, coaches, agents and entourages from around the world was a terrific challenge and one that was both daunting and exciting in equal measure. My years as the Wimbledon Referee saw much change in the sport, some for better and some for worse. The challenges brought about by the expectation of the professional sporting world, and particularly the advent of social media, are tough. The high-profile nature of The

Championships means that every decision is closely analysed by all. Being a small part of it was the most wonderful privilege and so for 20 years I completely devoted myself to all aspects of Wimbledon.

The years of playing make you very self-reliant. You have no choice. The skill sets required for coaching and officiating are quite different. As a coach you're judged on the success or failure of others and you often sit courtside with a real sense of helplessness. As an official you can only show your worth when things are going wrong. You never wish that on yourself or the event you're working. If you prepare properly then you minimise that risk and, from the outside, it can seem straightforward. Others will also think that and so when it comes to the critical promotions or selections too much is still done on hearsay and whether your face fits or not. Most of the time my face fitted in the world of officiating, though others aren't necessarily always so lucky.

Whether playing, coaching or officiating I've tried to separate my personal and professional life. I'll work very hard when it's the time to do so but tennis has to stay in its box as far as I'm concerned. It's not my total world much as others like to pigeonhole you. Playtime has to be enjoyed as well. Too much work makes Andrew a very dull boy!

The sport has changed dramatically over the years I've been involved and standards are far higher. Players are fitter, faster, stronger and hit harder with better-quality rackets and equipment. Modern training methods are more scientific and produce a better quality of athlete. Stars have a presence and a confidence that comes from winning so many matches and there's no doubt that yesteryear's top players would have been contenders today armed with the same opportunities that the current players have. They would have adapted. Nonetheless, the tennis played now is the best ever and I've been lucky to be involved at Wimbledon during a golden period for the sport when Federer, Nadal, Djokovic and Murray have been at the summit. When I played a British winner at Wimbledon seemed light years away. But it finally happened when Murray broke the

77-year drought since Fred Perry's win back in 1936 and it was marvellous to be in the stadium that day. It was a great moment in sport and one that those who were there will always remember.

Fulfilling the ceremonial part of the Referee's role on finals day at Wimbledon was marvellous. Walking on to the Centre Court for the coin toss prior to each final was very special and I appreciated it all the more for knowing that I never got close to doing that as a player in the main singles event there. The occasional second-round match on the outside courts was to be my personal summit. Being a small part of the Wimbledon final was thrilling but, for me, it all started back in 1965 as a seven-year-old walking on to the shale courts at Crewe Street in Derby for my first-ever tournament. Believe me when I say that was far more nerve-racking! And then ten years later came the first tentative steps at the start of over 40 years' involvement in professional tennis.

Part One
The Playing Years

Chapter 1

The B Squad – It's Now a Job

I knew I could play but could I do it for a living? I'd grown up with tennis and junior tournaments were a regular part of my calendar. I'd done consistently well in these and was one of the best junior players in Britain. But I'd also played overseas enough to realise that there were many around the world who were as good if not better, and that was just my age group. If I'd known then what I know now I'd have been petrified at the prospect of committing myself to such an insecure way of life. But at that time all I knew was that the LTA was setting up a full-time training squad at Queen's Club in London and I was invited to be a part of it. Without any real thought process or consideration for the future I joined. There was no real decision-making or discussion as to other options. I never considered the university route that my brothers had taken. I was leaving school, it was 1975 and I was just going to play tennis.

And so a small group of young, hopeful tennis players, all of us well known to each other, took up residence at the Wimbledon YMCA for two winters and commuted to Queen's Club to practise and train daily Monday to Friday. Occasionally, we'd go off and play events both in Britain and also overseas as we cut our teeth in the world of professional tennis. We were called the B Squad and above us in the pecking order were the A Squad. Not only were they older but they contained several already well-known players such as John Lloyd, Jonathan Smith, Mark Farrell, Robin Drysdale and John Feaver. They were who we aspired to become and they sat at a separate table to us in the lunchroom at Queen's. Sometimes we'd get to hit with them and it always seemed to be a major test and one to really be up for.

So what of my fellow B Squad members? For a start there were two others that had come from my own Millfield School, a testimony to just how strong it was then, Chris Kaskow and Nigel Sears. Chris was an early doubles partner of mine; we'd won the British Junior Championships doubles together at Wimbledon on the shale courts and he was a good player who played a fair game of cards as well to supplement the meagre earnings on offer. If we'd have needed a rogue trader in our pack Chris would've been our nomination as he was always on the lookout for a deal. Nigel was destined to become a top coach working with many leading female players. He always looked the part of the bronzed Adonis pro tennis player and his strong work ethic and good humour were good qualities for his future role. Chris Bradnam was a wonderful player with a natural feel on the doubles court. We teamed up, played well and I felt we were on the fringe of making the Davis Cup team together when he suddenly gave up full-time tennis. He would make me laugh and our matches were rarely filled with the tension you usually associate with competition. We travelled a lot together as we frequently played doubles and were expectant of doing well, often overshadowing our less impressive singles matches. That left Neil Rayner, a wiry, talented player from Essex, Martin Smith, a tall left-hander from Norfolk who became a leading coach, and Bill Gowans, who was very different from the rest of us. He was more cerebral, very laid-back and disparaging about his own abilities. What a lovely man. He eventually became a GP (doctor) and did real work to his credit, using his considerable brain for higher purposes.

Each morning for the B Squad would start at 6.50am when Paul Hutchins, the Director of Men's Tennis at the LTA, arrived in his blue Triumph Stag to take us from Wimbledon town up to the Common. It was typical of the man to show such dedication to the cause; now there would be an army of underling LTA coaches to take on such a thankless task. As we climbed out of the car local dog walkers would have thought it very strange to see so many bodies climbing out and lining up ready for our timed mile run around the Common. Decades later, while working as Referee for The Championships, I stayed at a house where I overlooked this scene and remembered how I would race into an early lead, hold the advantage for a few brief yards and then see all my colleagues overtake in turn. A few hundred yards before the finish Chris Bradnam would go into overdrive and surge past Nigel Sears to win comfortably and prove that he could have been a decent middle-distance runner. At a similar point Bill Gowans would overtake me to leave me last in the group, giving me a daily reminder that athletics really wasn't my sport. After a few minutes to regain our breath we went through a series of exercises including press-ups. Leaving handprints in the frost of winter reminded us that if it hurt it must have been doing us good. Amazing what you can believe, isn't it?

The tennis training took place at Queen's Club in West Kensington under the guidance of Roger Becker, the former Davis Cup player and then Davis Cup coach. He was a wonderful, positive character who oversaw not only our group but also the older lads as well. Though he had a wide-ranging brief his infectious grin plus bulldog spirit meant he always gave off a winning attitude. He loved a story, enjoyed a laugh and was good company. One day he offered the B Squad players the chance to work on his garden. He had a job to be done, we were willing labour in need of a fiver and so we spent an afternoon at his lovely home. He was a fixer with great contacts and he loved a deal.

The setting up of the squad was well intentioned. It was a real attempt to address the concerns at the time that our young players didn't work hard enough and weren't professional enough in attitude to make it as Tour players. The regime put hard work and physical fitness above the ability to play the sport. Consequently, our bodies were tired and aching most of the time when it came to improving the necessary skills needed to perform at the highest level. This is no criticism of the regime itself or of the people involved. It was a fine and laudable attempt to change the existing status quo and was state-of-the-art thinking back then. What we see now, though, bears no relation to what we were doing, which was more likely an invitation to long-term injury.

Being a disciple of Brian Clough, the legendary Derby County manager who employed unusual methods when getting the best out of his teams, I wonder what his tennis equivalent might have made of me. Undoubtedly, I had some talent, could work on occasion, was definitely a bit independent and rebellious, but had other interests that deflected me from a single-minded approach to becoming a better player. Would Cloughie have used the carrot or the stick with me? I'd have loved his unconventionality and the humour he could bring but would he have been too tough for me? One thing he used to do that I admired was concentrate on the positives. He emphasised what a player could do and didn't unduly worry about what he couldn't. I was surrounded at the time by the mantra of hard work, repetition, hours on court, etc. to the point of boredom. I think I needed more of a take it on, hit through the court and show everyone what you can do type of approach. There is something gloriously simple about 'Defend when you have to; attack when you can. Otherwise, don't miss'. The nearest thing to Cloughie in the British tennis coaching world at the time was Alan Jones, a Londoner who had a sense of humour and could talk endlessly, and a man who just might have made me a better player. I never really worked with him properly and in some ways I wish I had. If we hadn't driven each other mad it just might have worked.

Some years later I played a guy called Gabriel Urpi in Spain on a clay court. I was OK on the slow stuff and was prepared to rally and chase. But that day I got a lesson. It was that I was technically unable to compete against the new types of weapons, specifically the semi-western forehand hit with high, heavy topspin from all over the court, running me into the ground. No matter what I tried I couldn't keep it away from the dictating forehand and I lost in two long, but ultimately unsuccessful, sets. When I started out my two-handed backhand was a relatively unseen-before weapon and it had served me well but here I was some years later on the receiving end and I was now a technical dinosaur that had no answer on this particular surface. The B Squad taught me to try hard, to run all day but not how to combat and develop my own way of playing that would have been competitive against this continental onslaught.

Twice a week the squad would go to the west London track in the shadow of the prison at Wormwood Scrubs where we were trained as athletes by Ken Woolcott. Ken had been employed by the LTA as the first of the formal physical trainers. He was a delightful character who had expertise in athletics, though little in tennis. The methods he used were familiar to 400-metre runners but were alien to us. We tried, very hard, and I'm sure that we did improve. But it must have seemed an impossible task for Ken who did at least have the long-legged Tina, his high jump protégée, alongside to brighten our mornings and provide a welcome distraction. One morning I even threw up at that track, completely exhausted at the end of one particular session. Once the training had finished, we'd make our way to Queen's and start a day on the courts, perhaps not the best way to ensure quality tennis skills training. But it was early days, we were LTA guinea pigs in the pioneer LTA National Training programme and we had events to look forward to.

Socially, we were accidents waiting to happen. Six boys staying together at a YMCA and with London on their doorstep are not going to be angels. Even though we were tired at the end of each day we had the tube network and also Betty the Bus. Betty was a present from one of the great characters of Queen's Club, a wonderful man, originally from Poland, named Stefan, who was to become a personal friend over many years. He donated the minibus to the LTA for our use and now we had real freedom. Officially, it was to transport us to and from the YMCA from Queen's but in reality it meant Nigel and I could go anywhere we wanted to go since we were the only ones with driving licences. We had a technical friend fit Betty with a loudspeaker close to the radiator under the bonnet and this was connected to a microphone in the main cab. Now we could broadcast to the world, which meant we could offer opinion on everything: the lady crossing the road in front of us a bit too slowly, the dodgy haircut of the youth walking on the pavement, the couple holding hands at a bus stop or, most likely, the contents of the tight T-shirt of any attractive girl that had the misfortune to catch our roving eyes. How we didn't get stopped by the police or reported shows how tolerant people can be. It was mischievous and good-natured, though, and it meant that every journey was anticipated with great relish as a highlight of the day. Betty met a sad end on the streets of Fulham one day when I wasn't present. Nigel was at the wheel when something got in the way, there was a collision and Betty was no more. Chris Bradnam was left a bit dazed but otherwise no one was hurt. But it was the end of our frivolities and it was a great day for the people of west London now that the menace of Betty was off the roads.

Our group had three rooms up on the seventh floor of the YMCA. I shared with Chris Kaskow and we overlooked the main street down below. One evening a water fight broke out, which was inevitable at some point, and things got out of hand. At one point a metal wastepaper bin was filled with water and brought into the room. After the trivial paper cups of before this was seen as the nuclear weapon of water fights, the container to end all future argument. It was brandished around waiting for its victim when somebody spotted the girl down below on the street dressed up to the nines on her way out for the evening. It was wrong, and we shouldn't have done it, but the communal intelligence of six lads with only one shared brain cell, at the moment when a bin filled with water and an irresistible target appears, means only one thing will happen. And it did with spectacular results. A direct hit, a sudden drenching from the sky, completely unprovoked and undeserved followed by the awful realisation of 'what have we just done?' We could hear commotion downstairs at reception as the girl rightly lodged her fury but we were hidden away quietly upstairs and amazingly managed to get away with it. Another time we weren't so lucky.

We'd decided to celebrate the end of 1976 with a party on our floor. Chris Bradnam and I were going off to Florida for some junior tournaments together with Jo Durie and Anne Hobbs the following day, so this was the excuse since the girls were staying at the Y as well. A few extras connected with our tennis world also arrived and, with alcohol thrown into the mix, things got a little out of hand. We were warned about noise a couple of times, the game of strip poker wobbled precariously between those who would and those who wouldn't and finally the usual sleeping arrangements had to be changed to accommodate the extras, charged with all the associated tension of youthful mixed-sex insecurities! Such were the problems of a social life with your friends as they were also the same people you would be competing against regularly and who consequently you didn't want to show weakness to. It's an odd situation that each must come to terms with on the foothills of professional sport. The repercussions for the shindig came soon afterwards. The party was reported to the LTA together with the fact that somebody had thrown up all over a carpet and it hadn't been cleaned up. It wasn't good. All who were still in London were called into Paul Hutchins' office at the LTA and the price had to be paid. Chris, Jo and Anne were with me in Florida by this time, so the first we knew about it was a letter advising us that it had been decided not to recall us from the events there but that we were to be suspended for four weeks from the YMCA on our return home. It was a fair cop!

Chapter 2

The Transition from Junior to Senior Tennis

The school holidays were dominated by various events, first locally and then, as I progressed, at national level. The Derbyshire Junior Championships, held at Crewe Street in Derby, had been my introduction to competitive tournament tennis and also to a lifelong friendship with Big Dennis Archer. Together we moved further afield to the foreign lands of Nottingham where we played many events, sometimes in awful weather, while forging friendships and rivalries along the way. As I was several years younger than many of these other players it made for some odd sights as I was by far the smallest. Dennis was very patient to put up with his young friend even if we were starting to win quite a lot of the time.

One of our fellow competitors was Mike Elvin who, like Dennis, became a lifelong friend and godfather to my daughter Jazz. He also towered over me and still does. It was these friendships that underpinned my love of the sport. Winning and losing were, and remain, important but are as nothing compared with relationships like these that go back for decades.

Those of us playing and winning regularly started to become involved with national events, first at Exmouth then Eastbourne and the British Junior Championships for Under 18s at the All England Club, Wimbledon. These seemed very important at the time as there were official people like LTA councillors and national coach Tony Mottram around. I also got to see players like John Lloyd, Buster Mottram, Michael Wayman, Richard Lewis and Fred Whittaker for the first time. It was a step up in terms of level but I was encouraged not intimidated.

Fiery Fred Whittaker was one of the first of the 'bad boys' by reputation and his matches always attracted attention. The LTA councillors would lurk to see if he'd 'go off on one' giving them something to talk about over their gin and tonics. In those days the umpire was another competitor as all of us were expected to umpire another match each day for which we'd get a tea ticket. Looking back now there was plenty wrong with the system but it was a different era and was entirely normal at that time.

I attracted some attention as well but mainly because of my size and age. I was way younger than others in the draw by several years so I looked pretty ridiculous against most of my opponents. I was accepted into Junior Wimbledon at the age of 11 meaning I was competing against 17- and 18-year-olds in my first year there in 1969. A big treat about being accepted then was getting to go to the Fred Perry office, a small place tucked away in Vigo Street just behind Piccadilly Circus. There you'd get, free of charge (!), two shirts and a pair of shorts. What a treat that was and I sometimes think of it when I see today's stars opening up another carton of new gear with little real appreciation. My own experience still had humiliation, though, as Fred Perry didn't make shorts small enough to fit me! I had to wait until my second year before I'd grown a bum big enough to fit into their smallest size!

The national junior events came and went each year and I got steadily older. Sometimes I won and sometimes I didn't but I stayed in the forefront of each age group and so was usually considered for any junior internationals that were staged at the different levels. There weren't many of those then so each one seemed like a major treat, particularly if it involved going away to another country. I always loved the travel side of playing and seeing new places was exciting. I knew it was important because I was now playing for my country but there was also the feeling that if we were overseas we must be on holiday.

Strangely perhaps, the actual tennis in most of these events has faded into the background and few events and situations come readily to mind. One time I was sitting on the tarmac at Heathrow in a British Airways plane waiting to take off for Oslo for a junior international in 1976 with Chris Bradnam, Jo Durie and Anne Hobbs. Anne later became a Tour player and British number one but this was her first-ever trip abroad and she had little flying experience. As we waited she announced that she was a bit hot so I suggested she call the flight attendant to open her window and showed her the button to call for attention. On went the button and we tried hard not to giggle as we waited for the conversation to take place. The stewardess was very kind and explained why windows on a jet didn't open. Anne got a bit embarrassed and we enjoyed reminding her of it for years later.

Chris, Jo, Anne and I were the leading British juniors and often found ourselves playing the same events and in each other's company. We were now competing at international level against the world's best juniors. We became familiar with the likes of Peter Elter (Germany), Heinz Guenthardt (Switzerland), Lorenzo Fargas (Spain), Yannick Noah (France), Gianni Occleppo (Italy), José Luis Clerc (Argentina) and a young American, John McEnroe, amongst many others. It's interesting to see now that this group of players did produce some who went on to great things but also others who fell by the wayside, despite all being excellent players.

It's a long journey to become a player. It's a marathon and not a sprint. Those who look potential world beaters sometimes just don't make it while others, usually those with more stickability, steadily progress and one day find themselves in the upper reaches and regular Tour players. It's easy to think that each day, each match, each opportunity, is the most important and to invest so much emotional effort into it that anything less than triumph is a terrible calamity. It's not. Just take a longer-term view and keep going. Those who have a body and a mind capable of withstanding the stresses and strains of prolonged months and years of taking knocks and bouncing back will one day seize the opportunity to climb to a new level. It's a little inspiration and a lot of perspiration.

For my part I only coped with this moderately well. I was caught up with the immediate need to win but a different approach is needed when you become professional to that of casual sporting endeavour. I was perhaps never fully able to absorb this way of thinking. As for coping with the demands and expectations I had of myself as well as those of others I found release away from the courts. Sometimes I would just go away and do something else! It was my escape. I would say 'it doesn't matter', and believe it, much to the frustration of those, like Paul Hutchins, who had to deal with me. This approach did allow me to keep playing but not in the hard-nosed professional way that might have been more successful. It would have sacrificed some of what was, and remains, me.

One example of this came when Rohun Bevan and I were playing together in an obscure competition called the Pernod Trophy in October 1977. This involved three individual events linked by a points system to a team event in which he and I were the British team. By the final week Rohun and I had just secured the team victory by both qualifying for the singles final against each other, so nothing would change that. We were only playing for pride in the final. Sadly, the final was in Washington, Tyne and Wear at 1pm on a Saturday lunchtime and Derby County were away at Newcastle, kicking off at 3pm just down the road. Quick calculations meant that a two-set final would be OK but three sets would not. With my mind on the clock I lost in a speedy one hour and made it in time for the kick-off. Was this professional? Of course not. On the credit side, though, I was there for a wonderful 2-1 win at Newcastle with one of my great heroes, Roy McFarland, on the scoresheet. It was an afternoon I've fondly remembered ever since.

The summer season of British open events brought together some marvellous characters. It was a different era to today and one that's remembered with fondness by those who were part of it. Here you would find some seasoned pros from overseas who were honing their games ready for Wimbledon; the best of the British players with the exception of those good enough to be playing a level higher at the German, Italian and possibly French Open qualifying; the leading British juniors (including me) who were starting to make inroads into senior tennis; and then some assorted odd bods who just wanted to play tennis and somehow found the means to get from one event to the next.

Cumberland, Sutton, Lee-on-Solent, Guildford, Chichester, Worthing, Sunderland, Norwich, Torquay, Manchester, Ilkley, Sheffield, Bristol, Frinton, Felixstowe, Newcastle, Glasgow, Edinburgh and others all featured on the calendar providing top tennis together with some marvellous social shenanigans. Each of these was independent. Later they became linked as part of satellite, futures or challenger circuits in a world ruled by computer ranking points. I played when this process was starting but the events still contained much that was gloriously idiosyncratic of the age. There were plenty of wins, plenty of losses, much counting of the pennies to get to the next event and plenty of wonderful tales, some of which were even true!

Chichester featured my favourite match of all time, not between Roger Federer and Rafael Nadal as many might think, but between Dale Collings and Victor Eke, both of Australia. These guys were part of a strong group of Aussies who would bring great colour, character and no little ability to the British shores each year. Dale was known as 'Animal' because he just was. He was a huge, intimidating presence on the court with a massive temper and a liking for hurling his racket, together with short flashes of minimalist vulgarity that meant his matches were always pure box office. At the other end was Victor Eke who wore spectacles, had the physique of an IT specialist, reminded you of the local librarian but also possessed the mouth of a merchant navy seaman that completely belied his otherwise mild impression. The match was assigned to a distant outside court of Chichester tennis club. An unsuspecting old British official was given the job of umpiring and the rest of us rubbed our hands in glee and went to watch the fun. It didn't disappoint. I recall the umpire hopelessly asking both players to mind their language and their behaviour in the days before the code of conduct. No chance! Friendly as they were off court both players fought the whole way, disturbing other matches near and far with regular bursts of outrage. The highlight or lowlight finally came when even the Animal was reduced to open-mouthed admiration as a racket launched by the mild-looking Eke from the far end flew high over his head, over the back fence and came to rest in a neighbouring garden. It was an awesome throw, probably some 50 metres, and it was fully appreciated by all of us watching. Who won? Who cares! It had truly lived up to the expectation of it being 'match of the day'!

The Aussies brought their work hard, play hard ethic to the courts and were great value. Others included Keith Hancock (first bloke I saw wearing pastel-coloured clothing, at Cumberland), Greg 'Blue' Braun, Warren Maher, Chris Kachel, John Marks, Noel 'Fatty' Phillips, Bob 'Nails' Carmichael, Alvin Gardiner, John Trickey, David Carter, Noel Jensen, Ernie Ewert, Wayne Hampson, Cliff Letcher and Paul Kronk. Better-known ones were Peter MacNamara, Paul McNamee, John Fitzgerald, Ross Case, Geoff Masters, Wally Masur, Rod Frawley, Mark Edmondson, Kim Warwick, Brad Drewett and Pat Cash. What a group they made and some of them could really play.

But still it was the off-court events that dominated much of the discussion and fun around those tournaments. One of the best was Newlands in Glasgow, which hosted the West of Scotland Championships each year. It became my favourite tournament and only partly because I seemed to do OK there most years. It went under the sponsorship of various companies but was perhaps most famously sponsored by the Red Hackle whisky company. This meant a trip to the distillery at some point in the week and in 1976 this visit directly led to another of the famous matches I remember. This one featured two travelling Aussies (of course) up against two locals in a doubles match staged in the evening to allow the locals to finish their regular day's work and then to come to the courts ready to play. The Aussies were vastly superior players but were under the substantial handicap of being a bit worse for wear having enjoyed the distillery trip earlier. A good crowd was there to watch as the match went deep into a final set in the gloaming of a surprisingly warm and pleasant Glasgow evening. Once again those in the know were there to enjoy the occasion and offer some vocal encouragement as the local lads smelled the chance of a major upset and a good write-up in the *Glasgow Herald* the next day. In the end the Aussies came through but only after the Scots had snatched defeat from the jaws of victory and produced another of the glorious Scottish sporting failures that are so loved by the English!

The Scots were marvellous hosts and had a great social programme running alongside the tennis. Two squash courts were transformed into additional bars for the week, one for the more sedate and the other for the singing, rowdy crowd. After a year of settling in you were expected to take your turn helping out behind the bar and so I joined John Watson, my housing host, as a barman. John, together with his marvellous wife Moira and their two sons Trevor and Gordon, provided another home from home for me within walking distance of the club. John quickly initiated me by serving an overseas visitor who'd asked for some fancy cocktail, only to be told by John, 'Here you can only have heavy (the local brew) or whisky, or you can have heavy and whisky!'

Meanwhile, Mark Farrell, of legendary status in Glasgow for his drinking and his singing as well as for some excellent tennis, was up on the bar leading the community singing in 'Flower of Scotland', which boomed out several times a night together with other favourites. By the end of every evening everyone was well pissed and so when someone announced that there was going to be a wedding in the next bar in five minutes' time and we were all invited it seemed very normal. It turned out to be another two of the travelling Aussies who were shacked up together in a combi van playing the tournaments. They'd been chatting to a minister who'd claimed to be licenced to marry people and asked if they wanted to do it now. A few minutes later it was all set up and so an impromptu wedding took place blessed with heavy and whisky (or a combination!). I wonder if the happy couple stayed together, or if they even remembered having got married when they woke the next morning?

One year a young Pat Cash and Wally Masur were there while making their first trip to Britain as part of a young Aussie touring team. They were also billeted with John and Moira as the house was large enough for more players apart from me. One day Pat came into the lounge where John and I were sitting with Whisky, the black family cat. Making conversation, he asked John, 'What's the cat's name?' John had a lovely sense of humour and leaned back in his chair, took a puff on his pipe and considered this tricky question carefully. After a few seconds' thought he replied, 'It's Cooking Fat ...', and then added, 'but I think it may be a spoonerism'. I don't think Cashy had heard of a spoonerism before so he looked blankly back at John while I nearly fell off my chair laughing. John and Moira are not with us any more sadly. I still miss them both.

In amongst the social there was some surprisingly decent tennis played and I managed to win the West a couple of times so it earned me a few bob along the way. The courts there suited me perfectly. They were blaize, a Scottish version of the English clay that we knew as shale. They allowed me to rally and counter-attack in a way that seemed to work for me. Wherever you play you need to find a method that is both comfortable and natural and Newlands felt like my home courts whenever I played there. Perhaps that's why I used to disagree with Paul Hutchins each year when he was correctly encouraging me to go to Paris to play the French Open qualies during the same week but I preferred to play the West with all of its many attractions!

The British tournament scene used to be stronger than it is

today. Many of the events were on grass leading up to and following The Championships. They would be huge, multi-event festivals of tennis staged in towns around the country that would attract a whole host of different-level players. Top county players would mix with the overseas Tour players in the hope of getting a good win or perhaps just the opportunity of sharing a court with a well-known player for an hour or so. The John Player event at Nottingham was a good example of this. It would attract some really good players and the local lads (all of whom had daytime jobs) would ask for their matches to be in the evening after work. If they were lucky they'd finish work at 5pm, wander down to the courts and have a couple of sets with an Ilie Nastase, Stan Smith or maybe a young Jimmy Connors, for example. It was a different era. Nowadays, you need computer ranking points to even get into the qualifying for the lowest-level pro events and these would certainly not involve the top players at all. It's the inevitable result of progress and of competition with the rest of the world. Everyone wants to have the top stars at their events and the number of pro tournaments that form the whole ranking system runs into the many hundreds. But it comes at a price because there's no chance of putting in an entry for a local open tournament now and playing Roger in the first round!

Chapter 3

Finding a Way to
Earn a Living

Paying my own way was always important to me and I was keen not to rely on my parents for financial support. They'd done enough when I'd needed transporting from place to place as a junior and they'd invested not just money but also much time and love supporting me along the way. Finances for players are a constant problem at lower levels and so I was well aware of the incomings and outgoings. You must do what you must do to pay your way. Don't expect handouts. I would play where I thought I could cover expenses and hopefully a bit more and was not afraid of settling for hotels and hostels well removed from the fancy places the players are used to these days.

As I tried to make a living playing tennis I didn't want to be a burden. So I looked to play other events apart from the usual British tournaments plus the junior events that paid no money. One source was prize money events on the continent, particularly France and Germany. The French had weekend tournaments held on a regular basis and these involved going across the Channel by ferry on a Friday night to be ready to start play on Saturday morning. They had a staggered draw, which meant that being reasonably ranked I only joined the draw for the final weekend. I'd play two, three or four matches over this time and then return to England on Sunday night, hopefully a few pounds richer and with some match practice under the belt as well.

Jacques Dorfmann, the French Open referee at the time, was often the referee for these events and he would apply local rules whenever needed. One time I went on court, played and won my first match and then looked at the draw to see who I played next. My entire match had been subject to Jacques' pencil and eraser and been moved to a completely new section of the draw! No point in saying anything; it was Jacques' event and what he said went. If you had have complained he might have found a way to make life difficult in the future. Never forget: don't piss off the referee as they have the final word, not necessarily today but at some point in the future!

Jeremy Dier (later to be father to Eric, the England footballer) and Mike Appleton were regulars at these events and they became expert enough to copy the rating system used by the French and set it up in Britain on behalf of the LTA. Clever boys. We stayed in some grim little hotels in Paris but one time there was a funny night to remember when we woke to the ecstatic sounds of a woman in the next room approaching orgasm. We crept out into the corridor, waited for the grand finale and then burst into raucous cheering and loud applause. There was instant stunned silence from the room and we crept back to our own room giggling like the little schoolboys we undoubtedly still acted like. Next morning was fun trying to spot the embarrassed couple at breakfast, though.

Germany was also a good source of additional income as they had a series of good prize money events that attracted some of their best players. They would buy a big fat Mercedes and then drive around the country at weekends playing for the money on offer. Midweek they'd give a few lessons at a club and make a steady income without the need to travel internationally. If you add to that the excellent money paid to play German club matches then it was possible to make a very good living. At the time this easy way of life was given as a reason why Germany didn't produce top-level players. Then came Becker, Graf and Stich and the argument ended!

Though I did play German league it was not until much later in the Vets. Well before that came a wonderful four years of playing for De Manege, a team based in Apeldoorn, the Netherlands. The opportunity came when I reached the final of a decent event in Amersfoort in 1977 and afterwards chatted with Auke Dijkstra, the coach of De Manege. He explained that he'd like me to come to play for his team in early May and that they were aiming to get promoted to the Eredivisie, the premier Dutch league. The money would certainly come in handy. I visited the club and everyone seemed very friendly so, as a 20-year-old, I signed up and started a great liaison.

Matches at Manege were events in themselves. We only had four courts including a marvellous main court that was surrounded on three sides by very limited, crowded seating. The court surroundings were too small, next to the clubhouse bar, and the locals were very supportive, loud and, by late afternoon, drunk! It was the next best thing to playing in front of a football crowd and I loved it. It became my home court and I never lost a singles match on it over the four years. The format was vast: four men and two ladies would play six singles, two men's doubles, one ladies' doubles and two mixed doubles. The team winning six or more matches were the winners. As the number one player for Manege I was required to play singles, doubles and mixed on the same day every match. No problem; I loved it!

We had some memorable matches, the best of which was probably the final of the play-offs to win promotion. We had to play Hilversum who featured John Paish as their foreign player (each team was allowed one import), someone I knew well from Britain. My parents had come across from home to Apeldoorn to see the match and, while under pressure, I was confident that on my 'home' court I would have enough to win. The afternoon was tense with matches going both ways. I won my singles and doubles but by the time we came to play the two mixed matches Manege were only ahead 5-4. The other was quickly lost, leaving mine as the last on court. It was played on our back court sandwiched between woods on one side and a swimming pool on the other. With little or no spectator room the drunken and excited club members were standing wherever they could find a vantage point. I played with Sabine ter Riet, older sister of Hellas who was then a little girl but was later to play pro tennis and marry Jacco Eltingh, the Dutch Davis Cup player. Sabine and I started badly but then Auke came to the court and told me to stop being a gentleman and to hit hard at the girl at the other end. The match turned, we won and the celebrations went on into the small hours. The Hilversum team disappeared quickly feeling that our supporters had been too rowdy (probably true!) and cuing the start of what was to be a long, wild night. The celebrations started with a fully clothed champagne dip in the swimming pool and then moved on to an all-night drinking session with singing that went on until only Auke and a small group of senior club officials were left to have coffee and breakfast the following morning.

De Manege treated me very well and I think I did well for them too. It was a great fit. One year the team were sponsored by a local caravan trader who put a caravan in the club car park for my use. But mostly I would stay with the Van de Marels in their beautiful home close to the club in the delightful Berg en Bos area. Joost, one of their sons, was my doubles partner in the team while Jeroen, their other son, was a marvellous rogue who would turn his hand to anything and frustrate the hell out of his father while making me laugh. And then there was a girl.

Freja was this vision who occasionally worked behind the bar at the club. Any further connection to tennis was minimal, though, as she had little interest in sport at all. She was a brilliant academic, spoke many languages, had a calm and aloof manner and was simply stunningly beautiful. Unbelievably, she seemed to like me and soon we started dating whenever the chance came. I was completely besotted. She came over to England to stay and it provided a problem. How was I to find something suitable that would capture her imagination? Suddenly, it was obvious we shared little in common. My usual inclination of a trip to see a football match or perhaps a round of golf just wasn't going to cut it. I decided to go for the grand solution and bought tickets to go to Covent Garden to see the ballet.

Since it cost several multiples of what an afternoon on the terraces at the football would have cost I was hoping this grand gesture would be appreciated. So we got dressed up (you don't have to do that on the terraces, you know) and soon I found myself sitting behind a large hat, under which was a woman who was to keep me amused later. Well, the evening wore on and on. Freja was entranced by it all while I kept looking at my watch, which clearly had a problem since it was obviously running so slowly. 'What are you doing?' she hissed at me when I checked it for the 20th time in ten minutes. 'I think the battery's going dead' probably wasn't the right answer and the yawn didn't help either! Later on the woman in front provided some amusement when I noticed how she kept the bottom of her hands together and flapped her fingers together when applauding. 'What a lovely little ballet!' she exclaimed after yet another unexplainable piece of prancing about had finished. Freja quickly realised that I am a cultural desert (in fairness she'd got that idea long before!) and after what seemed like days I finally escaped the night at the opera (or was it ballet?!).

This relationship was also memorable for another faux pas on my part – the time I met her parents for the first time. I'd been elevated to 'meet the parents' status and was invited to spend a couple of nights at their house (separate rooms, of course) instead of staying with the Van de Marels. We had both arrived late the night before from London and had gone straight to bed as the rest of the house was already asleep. So the following morning Freja came into my room to say that the family were all downstairs and waiting for breakfast with me. I went down to find a beautiful breakfast table all laid out formally. The napkins, glasses and cutlery were all lined up perfectly and Freja's mother, father and grinning 16-year-old brother were all there waiting to meet me. They were formal but delightful and tried to make me feel welcome. I was desperate to make a good impression and was on my best behaviour. Her mother offered me a boiled egg from a basket and, as I like a boiled egg, I took one and popped it into the little egg cup holder in front of me. Now if you also like a boiled egg you'll know that you're either a slicer or a basher in terms of taking the shell off. I'm a basher and so I looked around for a suitable weapon with which to launch my attack on my egg. Sadly, nothing was immediately available and so, seeing a plastic spoon, I took it and put my thumb in to crack the shell so I could then peel it off. In went the thumb but, to my horror, the egg was soft and not hard-boiled as I'd expected. A jet of bright yellow yolk shot across the table and only just stopped short right in front of her mother. I was mortified. The 16-year-old brother howled with laughter and I wanted the earth to swallow me up! In fairness the family laughed it off and couldn't have been nicer but I reckon I'd marked my own cards at that point. Uncultured, unworthy, but looking back now it was very funny! Freja moved on to an outstanding career in her academic field and probably had nothing more to do with sweaty sporting jocks who were more interested in chasing balls around a playing field.

Club matches, money tournaments and even the occasional promotional trip were ways of filling in the gaps in the calendar when I could play for points and prize money, trying to rise up through the professional rankings. I went on two promotional trips for the International Tennis Federation (ITF) to help promote the sport in the Middle East. They were partly funded and sponsored by Dunlop and involved playing exhibition matches, conducting coaching clinics and doing press conferences across the Gulf States. These included Kuwait, Qatar, Oman, Abu Dhabi and Dubai, with a few days in each. We had a couple of Arabic speakers in the renowned players Ismael El Shafei and Khaled Baligh from Eqypt;

Chris Bradnam, Debbie Jevans and I from Britain; Tracy, a coach from the US; and Trish Faulkner from Canada to provide some coaching experience. The whole thing was organised by Barbara Wancke who worked for the ITF. Apart from being a great experience and very good fun it was an opportunity to see this fascinating part of the world. It also made the contact that later led me to go to Dubai to coach after I finished playing.

The various events I played were both enjoyable and necessary. They helped to pay some bills and as I'd just bought my first flat I needed to find ways to cover the expenses that come with property ownership. As I improved it meant that the chance of playing team competitions came into view. The King's Cup was a European team event played in the depths of winter and involved matches home and away against other nations. It was a representative honour to play, a step up from the various junior internationals of the past, and took me closer to selection for one of my great tennis goals, that of playing Davis Cup.

One year we were drawn to play against Russia, Sweden and Hungary in our group for the King's Cup. I was excited because I hadn't played in eastern Europe before and it was still prior to the fall of the Berlin Wall and the advent of the post-Cold War period. The trips to Moscow and Budapest were definitely more off the beaten path then than now. They also carried the thought of spies, secret police and special agents that boys the world over love. The matches themselves consisted of two singles and a doubles all on the same evening, which could, therefore, mean a late-night finish. As we played two matches each week there was then travel each way so it made for a fairly hectic three weeks.

We played Russia at home in Huddersfield, an unlikely venue really but it was an opportunity to take international tennis to some smaller places. Besides, the players themselves were hardly household names so crowd control wasn't going to be needed. Russia at the time restricted travel for their players and sent out KGB minders to accompany their team to ensure they didn't apply for political asylum

41

while away. Stories of the dancer Rudolph Nureyev and his defection were uppermost in our minds as we heard the plight of Vadim Borisov, a very gifted Russian number one who eased past his opponents with real class. His modest world ranking was explained by the fact that he could only play a handful of events such as Sofia in Bulgaria, which was behind the Iron Curtain and so allowed for the Russian players. He was runner-up there in 1980 and he'd put together an impressive Davis and King's Cup record that suggested his true standard was more like a world ranking of 30. Vadim readily agreed to meet up for drinks in the bar after the match and it was fascinating hearing of the tough life of the Russian players in those days. He was a nice guy and a good player who would have become a multimillionaire in another era. Bad luck, wrong time and wrong place.

The return match in Moscow came immediately after we played Sweden at home in Cardiff. It was January 1981, Russia had invaded Afghanistan and the world was outraged. In our team was the great character David Lloyd. He had formed a very effective doubles partnership with Mark Cox who was now coach to the British teams under the captaincy of Paul Hutchins. David and I had just finished the final doubles match when an argument started in the locker room after David announced he wasn't going to Moscow the following day. It was a highly charged dressing room as strong views were exchanged on the subject between the former doubles partners. At the end of it Paul was left to make new plans for the trip to Moscow. It was to be David's last international match as a player and before his stellar success in business where he founded the David Lloyd Indoor Tennis Centres.

On my way back to London from Cardiff in the early hours my old banger of a car broke down on the M4 and so I completed the journey on the back of a tow truck. All in all it had been a night to remember. Later that day it was a subdued team that met at Heathrow, one short without David, and the events of the previous night were still at the forefront of everyone's minds. On landing in Moscow we were met by a ludicrously large 52-seater bus for the five of us, together with a 24-hour duty driver and a guide who was also there to keep an eye on us. After practice in the afternoon we returned to the Metropol hotel and managed to lose the guide to go for a walk to nearby Red Square. Being January it was freezing cold and snow was still falling on the white carpet that already covered the Russian capital. We enjoyed a snowball fight with some university students before continuing up some steps and into a deserted Red Square. There we saw a man wearing the most magnificent Russian bearskin hat walking briskly across the famous landmark. It was an irresistible target. My aim was true and the snowball caught him smack on the head. Both delighted and appalled with what I'd done we continued walking away pretending that it hadn't happened. Then I heard steps behind me and felt a tap on my shoulder. I turned around to find the man shouting at me in Russian for a few seconds before opening his coat to show me his police badge. At that point all the spy stories about the KGB headquarters at Lubyanka came to mind and I expected to be arrested. He shouted some more but then realised we were foreigners and no doubt that would have involved a lot of paperwork for him. With a final huff he turned, walked away and I lived to play in the tennis match the following evening.

Any opportunity to play bigger events also meant the chance to compete for bigger prize money and the Wembley Indoor Arena in 1977, at the old Benson and Hedges (in the days before cigarette sponsorship was banned), was one such potential payday. Only problem was I always seemed to play badly there on the supreme court they laid down for the event and so I moaned and grumped my way through a horrible first-round loss to Ferdi Taygan, an American who had long hair and a decent enough game but not one that could regularly trouble the best. It was a poor performance and I was completely undeserving of the more than reasonable pay cheque that came afterwards. My usually totally supportive mother obviously thought the same as she delivered a damning verdict with her comment in the car as we left the site. 'Do you realise you were just paid more for that than your grandmother has in her life savings?' I couldn't have felt worse and I've remembered it ever since. How could I be so immersed in self as to miss the bigger picture?

I think many players have a love–hate relationship with the sport and find that the rewards, or potential rewards, of tennis keep them playing even when it's hard to get out of bed to practise, train and play matches day after day, week after week and year after year. Anything you do full-time can drain the enthusiasm for the task but when it includes being stretched to the physical and mental limits on a daily basis the option to drop off the treadmill is always there. It certainly was for me, particularly when you hit a rough patch of form and the wins are hard to come by. And those wins are never easy since you've got a professional player at the other end doing whatever he can to stop you. It's a tough way to earn a living but nothing worth having is easy and the rewards for those who make the top are vast. Just try reminding a player of all that who's just lost, though. Losing matches sucks!

Chapter 4
Playing Overseas

Perhaps I was more a full-time tennis player than a professional tennis player. I travelled widely, played a lot of tournaments and matches but never made the big time. I got to share a court with a lot of good players from time to time but was never one myself. Could I have been? I don't know but I found it hard to commit in the way a Lendl or a Courier, or in more recent years a Murray, have done. Perhaps it's easier when you are being rewarded with fame and fortune but I actually wasn't particularly motivated by money. I loved the diversions that travel would bring. The opportunity to see places around the world that I'd only read about in books and magazines. I wanted to visit every country in the world (not any more these days!) and would take time out from the practise–train–play–travel routine to make sure I took in the major sights of wherever I was. I also loved the fact that I was away, was on my own and could make my own decisions, both good and bad. I loved the independence of it.

The constant juggling of finances and decisions of where to play, whether I could afford to get there and what the odds were of breaking even or making a profit were ever-present. Cheap travel and living expenses were researched carefully. Some players managed to get a supply of the little yellow stickers that were used by airlines to change a ticket. It didn't supply the necessary stamp that an airline office would add but it did give you a chance of getting on a flight that might otherwise involve an additional charge. These days everything is done online so no chance of getting away with that trick now!

Over the eight years that I was a full-time tennis player after leaving school in 1975 I played in many countries. And I reckon I lost in all of them apart from Norway where I once went undefeated in a junior international and then never played there again! So there you go – never play me in Norway but everywhere else you should be OK.

Tennis is a tough sport in that after two days of competition 75 per cent of the players starting in the draw have lost. These are the statistics that face every player. Only one player remains undefeated at the end of the week, leaving everyone else feeling that they could and probably should have done better. Typically, you go from junior events where you get used to winning very regularly to events where you might go weeks without winning a match. When I started to go overseas for events in the senior world the pressure to win started to rise.

They say you always remember the first ATP point you win. Curiously, I don't! It's the time you get far enough in a point-scoring event to get yourself listed on the ATP rankings. From then on it's a question of adding as many more as you can as quickly as you can so that you can start rising up the ladder. Initially, you'll have a world ranking close to 2,000, which is probably not worth shouting too loudly about. More wins bring more points so that by the time you get sub 1,000 you can at least start to believe that you're a pro player even if the truth is very different. Each jump up the rankings is harder than the previous one. Initially, a decent tournament performance can move you tens and maybe even hundreds of places up the rankings. Later on the move becomes much harder. You also face the task of defending points once you've been playing more than a year. Because you lose the points you earned the same time last year and add on the points you gain from the current week it means that you might get to the final and still fall in the rankings because you won the same event the previous year.

One of the most spectacular falls was from Chris Lewis, the excellent New Zealander who got to the final at Wimbledon in 1983 where he lost to McEnroe. He then struggled badly, lost a few early-round matches and so returned to Wimbledon the following year with a finalist position to defend. It didn't happen and Chris' ranking disappeared over a cliff the following Monday when the new rankings were issued. More recently, Emma Raducanu won the US Open in spectacular fashion in 2021 but then lost in the first round in 2022. Most second-year pros don't have to deal with such a dramatic fall but many face coping with a similar, though smaller, mental challenge.

The British events I played gave me a modest ranking but one good enough to start to play in satellite events (a small circuit of events leading to a Masters in the same country – now defunct) and futures (slightly larger stand-alone events). The trick was to identify events where you could get in and have a chance to both win and also earn enough to cover your expenses. It was hand-to-mouth stuff most of the time financially. Cheap airfares, housing and restaurants were the norm. One benefit of this is that I've been completely used to travelling independently and cost-effectively around the world ever since.

The first time I went to play anywhere exotic was in 1978 at an ATP event in Calcutta where we, quite seriously, played on cow dung. I always wondered what would happen if it rained. Could smell stop play? My plane landed and as I exited customs I was greeted by a mass of people there to meet their friends and relatives. I pushed through all the people with my bag and rackets and then ran a gauntlet of those wishing to offer their services to carry my bags and drive me in their taxi. I'd never seen anything like it, and I was 20 and on my own. Eventually, I found myself in the back of a taxi with people still banging on the back as we pulled away from the terminal. The next 40 minutes I felt I learned more about human life than I had in ten years at school. The ride took me past villages on the sides of the road where vast numbers of desperately poor people were eating, sleeping, shitting, trading, shouting and just living loudly. My car window looked out on to a world I'd never seen before. Sometime later I arrived at a fancy five-star hotel with an immaculate doorman dressed in the most extravagant costume. It was a different world again as I checked into my large, comfortable room. But I knew what was just outside and so very close by. It took me about four days to pluck up the courage to finally get away from the hotel–courtesy car–tennis club routine. I walked into the crowded streets, ignored the fact that some were going to walk with me just because they had nothing better to do than follow me around and soon I had fallen in love with India. After ten days I'd gone full circle from hating the place to completely loving it.

India divides opinion. Many can't take it but I love the sights, the sounds and the people there. Craziness is routine and the Indian tourist board's catchphrase of 'Incredible India' is inspired. Many years later I was in New Delhi to teach at a tennis officiating school and was watching a motorcycle on the road. I'm not sure why I was watching the motorcycle but something about it just drew my attention. Maybe it was the fact that there were five people on it. It slowly drifted to the side of the road where it then fell over almost in slow motion. Four of the riders fell off but one had better balance than the others. I looked again and saw to my amazement it was a monkey! Incredible India!

One summer, in 1980, I went with doubles partner Jonathan Smith and his wife Vicky, who liked a cigarette, to Italy for a long satellite. It was seven weeks plus a Masters and we travelled in Smithy's blue Triumph all the way. With true Italian organisation the weeks didn't follow on in a logical way geographically but had us traversing the country north, south, north, south in a ludicrous fashion. We got to know the Italian Autostrada system pretty well.

We always seemed to get stuck on the ring road around a place called Firenze. Many weeks later, long after we'd returned home, we found out that this was what we knew as Florence and we'd never actually stopped there! Oh well, never mind … cultural desert and all that!

I would struggle through a round or two of singles but then Smithy and I would make the final of the doubles where most weeks we'd play Italian Davis Cuppers Paolo Bertolucci and Antonio Zugarelli. Sometimes we'd win and sometimes we'd lose but we played them nearly every week. Eventually, we won the circuit on the basis that they missed one week due to playing Davis Cup. Apart from that we were even. The week they missed we won the event, beating a young, loud, very excitable and very irritating Italian pair who used hand signals behind their back to indicate whether they were going to cross or not after each serve. We'd spotted this and organised Vicky to quietly change ends and put her cigarette in her mouth every time they were going to cross. We had them on toast and it was a set and a break before they realised! I've never understood why players use signals. Don't tell me we were the first to 'break the code'.

Another satellite I played was in Austria in autumn 1982. Once again it was multi-week and this time I had my own Morris Marina car with me as transport. This made life much more bearable and allowed little side trips such as to Mauthausen, the former Nazi concentration camp, which made a big impression on me. A fellow competitor on this satellite was Birger Andersson, a tall enigmatic Swede who had once been a teammate of Björn Borg. We played doubles together and I remember everyone being a little in awe of him, partly because he seemed detached and alternative. Off court, and in a different part of the world, Argentina had invaded the Falkland Islands and the news each day was full of the subsequent indignation and jingoism as Maggie Thatcher rattled her sabre and prepared for war. We had some Argentinians on the Austrian satellite and instantly we found we had foes on the other side of the argument. Vicky Smith was hissed at as she walked down the stairs at one of the clubs and things were a little heated. I'd arranged to practise with another English lad one day and was amused when he arrived ready to play in a T-shirt from the latest *Star Wars* movie advertising *The Empire Strikes Back*!

I had a couple of memorable car journeys back home from Austria. One coincided with an opportunity to see the first match of the football season in 1983 when Derby were away at Chelsea. We'd just signed John Robertson, Peter Taylor was the new manager and the *Derby Evening Telegraph* thought we were about to take Division Two by storm. I left Vienna on Friday morning and drove all day, evening and night to reach Calais in the early hours. The Channel ferry took me to Dover and I finished the journey to London in time to have a shower and a meal and then be off to Stamford Bridge excited and full of optimism. Ninety minutes of football later we'd lost 0-5. Such is the life of a football fan!

The other came a few years earlier when I had a wild card into the Bournemouth Hard Court Championships in 1978, an ATP point-carrying event. It was a good opportunity on my favourite surface and so I left my car in the Vienna airport car park and flew back to Britain half expecting to be returning only a couple of days later. As it turned out I had a good week, beating some useful players including Iván Molina and Wojciech Fibak, who was in the top 20 at the time, and reached the semi-finals. It allowed me to earn enough prize money to pay the large parking bill facing me when I returned to Vienna to collect my car and, once again, drive back across the continent to the Channel for the car ferry.

It was certainly a more successful outing in Bournemouth than in 1983 when I got there to find what I thought was a great draw. I was drawn to play an unknown young Swede called Stefan Edberg. He had never played at Grand Prix level before so this was a really good chance to win points and prize money. Unfortunately, I screwed it up, losing in the first round 4-6 4-6. I was so disappointed. I wonder whatever became of him as he seemed such a nice young man.

Occasionally, there were chances to play at a higher level. One such time was in Milan in 1979, a major indoor event, and I went to play the qualifying. On arrival there I received the good news that late withdrawals meant that I was now elevated at late notice to the main draw and had several days to kill while the weekend qualies took place. Then the draw was made and I had to play John McEnroe who was coming from the US and was granted a Wednesday evening match. It meant I was there for five days before I played and so had plenty of time to get used to the conditions. McEnroe, meanwhile, endured the red-eye flight and only had a short warm-up before he was on court in the Wednesday night match. Poor bloke didn't really know what day it was and I was playing well. After winning the first set against one of the best players in the world I sat down at the changeover pleased with my evening so far. I looked up to the players' box and saw Connors and Nastase entering to see what was happening and who this bloke was who was beating McEnroe. I remember thinking, this is wrong. I'm usually watching them and not the other way around! There was to be no happy ending. McEnroe raised his game and, though I still continued to play well, he ran out a comfortable winner in the end. But it was nice to play a major star for a while and not get embarrassed.

The Milan event also saw some off-court player fun. A group of players in the hotel reception were telling anyone willing to listen, 'If you walk down to the corner of the street there's an amazing-looking girl in a long coat. When you get close she opens up her coat and flashes you – and she's nearly naked underneath'. Solely as a social experiment of course I was one of several to go and check it out and, sure enough, it was exactly as the hotel banter had said and she was indeed beautiful. It seemed that she would find a customer, a car would draw up, she and her customer would drive around and then they would be returned to the same corner where the process would start again. On returning to the hotel the group of players were still in evidence, only now they were laughing and clearly loving the whole situation. 'What's going on?' I asked two of the older players. 'You're so young; you don't understand,' they replied. It turned out that it was a transvestite on the street corner and they were hoping that one of the players would make a bad mistake! Boys will be boys on tour!

A marvellous trip I made was to South Africa in winter 1977 to play the famous Sugar Circuit there. This started at Ellis Park in Johannesburg with the SA Open where I managed to qualify meaning that the cost of my airfare was covered straight away. A good start and exciting too in that I played against Stan Smith, a former Wimbledon champion and a delightful man, in the first round. I even held a set point in the first set in the high altitude they have there before the rightful order of things took over and I didn't win another game. With my airfare paid off so early in the trip it meant some of the pressure was off to earn money. From Joburg we went on to Bloemfontein, Durban, East London, Port Elizabeth and Cape Town, and I loved it all.

East London saw a shared room with Rohun Bevan where we were woken up by a cockroach scuttling across the bare floorboards of the local YMCA we were staying at. A plan was quickly made and we took it in turns to shoo it out from its hiding place under the wardrobe. When it shot across the floor the other would use his tennis racket to try to bash it, making the most awful noise in the process. It didn't take long for management to come to threaten immediate eviction if we didn't shut up. We did and the cockroach survived.

After the Sugar Circuit was over, I stayed in South Africa with Rohun at his relative's home near to the Kruger National Park to see the famous game park. What an opportunity tennis gives to see the world and to broaden horizons. Perhaps that's how I saw it all rather than immediately getting back to work on my body and my game to make myself a better player. It was a fantastic life experience nonetheless and I've always been aware of that.

Another year I played in India but then had some spare time before I was next due to play in the Far East ahead of still further events in Australia. This gave me the opportunity to plan a major trip taking in some more places I'd never been to. I went up to Kathmandu in Nepal for a few days and saw cows wandering unrestricted around the markets there because they were sacred. I'd also wanted to visit Sri Lanka, Bangladesh and Burma on the way through to Thailand. Sadly, this didn't happen but it was due to visa problems rather than the realisation that perhaps I should have been using this extra time to practise and train professionally for the next events instead.

The more exotic and far-flung trips always carried a greater attraction for me. Somehow the more mundane visits across into Europe never seemed quite as exciting. Over several years there were many indoor events in Europe and many of these merged into my memory to the point where I can now look at a map, see a place I recognise, realise I once played there but have no recall whatsoever of what it was like. It was just another airport–station–hotel–tennis centre kind of event!

Croix in northern France was one of those places. It curiously held the qualifying for the much larger Paris indoor event for a few years and the only reason I remember it was because it only had one court. The entire qualifying in 1981 was played on one court. The draw in those days was made immediately after the close of the qualifying sign-up which was at 9am in the morning. Then, if you were the first match scheduled, you'd be on court straight away. No warm-up time and if you hadn't had breakfast, bad luck! Alternatively, you might be last match of the day, eighth match on the schedule and you try working out what time that might eventually get to court!

The ATP qualifying sign-up was eventually changed to allow for better preparation. But in those days it was just part and parcel of life as a qualifier on Tour. Another time I'd been delayed on a flight in the US that had meant an early-morning arrival on a red-eye flight. A taxi to the club got me there just in time for the sign-up. Then I was scheduled first match just a few minutes later, lost quickly in two sets and was back in a taxi and at the airport again about six hours after landing there earlier. I never even got to stay the night there. Where was it? It was either Indianapolis or Cincinnati and I still have no clue which!

That particular trip in the States was so memorable that I can't recall where it was! But that wasn't the norm. American hospitality is second to none and I had many great trips and events there. It was one country where you would often get private housing, particularly at the smaller events away from the big cities. This opportunity to stay with families gave an insight into the way of life there. It's true that travelling and experiencing different lives and cultures overseas is the most wonderful education. It's true and I never lost my appreciation of it, even if it probably did come at the cost of some dedication to my playing career.

Chapter 5

Chasing Points and Prize Money

Every budding professional player at some stage looks to gain much-needed computer ranking points and prize money by going to an out-of-the-way place where you think the draw will be easier. In 1981 four of us (Richard Lewis, Jeremy Dier, Debbie Jevans and I) decided that Benin City, Nigeria was the place and so we booked airfares with Balkan Air (because it was cheap) and organised injections in readiness. A proper darts match it was with four different beauties being pumped into the arms of us all.

The Heathrow flight left and took us first to Sofia with a three-hour stopover. Sofia is not on anybody's list of favourite airports and after three hours in hard seats with nothing to do we were ready to move on. The next stop was worse – Tripoli, Libya, with some rather suspicious-looking characters just staring at us. Travelling with a bundle of tennis rackets under your arm always attracted attention. Then finally there was the last leg that brought us to Lagos in Nigeria. It was a really fancy, brand-new airport so we wondered why we'd been apprehensive. We soon found out! The health check came first. Three of us went through no problem but Richard Lewis was stopped even though he had the same documentation as the rest of us. 'Your yellow fever is invalid,' he was told. 'You have three choices: you can either return on the next flight to London, stay here in the airport jail until tomorrow when your yellow fever will be valid or you can pay me $100!' 'I haven't got $100,' he replied. 'How much have you got?' '£5,' said Richard. 'OK, that will do,' came the reply and Richard was let through! It was as blatant as that!

Next came the passport control. The deal was that everyone on the flight had to hand in their passport and wait to be called forward. Well, there were only about 12 non-Nigerians on the flight and guess who were the last 12 to be called forward! At last it was my turn and I approached the man in glasses behind the desk. He looked at me briefly and then typed furiously on to his very impressive-looking computer terminal. After quite a long time I looked again at him more carefully and realised that there was no reflection from the screen in front of him and that it wasn't even working. While he might have been tapping away it was all only for show. The whole thing was just a sham! However, on the credit side at least he didn't demand money from me. Eventually, my passport was stamped and I was into Nigeria.

We then battled to get a taxi to the domestic terminal with the assistance of a 'helper' who had suddenly appeared. He aided us in getting our bags on the correct flight by bargaining with the check-in staff to actually put the bags on the correct flight for a suitable bribe – otherwise your bags would be headed for another destination. This 'friendly' businessman then demanded payment for his 'fixing' services! As this type of transaction apparently needed to be done in secrecy, he said to follow him. Stupidly, we did as he said and so Jeremy and I followed behind him. He led us to the men's toilets where he suddenly demanded his payment. We protested at the amount and suddenly two 'strangers' behind me advised me to 'pay the man'. So once again we were parted from a little cash and we hadn't even left the airport!

Benin City turned out to be awful even though we stayed in a hotel that was fine. It had recently been completed by the owner who had returned from the US – but the only things we trusted from the kitchen there were well-cooked omelettes. After a few days we were completely egg-bound but, together with the large supplies of Pot Noodles and other food we'd brought out with us, we managed to stay healthy. Night times were scary because you didn't trust security at all and so when you woke up in the morning it was part-relief you hadn't been mugged in your sleep and part-apprehension at another awful day ahead.

The club was the ultimate in basic. The courts looked familiar enough but the difficulty was finding anywhere comfortable where you wouldn't be harassed by little kids begging. After dark and under floodlights, prehistoric-looking flying bugs would buzz around until they got dizzy. Then they'd crash down to the hard surface where they'd be gathered up by the ballboys who put them into plastic bags. I was glad I didn't have to deal with them as they wriggled around. Not long after the match when I walked past the same group of ballboys I saw them eating the bugs, crunchy shell and all, behind the stands!

Very few spectators came to watch the tennis during the week but this all changed on finals day. We were told that a local dignitary was coming to watch and a large armchair was put courtside for his VIP bum to sit in. Though the stands were full the matches couldn't start until he arrived. Then he was two hours late so we were left waiting, waiting, waiting …! When he did finally appear there was a sort of ceremony with all the remaining players. Each of us in turn had to walk on court, bow in front of him and then move to our set position. Only problem was we were a group of tennis players not used to quietly doing as we were told and we were pissed off at being kept waiting. So we quickly arranged a competition between us to see who could perform the lowest and most impressive bow. There was much chuckling going on as we all tried to outdo the others in the low-bow stakes!

While in Benin City we befriended an English family who

were kind enough to invite us round to their house. Maybe they sensed our apprehension about Benin City because they went to great lengths to justify why they were living in such a terrible place. I hope they were earning a lot of money or whatever made them happy because nothing could have tempted me to stay. They very kindly offered us their driver to take us back to Lagos airport at the end of the week. On the drive back we were on a deserted dual carriageway when we came across a large lorry jackknifed across the road. There was no chance of getting past it so we turned around and went against the flow of traffic (not that there was any!). At the next gap in the middle we crossed to the other side and made our way back past the stricken lorry. As we slowly went past the accident we looked on in horror as we realised the driver was still hunched dead over the steering wheel. 'How long will he be left there like that?' we asked. 'Oh, probably a few days, maybe a week,' came the reply.

Some miles further on there was a solitary man wearing military uniform standing in the middle of the road holding a rifle and gesturing us off the road. This was scary as, again, there was no one else around at all. At no stage did he say a word to us. He merely gestured with his rifle. First to get out of the car, then to open the boot, to take out the bags, to open the bags, to close the bags, to put them back in the car, to get in the car and finally to drive off. We had no idea why the incident took place and spent the rest of the journey discussing it. I don't know if he was a soldier, policeman, bandit or vigilante! We all knew he could have robbed, mugged or even killed us and it was scary to think that no one would have known or cared at all. The first anyone would have known would have been when we didn't arrive back in Britain; questions would have been raised, contact made with Nigeria and no one would have had any idea what had happened to us or why or where. We would have simply disappeared.

It was a lovely feeling when the British Caledonian flight left Nigerian airspace. When I got home I made a note in my diary reminding myself that no matter how much I needed the ranking points or prize money I must resist the temptation to return the following year. The poverty and the poor conditions I could handle no problem. What I didn't like was the feeling of needing to be on guard against being isolated and possibly attacked. I couldn't guarantee my personal security. It felt intimidating and I didn't want to return.

Chapter 6

Choosing a Doubles Partner

The best way to guarantee a bit of success is to make sure you have the best people on your side. That's why choosing your doubles partner is vitally important. It then doesn't matter how much you screw up because your partner might get you out of the shit! Often you arrive at a tournament site, and if you haven't made a prior arrangement, you'll find a doubles partner from one of those also practising on site. Sometimes, these scratch partnerships can work surprisingly well.

I was lucky to have not one but several great partners over the years and I teamed up at some time with all the other Brits of my era. I played with Buster Mottram at Wimbledon, won professional titles with John Feaver, Colin Dowdeswell and Richard Lewis, reached an ATP Tour final with Robin Drysdale and rather curiously partnered all of the three Lloyd brothers while playing for GB, John in the Davis Cup, David in the King's Cup and their younger brother Tony in a junior international.

There were also numerous other overseas partners at various times, plus many more at county and club level, and each of these brought a wonderful sense of teamwork and shared goals. I loved my doubles and attached great importance to it. If you played regularly with a particular partner there was a great comradeship that was more enjoyable than the rather lonely place that is the singles court. I'll highlight just three of these: Dennis Archer, Chris Bradnam and Jonathan Smith. I played many, many matches with all three and enjoyed some memorable times.

Big Dennis Archer

Dennis was my childhood, teenage and adult partner all the way from county Under 14s through to playing County Week for Derbyshire. Tall, strong and with hands like a couple of buckets he used the biggest grip I've ever seen. How he played with those rackets I'll never know. But play he did, in his own style, and highly effective it was. All over the net he'd take people by surprise with his outstanding crossing. But it was his highly competitive nature that made him such a formidable opponent and supportive partner. Nothing was impossible and he wasn't afraid to win. Somehow, he'd find a way to beat better players than him and with him by my side I came to believe it too.

Occasionally, his frustration would come out, much to everyone's delight. Playing against a very short lad from another county one day his attempted lob ended up being an easy put-away for the vertically challenged one. Holding out his massive hand at waist height Dennis then berated himself to the delight of all several courts away. 'Come on, Dennis – lob him. He's only this high.'

At Bournemouth in 1979 we were struggling to win a match that should have been much more comfortable. We'd dropped a set and were 2-2 in the final set, making life a little too difficult for ourselves. It was against a third pair from one of the Scottish teams and Dennis has always enjoyed joking about the Scottish, and also the French, for being, well, just Scottish and French I suppose! I was returning at 30-40 and hit a shot cross-court past the server straight on to the line causing a reassuring puff of chalk. 'Out!' called the server at which point Dennis turned to me and simply said,

'Follow me!' He marched around the net with me right behind him (honest!) and walked up to the server, pointed to the end we'd just left and said, 'Get round there!' There was a bit of a mumbled protest but our opponents saw his point of view, did as he said and we'd got the decisive break of serve!

Another year we were part of a Derbyshire team thrilled to have reached Group 1 at Eastbourne. We checked in to the Grand Hotel on the seafront and found that Dennis and I were allocated to the honeymoon suite right over the main entrance. Fortunately, a more suitable couple of beds had replaced the usual double and we were set for another great week of the highly competitive tennis that is County Week. After three days we had punched above our weight and won a lot of matches surprising many much more experienced pairs. Come Thursday we faced Yorkshire, a strong team never short of a touch of arrogance, and a wonderful character called 'Bear' Armitage. He was something of a professional backgammon player, liked a gamble and had been enjoying the fact that we'd turned over some well-known Surrey pairs earlier in the week who he was friendly with. One of these had struck a large bet with Bear that he and his partner wouldn't beat us when we came to play that day. The bet was large enough to attract considerable attention as it was made known around the grounds and so there was a larger than average crowd to watch our match played in poor conditions due to the rain which had delayed play. We never really got started in this match and ended up a fairly distant second to the delight of Yorkshire and particularly Bear. Later on came his classic retelling of the story while holding court around the bar in the Grand Hotel when he proclaimed that, 'Archer and Jarrett were good on paper but rubbish on wet grass!'

Dennis and I played together for years, won more than we lost and had many great times. He's become the closest of friends and he's undoubtedly one of the greatest sportsmen I've ever known with his good humour and encyclopaedic knowledge of so many sports. Top man!

Chris Bradnam

Later to become an outstanding tennis commentator, Chris was another top British junior at the same time as I was progressing up through the ranks. As a fellow National Training B Squad member staying at the Wimbledon YMCA we had ample time to get up to mischief together as well as play doubles. It was hand-in-glove stuff immediately. We just seemed to know instinctively what the other would do and our partnership matched up to be better than the sum of the individual parts. The only problem was that we were so used to being in the final of the doubles every week that our singles games paled in comparison.

Satellites and lower-level professional events were our standard at the time for singles but we were better than that in doubles so we were winning those events and pushing on to higher levels very quickly. We also had fun on court. Chris was a clown and could make me laugh and that helped when it came to matches where we might otherwise have lost our way as it kept us light, loose and able to play. He'd do crazy stuff like when we'd dropped serve in the first game of the final set and had failed to get the break back, until we were now 5-4 down with the opponents about to serve for the match. We sat down, towelled off and as we got up to walk to our end Chris burst into song with a quick round of Elvis Presley's 'It's Now or Never'. We laughed, thought about breaking back and then lost the match anyway!

Another time I reduced him to rubble as he prepared to put away a very short, high lob that had bounced just over our side of the net. Just as he was moving into position to complete the formality I let go the loud fart that had been brewing at just the same moment. It was a cracker and he collapsed in laughter, leaving us both completely helpless as the ball bounced twice with our opponents winning the point. Since it was a quarter-final of a satellite event it was meant to be of some importance, but this was just too funny and so we both enjoyed the moment. I think the only other person to hear it was the umpire so our opponents and the handful of spectators looked very puzzled until Chris took great pleasure in letting them know what had happened.

We were seriously pressing to be the Davis Cup pairing for Britain and arguably should have been selected together. Certainly, if Chris had kept playing I think we would have gone on to play together many times for Britain, as he was such a wonderful talent on the doubles court. He never fully believed in his singles, though, and couldn't make enough from prize money to set up he and Lee, his then girlfriend and now wife of many years, in a house of their own. He stopped playing and I was mad with him (still am really and I tell him so occasionally!) as it ended a great partnership too early.

Jonathan Smith

Curiously, Smithy and I were at school together but only just. Being a few years older than me he was at the top end of the school when I was starting as a very little 13-year-old. He cut a very grown-up figure in comparison especially as he took advantage of the school rule that allowed seniors to smoke a pipe! He kept this up after he left school and this was one very memorable reason why he was always an individual that stood out from others.

He was involved with the National Training A Squad at Queen's when I joined up with the more junior B Squad and our lot were a little in awe of this group. Of course, we all often played the same events and the lines between the groups soon blurred and eventually, with Chris now off the scene, I was looking for a new partner. Smithy and I teamed up together in 1978 in Sydney, Australia and then moved on to Melbourne for the Australian Open where we immediately hit it off and had the most incredible run. We beat Wimbledon champion doubles pairs in Ross Case and Geoff Masters and then Peter McNamara and Paul McNamee, as well as Ismael El Shafei and Brian Fairlie, to reach the semi-finals. There we lost to the relatively unknown Paul Kronk and Cliff Letcher; otherwise we'd have made it to a Grand Slam final. In 1982 we had a great start to the year reaching the final in Adelaide and then winning the ATP event in Auckland the following week. Briefly, it put us top of the Grand Prix standings and we made the Tour doubles finals that year, which were held in Sawgrass, Florida.

Our Davis Cup matches together were special after we first made our debut at Brighton against Italy in 1981. The run through to the semi-final that year against Argentina in Buenos Aires remains a fond memory from our time together. Playing for the country meant playing on some big stages and we couldn't have given any more to the cause.

This doubles partnership had a constant presence since J's wife Vicky was always there too. They had a very close and yet unusual relationship, making them an amazing pair. Vicky was totally supportive and would get involved as well. She was frequently to be seen out on the practice court instructing J what to do with his serve and would sit suffering through our matches from first point to last, chain-smoking throughout. Sadly, the cigarettes may have played a part in her health issues leading to her early death. Smithy lost his wife and his greatest supporter and I a friend.

The three of us spent a lot of time together socially at events around the world. In 1981 we were away at an event in Stowe, Vermont in the US and decided to entertain ourselves with a round of golf. Vicky was happy to follow us round for the walk while Smithy and I took a golf cart. Fortunately, she was about 50 yards behind us when I was driving down a steep slope as Smithy suddenly pointed out where one of our balls had ended up. I quickly pulled the wheel round and the cart turned over with both of us managing to leap clear in time to avoid injury. Vicky came running up to give me hell, Smithy went into peacemaker mode and we thought it best if he drive the rest of the way to let Vicky calm down.

Doubles has always had its specialists and has also provided a chance for the major stars to just have a bit of fun. I was a specialist to a reasonable level but it was always great to take on those at the top of the sport. Bob Hewitt and Frew McMillan were serial winners in the 70s and I got to experience a little offhand sledging that Hewitt threw my way while in the warm-up before a match in Sydney. I'd moved up to the net to play some volleys with Bob on the baseline but overhit my first one which he then in turn took on the fly and volleyed back to me. My next volley was the same at which point he simply caught the ball, pointed to the sky and said, 'Ok, I've had enough volleys now – can I have some smashes please?!' As a casual put-down it was great!

Another warm-up story involved Ilie Nastase who was at the net with me feeding him volleys from my position at the back while Smithy next to me was doing similar for Yannick Noah. It was in Paris in the 1981 final of the doubles of the ATP event there. Noah was the local hero, Nastase was world famous and I think we only had one supporter there, Vicky. Nasty asked for some lobs and when I did he moved into position, then in an exaggerated gesture spun 180 degrees before flicking the lob away with a perfect backhand smash. The crowd loved it and were laughing and cheering as he repeated it several times. I just smiled and played the straight man to his brilliance. I tried the same trick in practice a few days later and struggled to make any kind of decent contact!

Chapter 7

A Wimbledon Player

Growing up in Britain meant that the highlight of the tennis calendar was Wimbledon. It dominates the tennis scene, is one of the crown jewels of British summer sport and has the world's focus each year on the leafy London suburb of SW19. From my earliest tennis days it was a twin ambition to play at Wimbledon and to play Davis Cup. These would have seemed pretty unlikely when I first started my assault on the practice wall at Derby's County Club in Crewe Street, but in the end I was lucky enough to achieve both.

As a leading young British player I'd played my way into contention with some decent performances but it was still a moment of pure joy and excitement when I found out I'd been wild carded into the Wimbledon singles for the first time in 1977. I also had a lovely experience that kept my feet firmly on the ground in the days leading up to that debut at The Championships. It had been raining in London (there's a surprise!) and so I was scratching around trying to find somewhere to practise with a fellow young player Chris Kaskow who I'd been at school with and also had played some doubles alongside. Chris and I went to a public park in Queen's Park, north London (not to be mistaken for Queen's Club in West Kensington) where we rented a court for a couple of hours. An old lady came by the court, stopped to sit on a park bench and watched for a few minutes before coming across to have a chat. 'You're very good,' she said. 'Thank you,' we replied, and then came the killer: 'You should join a club!' It was so warm and generous of her, and we didn't have the heart to say anything other than offer our appreciation at the compliment.

When the draw came out it was on the Tuesday six days before the start. Nowadays the draw is three days later, on the Friday, but this meant I had six whole days to imagine my opponent at the far end every time I practised. I was to play Ray Moore, the long, bushy-haired South African who had been around pro tennis a long time, was a seasoned campaigner and was one who I knew would be a tough challenge. I'd played him before, at Lee-on-Solent, and lost and this was to be the same result. It was three fairly straight-forward sets on the old Court Six (now no longer), a court I was to become familiar with over the years as I was scheduled quite a few times there.

In those days I used the men's changing room under the old Court Two stands. The seeded players were in the main changing room which was part of the main clubhouse and had a side door straight into the walkway that used to run between Centre Court and Court One. With no escorts to help it was a bit of a struggle to get through the crowds but my commute was only a few yards along to Court Six and it seemed strangely peaceful once on court and in your own little bit of space in the chair to one side and behind the umpire's chair. There was something of an 'us and them' feeling with a bit of camaraderie when a Court Two challenger was going out to play someone from the main changing room. I do recall feeling a bit overawed when I was eventually upgraded to the main changing room, after selection for the Davis Cup took me into the more privileged territory. It felt strange looking across the room to see Borg, McEnroe, Connors and the other leading players and it took a while to get used to. Now players have their coaches in the men's (though not the ladies', reflecting the differing policies of the two Tours, ATP and WTA) and so perhaps that helps. But then we had to manage these feelings on our own.

One different thing about being a player at Wimbledon then was connected to the draw. When the draw is made now it's instantly transmitted to the players' phones and the entire world at a touch of a button. But in those days it was much slower getting the message out to everyone, and that included the players. You would frequently hear just a snippet of the draw on the radio, or perhaps have to wait for *The Daily Telegraph* to publish it the following day. And then they would concentrate on the leading players and who they were playing in the first round. You had to dig much deeper to find Jarrett somewhere in the small print. And so here's a confession: I would look to see who Jimmy Connors was playing before looking for myself. Why? Because he was much easier to find since his name would likely be in bold print, and, more importantly, I feared playing him because I had this horrible feeling he would eat me up on Centre Court and it would be an embarrassment! Jimmy had the game that would possibly have just destroyed me. I didn't have the weapons to hurt him and he was much better in every aspect of the game. Plus he had the determination and the drive to beat someone badly and I really didn't fancy a 0, 0 and 0 at Wimbledon thank you very much. Fortunately, it never happened! Borg, McEnroe or any of the others would have been fine; I just didn't fancy playing Connors in the first round.

As an occasional visitor to the main Tour the chance to play at Wimbledon was always even more special than it would normally have been. It meant a rare chance to compete with the world's best with a pay packet that was a lot better than normal. Of course, it meant that I was batting a little bit out of my league and so wins were rare on the singles court. I did manage to find a couple of poor souls who were worse than me and so I did have a couple of main draw singles wins but these were the exception and not the rule. Doubles success was a little better and in 1983 I'd got through a couple of rounds in partnership with Buster Mottram including a decent win over the second seeds Mark Edmondson and Sherwood Stewart but then screwed up a good chance to go deeper in the draw by losing a third-round match to Sammy Giammalva and Henrik Sundström. It was a frustrating match since I managed to find my rackets seemingly strung too slackly for my liking. As someone who was usually very particular about things like racket-string tensions I don't know why this match was different. But it was and we lost. If it were to happen now it would be 20 minutes or so before I could get a racket strung during the match. Rackets regularly fly back and forth from court to stringers. But then it was going to be overnight at best and by that time we were out.

The mixed doubles was another chance to play and I made sure to take the opportunity, in partnership with (first girlfriend, then fiancée, then wife and finally ex-wife!) Debbie Jevans. It's fair to say we did better together while in the dating phase than we did as the relationship progressed. In 1978 we got through to the quarter-finals, beating Wendy Turnbull and Marty Riessen on the old Court One. Debbie was serving for the match at 6–5 and 40–30 when the most amazing conversation took place in the middle of the court. 'Serve on his backhand and I'll cross on the first and stay on the second,' I said to my partner. 'No, can't do that,' she replied. 'Why, what's wrong?' I persisted, convinced it was a decent plan. 'I can't serve on his backhand; I just aim for the box so don't know where it's going,' came the unexpected reply. I suppose it made for good disguise. If she didn't know where it was going I guess no one else could read it either. But it wasn't the best time to find out this fairly critical piece of information! In the end it mattered not as we won the game and the match anyway.

In one of the earlier rounds that year I didn't cover myself in glory in the politically correct stakes by taking exception to a female opponent and I can't even remember why. We were playing against an Argentine girl called Raquel Giscarfre and I became obsessed with the fact that I didn't like her attitude and also that she was tucking the spare ball up her knickers when she served. It was, and remains, a common thing to do and so I don't know why I suddenly decided to make an issue of it. At the change of ends I complained to the chair umpire that it was unhygienic and that I didn't want to have to handle them after they'd been 'up there'! What a little sod I was to do it; I'm glad I didn't have to field that complaint years later as a referee!

Later on, by the time the relationship with Debbie had become marital, the conversation at the change of ends had become a little different. 4–3 final set in one match saw one of the less impressive ones when she asked, 'Did you remember to bring in the milk this morning?' It made me realise that tennis was not really at the forefront of our thoughts. By the way I hadn't! We didn't win many matches after marriage.

In those days, well before Andy Murray's exploits, we British players were all part of the yearly statistic trotted out by the British press: 'No British male winner for X years' and also the annual tracking of how badly the British wild cards performed. Only Buster Mottram regularly made the main draw on ranking and a few others would have the occasional justified appearance by either direct acceptance or by qualifying without having to benefit from the tennis equivalent of welfare, wild cards. Did it add pressure? Maybe, but then you can only affect what you're in control of and this was not something we could do much about. Tennis is an individual sport and while the fortunes of any nation may ebb and flow the only thing I could try to do was win my own matches. In those days as part of the British Davis Cup team I had more of a nationalistic feeling. Now based overseas and with a reduced feeling of belonging to my country of birth I feel quite differently. It's an individual sport and every player needs to know that very quickly.

It's special for any player to play at Wimbledon. The heritage and tradition of the place does get to everybody even though some will claim otherwise. When you're used to seeking perfection and perhaps to complaining a lot then it's difficult for them to say, 'This is as good as it gets and it's a privilege for me to be playing here'. For many you have to wait until after their career is over before they'll acknowledge that Wimbledon was, and most likely still is, a major part of their life. Certainly, any player will get the question from those who have just found out that they played professionally, 'Did you play at Wimbledon and what was it like?' The crowds, the attention, the perfectly manicured grass courts and the general excitement are infectious. It might be good to be a spectator, a coach, an official, an agent, a casual worker, perhaps even a weather forecaster at Wimbledon, but being a player is the best.

Chapter 8

The Davis Cup Ambition Fulfilled

As I climbed the ranks of the juniors and then made my way in the senior world two major tennis ambitions always stood out. Playing at Wimbledon was the first and playing Davis Cup the second. My dad had always been very impressed if anyone had played Davis Cup for Great Britain and names like Graham Stilwell, Billy Knight and many others were rarely uttered without the adage of 'Davis Cup player' afterwards. With two elder tennis-playing brothers it was worth something in our house. As I got closer to those in the team they also became something of a target. If I could beat them or do better than them at events then perhaps I could force myself into contention.

Paul Hutchins was the Davis Cup captain and he was also responsible for overseeing our development as young British players. So he knew all of us pretty well. The team of 1978 had reached the final against the US and in Buster Mottram we had a player who was competitive at the highest level. After that, though, things were not so rosy. John Lloyd was the second player and he continued to play but he also had other things on his mind, not least his marriage to Chris Evert and the international lifestyle that came with it.

His own playing career stuttered, he slipped down the rankings and his motivation to play was being questioned. Meanwhile, his elder brother David and Mark Cox, the doubles pair for some years, were nearing the end of their own involvement and suddenly a changing of the guard seemed likely. Richard Lewis, John Feaver, Robin Drysdale, Jonathan Smith and I were the next most likely and with Smithy and I having reached the Australian Open doubles semis in 1979, plus numerous other decent performances, we knew we were close. In addition, I was seen as a player who could play on clay, something of a rarity amongst Brits who in general were pretty allergic to the stuff. It was probably fairer to say that I was confident that I would beat any other British player on clay, except Buster, but if faced with a genuine European clay-courter then I would likely get a lesson.

Two or three ties came and went and I wasn't selected. While disappointed I remained understanding. It wasn't my time. Then came a tie against Romania in Bristol in June 1980 and I was in the best form of my life having just won again in Glasgow and beaten some decent players en route. I was convinced that I'd be selected. So when Paul and Mark Cox (by now the new coach) told me that they were going with John Feaver and that they'd like me to go to Bristol but only as a practice partner it was tough to take. I had to watch as Feav went two sets up against Andrei Dirzu only to lose in five sets in the first match, and then lost another five-setter to Ilie Nastase in the deciding match. Beating Nastase would have been a great win but losing to Dirzu was realistically the match that cost the tie. I couldn't help thinking that I would have won that match and now I had to wait until the following year. It seemed like a long time to wait and I felt pretty low at the time.

When 1981 came around it finally seemed all my Christmases came at once. The tie was against Italy, indoors at the Brighton Centre, close to my parents' home in Seaford, and only just over a year since I'd had a great night seeing The Who live in concert at the same venue! Smithy and I were selected for the doubles and we joined Buster and Richard Lewis in the team to face Italian idol Adriano Panatta, with his mates Corrado Barazzutti, Paulo Bertolucci and Antonio Zugarelli. Smithy and I had played in Italy a lot and had faced Bertolucci and Zugarelli before, but this time it was to be Italy's number one Panatta teaming up with Bertolucci and they were an experienced Davis Cup partnership. On the first day Buster saw off Panatta in four sets and then Richard lost a long five-setter to Barazzutti. We didn't see the end of this match as we'd gone back to the hotel to rest ready for the following day. But curiously, Richard's efforts in coming close to the higher-ranked Barrazzutti gave us inspiration and a belief that we could win the next day.

It's funny what you remember about special days like that. Things like the warm-up where everything is done to cater the practice to your exact needs and requirements, something so different to normal practice with others. I remember winning the coin toss and electing to pass the choice to our opponents – though very experienced they seemed confused by this and wondered if it was legal. It was, and we felt we'd got one over them before it had even begun. Then came the nerve-racking start, the relief when I held my first service game and the thrill as we broke serve to get our noses in front, realising that we could not only compete but possibly win. The first successful topspin lob (my trademark shot in doubles) over their heads for a winner boosted my confidence and there was always the constant encouragement from Smithy alongside me. He was serving big and dominating around the net in his usual familiar fashion and it all felt so exciting and good. All I could think of was to try as hard as I had ever tried in my life. By current standards the tennis wasn't great and the match was not particularly long as we traded the first four sets fairly quickly to be two sets all. As it wore on into the latter stages of the fifth it felt like we'd played for ages, though, such was the intensity of the competition. When we finally won the last point to claim the last set 7-5 it was the most marvellous feeling, and one I'll share with Smithy forever.

With our part played we could then enjoy the final day. And enjoy was certainly the word as we had Buster in our camp and there was never any doubt in our minds that he would win. Richard lost to Panatta but Buster drilled Barazzutti relentlessly in the deciding match to win in three comfortable sets for a 3-2 overall win. I was now a proud Davis Cup player, an ambition was achieved and it felt good to repay my parents a little for all they'd done for me for so long. It was great that they were both there to see it.

Just after Wimbledon that year came the next round, a quarter-final tie away to New Zealand, which involved all eight players from both sides plus support staff making the long trip from London to Christchurch for one week, only to return again immediately afterwards. Once again it proved successful with the same team coming away with a 3-0 win against the New Zealanders Chris Lewis (Wimbledon finalist in 1983) and Russell Simpson. Buster and Richard won heroic five-setters on the first day, which broke the spirit and resistance of our opponents. Smithy and I then went to work on the same two guys and won in three straight sets to set up a semi-final away in Argentina.

In October we all headed off again, this time to Buenos Aires for the semi-final. We'd gone first to Santiago for a warm-up match against Chile to give us clay-court match practice, and then crossed the Andes for the main event. Talk about a tall order! We faced two of the world's very best clay-court players in Guillermo Vilas and José Louis Clerc, who played both singles and doubles for Argentina. A football-type crowd sang, chanted and danced its way through proceedings while we got routinely hammered. Before the match we'd felt we had a chance despite what seemed like overwhelming odds. Once we started, though, it was all Vilas and Clerc. They supposedly didn't like each other and it had received much publicity in the media pre-tie, so in the middle of the doubles warm-up when they went up to each other in the middle of the court and warmly embraced it was a moment all the crowd enjoyed and cheered. Seen with the benefit of hindsight I like to say that we lost 5-0, and 13-0

78

in sets, but don't be deceived by the score because it really wasn't that close!

The following year, 1982, saw a repeat of the Italy tie with the exact same players representing both teams. This time it was in Rome, though, and it was to have a different result. We'd gone to Monte Carlo for clay-court practice before the tie and there we had the best possible practice partner, none other than Björn Borg. What a privilege, the world number one. He would arrive ten minutes early, ready to start at 10am, with his fingers already taped and all set to go. After the morning session he'd then go for his lunch, rejoining us again ten minutes before the afternoon session at 2pm, again with no delays. So professional. He played with all of us and just played sets, sets and more sets. Smithy came to watch one of my sets with Björn. It was on one of the beautiful terrace courts with magnificent views overlooking the Mediterranean Sea at the Monte Carlo Country Club. We'd started and I was playing yet another long, long rally against the Borg machine. Side to side, forehand, backhand, etc. we played until I got a slightly short ball, approached on his forehand and came into the net. Björn raced across the court and played a delightful topspin lob up over my head and into the court for a winner. I turned and walked back to the baseline trying to ignore Smithy's snigger. Next point it was exactly the same but this time I came in on his backhand side. Again came the familiar slide into the shot and another exquisite topspin lob up and over me for another winner. Came the comment from my doubles partner as I returned to the baseline, 'Just enjoy the view Chunks – just look at the view!' It became something of a catchphrase for us from then on.

All the time I felt that I should be pinching myself to believe that I was on the same court as my tennis hero. I even won a set on clay against Björn that week but of course it was only in practice. It did cause me to consider what my tactics had been, though. I decided that I'd brought him down to my level and then raised my game! I decided to store that idea away in case I could use it another day.

When we got to Rome it was to another passionate crowd. Buster thoroughly enjoyed being contrary and obstinate and he chewed up Panatta on the first day while irritating the crowd further by holding up play and slow balling from time to time, eliciting whistles and catcalls from the masses. It didn't bother him in the slightest. He just concentrated and won. Richard tried his heart out, as always, but came second to Barrazzutti in the second match, so we started the doubles with the tie at 1-1 as it had been in Brighton the year before. This time, though, there was no magic. We tried and we kept believing but it wouldn't go our way and we lost comfortably in three sets. It proved to be the decider as, though Buster once again produced the goods to win against Barazzutti, Richard was broken down by some typical Panatta panache to the delight of the Foro Italico crowd, and Italy were the tie winners 3-2. A vivid memory from Foro Italico in Rome was the crowd throwing coins at us. We'd sit down at changeovers and hear the sound of coins falling into the clay dirt around our feet. Paul would take time out from his role as captain to quietly go around to pick them up and give them to any small kid who was sitting close by. It was a good lesson in how to not react or provoke a bigger reaction from a crowd that could have turned nasty given any encouragement.

Our loss in Rome meant a relegation play-off against Spain in Barcelona where I played my only live singles Davis Cup matches. I started the tie against a player familiar to me in Fernando Luna. I'd played and lost to him before but I'd also beaten him in Italy where I'd set out to out-rally this most steady of Spanish clay-courters. Remembering this successful tactic I set out to bore him to death. Most people lost patience and made errors against him and I thought I knew what to do. Only it didn't work. It must have been desperate to watch as I slowly slipped to 5-7 2-6 2-4 in a match so tedious I think even I nearly fell asleep. Then I decided to change tactics in a final roll of the dice. I started to wait for my chance and then attack, coming in to the net when possible, and the match turned. After recovering to win the third 7-5 I went in for the ten-minute break that used to happen in those days. I showered, changed and came out to continue to force the pace, winning the fourth 6-0. The fifth also went my way until I found myself serving for the match at 5-3 and 30-15. It was then I hit the luckiest serve of my life. I was so nervous I could barely lift my arm up over my shoulder. My serve was rarely a point-winner and it was once said that I couldn't serve my way out of a paper bag, so aces were not on the cards. I tossed the ball up so badly it strayed off somewhere towards Madrid, but instead of letting it bounce I chased and hit it anyway. By this time the nice cushioned contact I'd planned had become a direct slap at the ball and it shot off my racket, cleared the net and landed halfway up the sideline for an unreturnable ace. How lucky was that? At 40-15 and with a little cushion of two match points Fernando also did the unthinkable and came to the net for just about the only time in his career. It was probably his first volley since he'd been a junior and he generously pushed it long to give me my most memorable victory. The match had lasted four hours and 20 minutes and I was physically shattered at the end. I made it into the shower and promptly cramped up in agony with my arms, legs and stomach all affected. Two of my teammates helped me out of the shower and on to the treatment table where they stretched me out and tried to persuade my body to get through the mandatory press conference 30 minutes later without letting the Spaniards know it had just about killed me off. By the time press was over Buster had almost finished his one-sided match and we were 2-0 up.

The next day I didn't know if I would recover sufficiently to play the doubles but perhaps ill-advisedly I did as we lost in four sets to Sergio Casal and Angel Gimenez despite winning the first. This had most definitely not gone according to plan and brought me down to earth again after the elation of the singles. My return singles on the final day was against José López-Maeso, a lovely man who smiled a lot, and he had good reason to smile as he went two sets up as I struggled to get going again. I managed to win the third and had the heart and desire to stage my second comeback of the weekend but it wasn't to be. Soon afterwards, we were back courtside to cheer on Buster as he took a very long time to complete what never seemed in doubt as he beat Luna to give us a 3-2 win and keep us in the World Group. Job done for the team and this time, unusually, I'd won a singles match.

My final year playing Davis Cup was 1983 and we started with another distant away match in Australia who had a young Pat Cash making his debut. John Lloyd was back in the team but he and Buster had to wait an extra day as rain wiped out the Friday play causing the tie to slip a complete day. We played on the grass at Adelaide and they even brought in a helicopter to hover three feet over the court to help the drying process. When we did play the Aussies jumped to a 2-0 lead with Cash and Paul McNamee getting the better of John and Buster. The next day John was my partner and we took on McNamee and the big gruff Mark Edmondson in a decent match that included an 11-9 set in our favour since it was before tiebreaks were introduced. Sadly, that set was our only successful one and the Aussies ran out 3-0 winners. Sir Cliff Richard was touring Australia at the time and, being a keen player himself and a tennis supporter, he came along to watch. We hit some balls with him and enjoyed his excellent company. One other thing that amused us all in this tie: we were sponsored by Coca-Cola but the Australian Davis Cup team were sponsored by ... British Airways! Go figure!

Once again we were in the World Group relegation play-off and so my final tie was a home match on grass at Eastbourne ... in October!. Now everyone knows that the home team has the privilege of selecting the surface for each tie and so as we were playing Chile it did make sense to pick something they'd be unfamiliar with. Only thing was we only just had enough daylight to play the matches and dew was becoming a problem by that time of year. But the tactic paid off and Buster and John put us 3-0 up with the loss of only one set. My own involvement was in a dead-rubber singles against Ricardo Acuña. As far as I was concerned it was still a high priority and so I was sad to lose a quick final set after two very long sets had been split 1–1. Buster was cross because he wanted to get away and had to wait until my match finished before he could get on court for his own dead rubber!

Shortly after this final Davis Cup match I went to play at a small event in Thessaloniki in Greece. First, I had to fly to Athens and then change planes to connect on to Thessaloniki. Unfortunately, the first plane was late and I missed the connection. No problem, I thought. I'll find a cheap hotel close to the airport and catch an early flight the following morning. A short time later I checked into a very basic little place but it had a single room available with a bed and a shower and it would do for the night. As I settled down to rest I took a last swig from a can of Coke, turned out the light and fell asleep. Sometime in the middle of the night I woke up with a dry mouth and thought of the unfinished Coke. Reaching out of bed in the darkness I took the can from the bedside table and took a long slug, and immediately found my mouth filled with little bits. Some were swallowed but the rest were in my mouth and now on my face. I turned on the light to see that the whole can was no longer red and white but black as it was completely covered with writhing ants from top to bottom. That was it! The final straw. I decided there and then it was time to move on from this life at the bottom of the tennis food chain. And so I did.

In the end my own fantastic, exhilarating involvement with Davis Cup finished but I'd loved every minute and every tie. The matches were so exciting to play in and it meant so much more to be playing for your country than for yourself. Motivation was always huge and quite different from some of the tournaments that I had to play to keep working on my ranking and give me the opportunity to play Davis Cup and bigger tournaments. These events could be a real struggle; I felt I was spending 48 weeks of the year trying to earn selection for Davis Cup in the other four weeks of the year. The imbalance was too great and it was time to move on.

Like the many thousands of former sporting professionals I had to find a way to earn a living. Life doesn't just stop when you finish playing and the realities of building up in a totally new direction quickly become apparent. Fortunately, tennis is a wide industry these days and it's perfectly possible to have a good career in one of its many areas. Some of these, including sports administration, medical or psychological support, and legal or player agencies can easily be transferred across various sports and so are not limited to just tennis. So, though it may be a little scary to leave the world you're used to it's also exciting and it provides new horizons. And there was one new sensation that I really appreciated just a few weeks later: it stopped hurting when I got out of bed each morning. Aching, sore muscles due to playing and training became a thing of the past. What bliss!

Chapter 9

What It's Like to Be a Player on the Tour

Despite having been in various parts of the tennis business I've always remained, at heart, a player. It's the area that is most visible, most recognisable and yes, the most fun of all. As you get older the ability to play anything like a reasonable standard becomes impossible and that's tough to take because mentally you still know what you want and should be able to do on a tennis court. The body won't allow you to get into position, the contact of racket on ball feels wrong and so all in all it's better to play golf!

Everyone holds an opinion of what professional tennis players should do and say and how they should behave. Very few have had the privilege of actually ever having been a professional player with all the doubts, fears, worries and concerns that go with it. They haven't experienced the joys of winning, the despair of losing, the nagging injuries that just won't clear up and the constant judgment that comes from all of those outside the bubble who just don't understand the pressure of having to perform every time you step on a tennis court.

I'm not alone when I see players that don't do it the way the outside world thinks it should be done. Those who misbehave on or off court, who don't apply themselves to the job and who don't give

100 per cent effort all the time, those who act like prima donnas or perhaps don't respect themselves or their profession. Like those others I sometimes wish it were different but you know what? It has never been different and nor will it be in the future. Why? Because we're talking about human beings here with all the strengths and the frailties that we all carry with us every day of our lives. Some days are better than others and on our best days we can be pretty good and on our worst days, well, just keep your distance!

When I started out I was just a kid who loved hitting, kicking, bowling, catching, throwing or chasing a ball. Later on that changed to something far more serious. It was my living and I had to produce peak performances on a regular and steadily improving basis while others would try to stop that at the other end of the tennis court. I had to make myself hurt every day in the pursuit of a stronger, fitter body and deprive myself of other far more enjoyable activities because I was told that that was the way to the top. But if I did all the right things there were no guarantees. There was no magic formula that suddenly meant I could simply walk on court, win my matches and reap the rewards. It was hard. Very hard. And every loss along the way was like an arrow to the heart. They talk of death by a thousand cuts and perhaps after a thousand losses it can feel that way. I worked hard but there are always others who will work harder and they do deserve rewards but they also require that special talent that allows them to reach the very top and that is something of an unknown. That's where the doubts come in. If you work hard enough you may still not be good enough. So do you have the blind faith to keep working hard enough anyway?

That constant, consistent effort is something that should come from within though there are countless examples of those who have been driven to success by others around them. These 'coaches' employ methods ranging from quiet encouragement to abusive practice to achieve their own goals. Are they correct to use such 'persuasion'? It depends on the individual case I suspect. In the eyes of the world the father who has bullied and driven his daughter to a Grand Slam title will be judged with almost admiration by many. When that same daughter falls by the wayside, never makes the top 100 and has psychological issues for life then the same father employing the same methods is seen as an obscenity to humanity. Which is correct? As they say history is always written by the winners!

Off the match court players need to prepare properly. The physical training and the practice are obvious but then there's also the more basic housekeeping. If a coach or agent is involved then they might help with the hotel and flight bookings but one thing that remains personal to each player is ensuring that their rackets are to their liking. Every player wants the best possible racket with grips and strings to their preferred tension. I was once seduced by the offer of a better endorsement contract by a rival company to my normal Slazenger brand. It didn't work out. Try as I might to find the right balance by using lead tape in various places, adjusting the strings and playing with different tensions, I never felt totally comfortable. The additional financial income wasn't worth the struggle.

Gripping and re-gripping rackets became second nature and was vital. Rackets came with standard leather grips which were fine in the colder temperatures of Britain but useless when you played in high temperatures with humid conditions. Playing with John Lloyd in the doubles at Flushing Meadows in 1980 I remember having to serve at three-quarter pace because anything more risked having the racket fly out of your hand as you hit the ball. This was before the new material overgrips came on to the market and we all became used to changing a grip in the 90 seconds allowed at the changeovers!

Getting the balance right between competition, physical conditioning, injury rehab and mental recharging is a vital part of a player's year. Help in scheduling from an older, wiser head can make a big difference, particularly in the earlier years of development. Planning time away from competition allows for any necessary work to be put in to improve. It's not easy to do this while out on tour. Any change in technique will likely feel quite different and may not give instant improvement. Ask any golfer trying to make a small change to their swing!

I could not possibly have tried harder than I did in the match against Big Dennis back when I was seven years old. And that same effort was repeated so many times down the years in so many towns, cities and countries. And yet with the repetition and the knowledge that there's always next week, or the one after that, there comes a feeling that it has become something of a treadmill. It's just another week in a faceless place where you go out, play some tennis then move on to the next stop on the Tour and do just the very same again, and again, and again, and again … Big events carry the excitement you once felt all the time but there's no denying that some places don't bring out the best in you. The routine that is drilled into you of chasing a ball and producing a quality shot in reply is challenged by the feelings that your shoulder hurts, the court is terrible, the umpire's shit, your opponent is getting up your nose and there's a flight this evening that you could take if you don't win. All of these thoughts are non-professional, shouldn't exist at all but undoubtedly do in the mind of every player at some stage of their tennis life! They're human after all; it's just that they're trying to be champions as well.

Players cope with these emotions in many ways. Some hide it well, get on with it and keep their mouth shut. Others will feign disinterest but you know that it's only a front and that they're hurting badly inside. Others will loudly berate themselves and everyone around them, make a show of their displeasure with their current circumstance and just become a right pain in the arse. They're all defence mechanisms to enable that player to live another day on the Tour. Somewhere, underneath it all, each must find the desire to win and this must exceed the fear of losing.

So in a perfect world every player does the right thing all the time, gives 100 per cent in every match, always says the right things in press conferences, is a perfect example of humanity to the next generation and, of course, is nice to puppies. Thank goodness for all our sakes they're not like that because how boring would that be? I do hope they're nice to puppies, though!

Part Two
The Coaching Years

Chapter 10
Dubai

Two coaching and exhibition tours of the Middle East with the ITF had taken me to Dubai as I neared the end of my playing days. This led to a job offer at Al Nasr Leisureland, where a few years before Sheikh Mohammed had tried to buy Wimbledon. Not literally, but he'd built a stadium, imported some of the top players and officials and created a very lucrative event that the players could not quite believe. Ilie Nastase had won and then, the story went, made a victory speech where he thanked 'some sheikh' and the sheikh had taken sufficient offence to withdraw his support for future years. So the site existed but now had no event and so I went in 1984 to manage the little centre and to teach tennis, together with first wife Debbie who taught squash there.

At this stage I had little practical experience of coaching other than a few lessons given here and there back in the UK or when playing club tennis in the Netherlands. My old doubles partner, Chris Bradnam, had entered the coaching world and was kind enough to help me with a problem I'd encountered when being too nice regarding payment. So keen was I to provide good value and to work hard for my fee I would frequently go over time and then be too embarrassed to ask for payment. When I mentioned this to Chris he put me right and I quickly got used to completing each session politely but firmly, asking directly for payment if it wasn't being paid. Once you've done this a few times you learn to be assertive without the embarrassment.

I quickly found that my role in Dubai encompassed virtually everything. Within days of arriving I found that my club was hosting the upcoming UAE National Championships and I was nominated as referee. No experience required but of course it would be fine since I presumably knew the rules. So I duly made the draws and did an order of play for the first time and off we went. I was mistaken in thinking that the Nationals would contain good players. The fact that they were the best in the country didn't mean they were anything above a poor club standard back in Britain. Matches were arranged around the work commitments of the participants and we only got a crowd if somebody's friend or perhaps their mother turned up to collect them. Nonetheless, it was the Nationals and so due spin had to be put on the proceedings in the local *Gulf News* or *Khaleej Times*, which had English versions as well as Arabic. Who was to do that? Me of course, and so I found myself the local tennis writer amongst my other responsibilities; it was a crash course in everything to do with running tennis tournaments and was great experience!

One of a referee's regular problems is a court that gets behind due to long-running matches. This event had its own version. I was wondering how one of my courts was going as it had been a couple of hours since they'd started and the players for the next match were waiting. So I went to see and as I got close I could hear strange noises coming from the court. Just my luck, I thought – I'm going to have to sort out some argument over a rules issue, so I hope there aren't local VIPs involved as I don't know people here yet. I turned the corner to be greeted by the sight of both players and the chair umpire down on their prayer mats facing Mecca! I considered the options quickly. Somehow 'Play shall be continuous' didn't seem to be appropriate and so I legged it back to the office and waited for events to take their course. The first rule in any rule book should always be 'Use your common sense' and this was a good example.

Days spent coaching in Dubai could be quite unusual. Temperatures there can be extreme and so my contract ran from September to May each year since the summers are too hot to play in any comfort. Even at the start and end of each season the middle of the day was roasting and so I'd rise early for a few lessons, escape into the air conditioning during the heat of the day and then come out again for more lessons once the sun had gone down and it became cooler. These would finish late after which I'd shower, go for dinner, relax and finally get to bed in the early hours of the morning. With the early start again the following day it meant I got used to sleeping twice a day. It was a few short hours at night and a few more in the middle of the day. It's amazing what the body gets used to.

There were some lovely people in Dubai and I enjoyed my time in this fine part of the world. It gave me the opportunity to learn about coaching and to find my own way of teaching. It's a totally different discipline to playing and I was very conscientious in trying to improve the games of my pupils. It was a new challenge and I tried to improve my skills rapidly as I knew this was going to be my focus for the next few years. My clients were typical of the breakdown of different nationalities, a mixture of local Arabs, western expatriates and those from the Indian subcontinent. One such interesting character was a young Pakistani lad who was a decent player and keener than most to improve. He disappeared for a month one year and when he returned he explained that he'd been to visit his family close to the Khyber Pass. I was always keen to find out about new and interesting places so asked what he did with his time there. It turned out that once he'd done his obligatory round of aunts, uncles and other family he met up with his friends. 'What do you do with them?' I continued. 'Oh, sometimes we run guns for the mujahedeen past the checkpoints,' came the answer. Different league of reply to going to the pub or what! Apparently, this was entirely normal, made them a few dollars and was just another practical way of making ends meet in a tough land.

Two of my favourite clients on court were Martina and Chris. They were middle-aged Indian ladies who would turn up for their lessons in their long, flowing Indian saris with tennis shoes underneath. They'd never played tennis before and, I was to quickly find out, they had never even played with a ball before. They were simply the most uncoordinated players I'd ever seen. I called them Martina and Chris because they reminded me of Navratilova and Evert but only because one was right-handed and the other left-handed! But they laughed and had fun and the hours with them were ones I looked forward to. One day we were doing the serve, which was a bit of a problem in truth and so I'd broken things down to the simplest of levels. It also helped matters if I passed the next ball to them rather than throw it on the first bounce. Their ball sense was very limited and one had an ample chest. Unfortunately, one time that I'd bounced the ball to her she'd missed the catch, resulting in the ball then lodging on the substantial platform that her chest presented. The lesson then had to pause as all three of us were laughing too much to continue!

In the evenings after dark bats would come to hunt insects around the floodlights. If my pupils came up to the net to work on their smash and I fed balls up into the air, the bats' in-built radar would lock on to the ball and they would go into fighter pilot-dive mode. My client would look up at the ball ready to attempt a smash only to see two red eyes bearing down on them as the bat pursued the same ball. It was literally a game of bat and ball! Maybe it wasn't very professional of me but it was amusing. Such are the ploys coaches will use to pass the time!

The working week in Dubai was six days with only Friday, the Muslim religious day, off each week. The choice of activities on the day off was pretty much sporting or bar/alcohol-related. Being not much of a drinker it meant I took my day off at the local Darjeeling Cricket Club where we only played home matches since we were the only club with a licence for alcohol. There we played on a sand pitch with a concrete wicket and not a blade of grass in sight. Other than that it was proper cricket with everyone dressed in whites and a decent clubhouse where many a happy hour was spent. After some weeks we started to foolishly believe that we could play a bit and as opening batsman I was making a few runs. Then I got a good lesson in the different levels of sport. A team turned up one day and asked if a lad could play who was out on holiday from the UK. He was a fast bowler for the Essex second team and fancied a game. We were delighted at the chance to see a county player at first hand and were definitely up for the challenge. As opener I padded up and went out to face the first ball. The lad came in off a short run, I saw his hand above the wicket at the far end just before he released the ball and the next thing I knew there was the loud thud of the ball hitting the wicketkeeper's gloves behind me. I wasn't even sure which side of my body it had passed and suddenly got a bit scared! Fortunately, he quickly realised the standard of batting he was up against and kept it pitched up. If he'd have dropped it short I'd have probably woken up in hospital, or perhaps not!

When I thought about it later I realised it was no different to the many tennis pro-ams I've been involved in where the pro merely plays with the amateur and completely dictates when they allow them to win points. Opportunities for the amateurs to win points are served up but then when a point is required to be won an extra bit of kick or direction to weaker sides allows the professional to always stay totally in control, usually without the amateur realising it.

The low standard in Dubai was not surprising since there were only a handful of locals who played, and the expats were there for other business reasons and only played for a bit of recreation. But it gave me a chance to try out my developing coaching skills and work out my own thoughts on technique and how to pass it on to others. Many retiring players think they can move easily from player to coach but it's a completely different skill set and while you have a considerable advantage in having played to a good level it matters not a jot if you don't have the personality and the desire to pass on tennis knowledge to others. If you are merely helping another Tour player then perhaps it's easier but to suddenly take on groups of beginners and organise and motivate them is much harder.

One day a group of schoolboys came along to play in a group lesson. My heart sank as they filed on to my court. I knew it was a group lesson but didn't know there were going to be 32 of them – on one court! I only had six rackets and a basket of balls and my young 12-year-old customers were wearing their traditional dishdash robes with the only concession to sport being their football boots sticking out underneath. It proved to be a long hour since they spoke little English and my Arabic was a non-starter. You quickly learn to mime and demonstrate while organising them into different areas of the court so that you reduce the risk of an early visit to accident and emergency at the nearest hospital. With much gesturing, shouting, smiling and demonstrating I got them in lines shadowing strokes, but then looked on in horror as one boy froze and a large puddle appeared under his robes and the others started laughing. Somehow I managed to ask the question, 'Why didn't you ask to go to the toilet?' After a bit of translating one of his mates supplied the answer: 'He thought you were a bit too busy, sir!' And so ended the first lesson!

My little tennis centre in Dubai only had three courts, two with some modest seating capacity and then a 3,000-capacity stadium court. This of course was vaguely ridiculous for the tennis that was played there and so on occasion they would have a concert there for the expats. Best of these was a rocking good night when Status Quo came to town and appeared on my tennis court. All the centre staff were reallocated into new roles and so it was that I can proudly claim to have been a bouncer for Status Quo under the leadership of our head of security there who had once been the body double for Jaws in the *James Bond* films *The Spy Who Loved Me* and *Moonraker*! We were able to recognise other similar 'heavies' by the yellow ties we all wore on the night. Even better was the fact that the Quo lads took over my office as their changing room and I was one of only about six to witness their soundcheck in the afternoon when they dressed up in dishdash outfits and performed 'Rocking All Over the Desert' as a variation of their classic 'Rocking All Over the World'. Francis Rossi and Rick Parfitt were just good lads, very approachable, and it was great fun having them break up the routine of another week's coaching tennis in the desert.

Another time we had a tennis exhibition at Al Nasr and one of the players dropped out at the last minute. Too late to arrange a replacement I stepped into the breach at short notice and beat Vijay Amritraj in front of my members and customers, which was great for business in the following weeks. Scott Davis and Tomas Smid were the others and I found that my being fully acclimatised to the local conditions more than made up for any feeling of being off the Tour pace. I wasn't fooled, though. Exhibition tennis is very different to competitive tennis.

Away from the courts there were many interesting people to spend time with. One was Peter Gordon, an excellent golfer, who joined me on a weekend in Karachi in Pakistan because Emirates airlines was just starting up and they had a promotional deal to advertise one of their first destinations. We stayed in a hotel and hired a horse and cart to take us around this busiest of cities. It was great fun seeing the sights from underneath our canopy as our sturdy little horse trotted his way to the black, crowded sand of Clifton Beach and then to the Mazar-e-Quaid where Jinnah was laid to rest. It seemed such an exotic way to spend a couple of days. It's one of the bonuses of being based in a different part of the world and I only wished I could have got to visit Bandar Abbas in Iran, only a short distance from Dubai across the Strait of Hormuz, and also Saudi Arabia, but they were still more difficult to enter even in those days.

And then one day part of my world fell apart. My dad died while I was living in Dubai. It was very sudden and a terrible shock. One minute he was alive and well and then he had an aneurysm and just dropped dead. With no time to consider even the possibility of it happening it was just a brutal reality. At some point in our lives we all have to deal with such realities, but you are never ready. I went back to Britain for his funeral of course as did brother Roger from Vancouver. My poor mum had had to bury a son (my brother Clive while he was at Cambridge University), and now this. She carried on as best she could and continued to live with good humour and dignity for the rest of her days. How sad she had nearly 27 years on her own though I never heard her complain even once. I was so lucky to have them both as my parents.

Dubai had been a good stepping stone for me into coaching. It was a good financial opportunity for a couple of years but then the shifting political sands came to bear and they realised they could make more money by employing a cheaper coach. I was offered a greatly reduced contract when it came time to renew and so I moved back to Britain in 1986. But it was better than the way the CEO was treated. A large, rather bombastic Englishman, he'd hit the jackpot by getting the job but then found out he was no longer required. Nothing was ever said but a local Arab was moved into position who only ever showed up for about an hour a day but was gradually taking on more and more of the existing CEO's role. After a few weeks it was clear that the Englishman was no longer needed and he would come in, sit around with nothing to do and then go home. This was the way things were done. If he didn't get the message, resign and move on they would eventually just simply stop paying him. No point in claiming industrial tribunals and contracts etc. because that just didn't work. He moved on as did Debbie and I. Back to England though by now to separate lives and a quiet divorce.

Chapter 11
Repton School

It was my old mate Roger Thompson who asked me to go to Repton in 1986. He'd been there many years, was well established and had put together a school programme that rivalled any school in the country since it had many players there who competed at top junior levels in the country. It was a good opportunity for me to continue cutting my coaching teeth and to work with better players than the beginner levels I'd dealt with in Dubai. It also meant a return to my home area and the many good friends I had, and still have, in the region. That was a real attraction.

I set up in Derbyshire, first with the Archers on their farm in Marston for a few weeks and then in a rather grotty little flat on the High Street in Repton. During the winter I would reach out of bed after waking up and turn on the little three-bar electric fire I had in the bedroom. I'd then wait until the ice had melted from the top of the inside of the windows before getting brave enough to get out of bed and start the day. It wasn't luxury but it was my own space and that counted for a lot in my independent mind.

The courts at Repton were in a block on an exposed site just away from the main cluster of buildings. The wind would whip across the whole area and tennis was frequently tough in the extreme.

Sometimes we had to sweep the snow from the court to clear an area we could still play on. There was definitely home advantage to be had when we played teams that were unused to tough conditions on the days when it got a bit wild. Players the world over have to learn to deal with adversity and that includes playing in less than perfect conditions. Some get on with it and don't complain while others will use it as an excuse. One thing doesn't change regardless of conditions: at the end of the match one player will have won and one will have lost. You have to find a way to be on the right side of that equation even though it can be tough to keep your cool!

I still played to a decent standard at the time and made a point of playing each of the team players every term. That was made possible by making guest appearances for any of the visiting county teams that would come to play against the school. So that meant that not only was I a Derbyshire county player but I also appeared for many other counties as well. I'd ask to play anywhere from number one to number six depending on who I hadn't played recently from my own school team. It was very useful since you find out a lot about another player when you play against them, and so it helped me to help them.

The team practised several days a week, trained physically, had a good fixture list and won the National Schools' Glanvill Cup event in a final against their rivals from Somerset, Millfield. It was strange to have a foot in both camps since Millfield was my old school. The final was played at Queen's Club, another of the venues with which I was very familiar from National Training days. We had seven or eight players who were in contention for the final six places available and I remember the discussion with Roger as to who would make the cut. There were various conflicting cases to be made but it came down to a simple belief I have in backing the best players. We had others who gave better team spirit, doubles ability and so on but I knew that the opposition would be happy if a top player was absent. I made sure they faced our top players. It was justified when we won.

A few years earlier Paul Hutchins had made a similar decision when he selected an out-of-form John Lloyd for a Davis Cup tie on the basis that he could imagine reading in the following day's paper that John had risen to the occasion and that he was capable of producing a winning performance. The opposition would fear him more than the journeyman player who might otherwise play in his place. It doesn't always work out of course but there's sound theory behind the thinking. Why else do we regularly find that when the top singles players do play doubles at Tour level they are more than competitive? It's easy: they are better players and can adapt. When Federer, Murray, Nadal and Djokovic step on a court with anybody they expect to win. And that includes when they play the Bryan brothers on a doubles court.

I enjoyed my time at Repton very much but then came a job offer from the Lawn Tennis Association, and more particularly from Sue Mappin who headed up the women's side of National Training. I had a lot of respect for Sue and was pleased to be part of her team. She was always honest, direct, fair and one of my favourite bosses. She wanted me to take charge of the Challenger Squad, a new group of girls who were making the transition from junior to senior tennis. All were world-ranked, aged between 19 and 22, and the LTA were prepared to support this group of four with financial assistance to travel plus the services of a coach when away at the events they would play. For me it was another step up in the standards of the players I was working with and the chance to work on the WTA Tour; it was January 1988 and a return to professional tennis.

At age eight at the Nottingham Junior Open – all I wanted to do then was play for Derbyshire. Nottingham Post

The Millfield School team in 1971. Ten years later Jonathan Smith (next to me) and I played Davis Cup doubles together for Britain. Millfield School

My favourite two-handed backhand was unusual when I started but now it's commonplace.

Len and Joy Jarrett (aka Mum and Dad) loyally sat and suffered through many of my matches. Frank De Jonge

Winning promotion with my Dutch club De Manege in Apeldoorn sparked wild and memorable celebrations. Frank de Jongh

Arguing with an umpire before I learned that referees are always right even when they're wrong! Frank de Jongh

Playing at Wimbledon with a wooden racket, an overload of colour trim and the shortest of shorts; it must be the 80s!

My first Davis Cup tie for Britain v Italy at Brighton in 1981. Yes, it was special. LTA

We reached the Davis Cup semi-final in 1981 v Argentina but Vilas and Clerc proved too strong. LTA

Seen here with teammate Richard Lewis, Cliff Richard was a very welcome supporter for our Davis Cup tie v Australia in Adelaide in 1983.

The Wightman Cup team of 1988 played at the iconic Royal Albert Hall v the United States. LTA

Smithy and I still together in 1994 as runners-up at Wimbledon in the old men's doubles. AELTC

I think Lady Di would rather have been playing with Sarah Loosemore and I at Nottingham. LTA

This was my business card for a while but I chose who I gave it to carefully!

Chapter 12

The Coaching World

It takes so many pieces of pie to make a tennis player and it's possible to break it down into as many little slices as you want. All players are looking for an edge in every single one of these and that's why the explosion of the number of coaches has hit professional tennis like a sledgehammer. When I played we rarely had a coach at tournaments with us, we would travel and organise ourselves alone and maybe occasionally we would get to touch base with a coach when we returned home, someone who we trusted to look at our technique and offer advice. Now it's very different. The players are paid vast amounts and 'invest' it in employing advisors in every possible field remotely related to the sport.

It's a problem for major events who are expected to give them access not only to the grounds but also the inner sanctum areas behind the scenes. Why? Because the other smaller tournaments around the world have an open-door policy to anyone connected with the players to make them all welcome and to ensure that the player has a good experience. After all, they want them to return again in future years. It's impossible to match this as demand is so high. Overcrowding of the main areas would soon happen with all the hangers-on being allowed in so restrictions have to be made.

Leading players may have a head coach with possibly sub-coaches, physical trainers, psychologists, nutritionists, PR bods and agents. And that's before we even start counting the various other assorted family members, friends and lovers. So it does mean some tough discussions when it comes to the whole accreditation process. And of course every one of these is important and absolutely vital to the whole business of a player so they will be 'very disappointed' if they can't all be accommodated. Those working at the player reception desks around the world at the majors have heard it all before and it's not easy.

As for the coaches themselves they come in all shapes and sizes. My fundamental belief is that players make coaches, not the other way around. It's undoubtedly true that there are many excellent coaches who have studied the game deeply, analysed their own teaching methods and come up with a set of principles that can then be tailored to work effectively with many different players and to help encourage them to develop in a manner that allows them to achieve the highest accolade any player can achieve – that of reaching their full potential. However, for every one of these outstanding individuals there are other jokers who turn up in an assortment of gear, stand around on the practice courts throwing balls to their latest charge and then sit courtside trying to look suitably concerned and supportive. As I neared the end of my own playing days I, like many, looked to coaching as my next form of making a living. And I tried hard to become a serious coach and not one of the jokers.

It meant learning the teaching fundamentals and putting my pupils before my own well-being, something I was happy to do. I attended the various LTA courses, passed the exams and took my place amongst the ranks of the professional coaches. This all happened at the time I was living and already working in Dubai as a coach so I had plenty of opportunity to practise what I was being taught and develop my own coaching style. I do hope I didn't make too many mistakes and ruin too many games but I doubt if there were any budding Rogers or Serenas out there who could look back now and say it was me who stopped them becoming famous champions.

Of course, many ex-players don't bother with the qualifications and the learning of the trade. They jump straight from playing on the circuit into working as a coach on it. These players know the Tour and the people on it and so take advantage of the fact that they have this huge benefit over the young teaching pro who works his way up the ranks and becomes an outstanding coach without the full Tour experience. It's sad but true; it's usually who you know and not what you know, but that's the same the world over.

There's a big difference between the roles of coaches working in clubs, schools and parks and those working on the Tour with pro players. I once shared a very scary ride in a VW Golf GTI with Jean-Louis Haillet, a charismatic French player with classic good looks and Gallic flair. We were at the French Open and he kindly offered me a lift back to the Sofitel Sevres where we were both staying. He drove at lunatic speed around the Périphérique, the multi-lane ring road in Paris, and I'd asked him what he was doing after the Open finished. He replied that he was giving a 'stage' in the south of France. I was confused and he explained that he was conducting teaching clinics and suddenly it made perfect sense. As a coach in that type of situation it's like being on show, or on stage. You demonstrate and use all the power of personality to present an enjoyable and educational show. If it's done well it's very powerful but it's quite unlike working closely one on one with a Tour player.

Coaches working at the high Tour level fall into different categories too. There are the high-profile super coaches, so beloved by the media because they are another storyline. They're usually happy to supply the sound bites the media crave. Indeed, many of these also work in the media and so double-dip in a way that maintains their all-important profile. Then there are the many lower-profile, well-respected coaches who have worked with multiple players on the Tour and get their next job by virtue of word of mouth and recommendation. The officials know most of these well enough but not necessarily who they are currently working with since it can change on a reasonably frequent basis. Then there are the family members, maybe a dad, who will be the constant driving presence behind the player and these may sometimes become a bit detached from reality. Some can border on being dangerous but they have provided some real amusement at their excesses from time to time on Tour.

Jelena Dokic's dad was one of the more famous tennis dads. He allegedly laid down in the road outside the Birmingham tournament once and also got ejected from the US Open after going nuts about the price of salmon. Another, the Williams sisters' dad Richard, wandered around Wimbledon holding impromptu press conferences while posing for photos with members of the public; Bernard Tomic's dad managed to get embroiled in various skirmishes that led to him being banned from the ATP Tour; Gloria Connors, Jimmy's mum, might have stolen the show completely if Jimmy hadn't been such a good player; Mary Pierce's dad was another who could lose the plot. And these were only at the top level. Beneath this were, and are, so many others who see their kid with some talent, see the huge financial rewards in top tennis and think, I'd like some of that and so dedicate themselves to reliving their lives through their offspring with a single-mindedness that the rest of us can only admire and deplore in equal measure.

I was motivated by coaching and keen to be the best I could be. I felt that with my experience I had something to offer and was sure I could help to improve those who wished to learn and to work at it. I'd had the experience of teaching in Dubai and had passed the professional qualifications by keeping my head down and ticking the LTA boxes that were necessary to get the certificate. The time I'd spent at Repton School had seen work with some national juniors but joining the LTA training department to work with some of Britain's best young female players meant that I was progressing to a new level. I was back into the world of competitive tennis once again, the world I knew best, and I wanted to contribute. I started working with a group of four young players, taking them overseas to events and helping to plan their schedules while working with their own personal coaches and fitness trainers for the LTA. The initial group were Julie Salmon, Valda Lake, Teresa Catlin and Clare Wood, who later became Assistant Referee with me at Wimbledon.

Becoming a professional tennis player is hard. I knew that from my own efforts but now I had to bring that experience to bear and try to help these girls as they faced their own challenges. Training, playing, tournaments, travel, injuries and more of the same week after week. The weekly challenge of facing the brutal cull of 50 per cent of players from the draw every day. These are tough stats and ones that mean that for almost all the last experience they had on a tennis court was a losing one. It takes real determination, courage and resilience to battle on and an inner belief is required that you will find a way and that you can be a successful player. All sorts of problems and pitfalls befall every player as they make their journey and it can be a very lonely place on Tour. The friends you have are likely to be the same people who will be at the other end of the court playing you for points and prize money. Can you cope with that? Many can't.

One thing I tried (and try) to bring is a sense of perspective to it all. I wanted my girls to take advantage of their travels, to be aware of where they were and the history of the places they visited. That meant that their memories of a place were not totally of tennis and whether they had had a good week on the courts. The reality of being judged by your ranking is harsh and it's hard to take a longer view of trying to improve as a player when all people think of is your numerical position in the world.

My own group of Challenger Squad girls did well without ever reaching the top levels of the sport. Some moved on to Fed Cup or other national team selection while others played at the major championships, itself a wonderful achievement for the majority of kids who start off on the long road to tennis stardom. For every Federer, Nadal, Williams and Grand Slam winner there are hundreds and thousands of others who make their own sacrifices without ever getting a fraction of the rewards. For these players the difficult thing is not to feel like a failure. They face huge expenses and are surrounded by great and often unrealistic expectations from those around them who wish them well but don't realise the pressure they are putting on with their support.

My girls as individuals, the squad as a group and myself as a coach were being judged on the ranking improvement or drop of each of them. Wiser heads may realise the wider picture but it's fundamentally true. The British press at that time were relentless in their condemnation of British tennis generally and so all at the LTA felt under pressure to deliver. I spent about seven years in this or a similar role and saw some strange goings-on at the LTA in that time. Since then new policies and personnel have been introduced on a regular basis, each asking for another five years before they could be judged. Of course, there is no magic formula and each plan in turn was successively tried and frequently found wanting by the cynicism that sometimes surrounds British tennis.

The role of the LTA, and indeed any national federation of any sport, is an interesting and much-maligned one. They are there to run the sport in their own country from the grassroots up to the high-profile national teams. How that's achieved is open to endless speculation. What's clear is that success at the highest level can disguise the failures elsewhere and so it's understandable when considerable resources are thrown at the top end, meaning reduced support to the base levels. Occasionally, you get times when initiatives are launched in one particular area of the sport such as clubs or parks but mainly the money goes where the press and public can see the instant reward of international success. Success can be fleeting, players and groups of players come and go, and those following may fail to live up to their predecessors. Then the coaches and administrators take the flak as they reap the rewards in the good times. In any case you can't just buy success. Coaches can improve players but they can't make average players great. That takes the little bit of magic stardust that is sprinkled on the very few plus a hell of a lot of hard work.

The LTA is like the Chelsea or Manchester City of the national federations. They have considerably more resources at their disposal when compared with just about all the others. Ireland, for example, operated for years with just a chief executive, a secretary and a national coach and did OK. Meanwhile, the LTA was able to buy a National Tennis Centre in Roehampton for a reported £44 million, fill it with administrators of every possible discipline and then had courts that they struggled to find a consistent use for. The upkeep alone of this place is probably more than most countries would have as a total budget for the year. As most organisations find once you have a human resources and IT departments you can add enormously to your staff numbers and salary costs overnight. But having the infrastructure in place means that support for players and their development can be competitive with the best in the world and success helps to bring greater expectation from all, and particularly from the players themselves in their own performances.

I spent seven years at the LTA and, by and large, managed to avoid most of what comes with being part of an organisation under pressure. I was lucky to be out on the road most of the time working with the players and trying to make their life on Tour a little easier by being there to support, to encourage and to offer what guidance I could. Put that way it's really very simple. You spend a lot of time with them, commit a lot of your own energy and will into them and genuinely have their best interests at heart. This then comes with a moral dilemma to wrestle with and I recognise this with all the national coaches I see now out on the Tour. You have a responsibility to do and advise what is in the best interests of the player. Many of the players you may be working with will have little chance of becoming a self-supporting professional tennis player. You can see that and statistically it is undoubtedly true. The best advice you might give that player is to quit pro tennis and, if they wish to continue with their tennis, go to an American university to get an education while still practising and training. That way they've hedged their bets and have something else for later in life. The trouble with that, from the coach's point of view, is that they are being employed by the federation to produce players and that advice runs counter to their employer's goal. If they continue playing full-time they will either become a pro player or they will become another that the next generation in that country must play through on their own way to joining the circuit. When that happens the depth of standard in the country becomes deeper and so it's better for the federation but not necessarily for the individual. I struggled with that dilemma.

I tried to get my girls to have some fun as well as put in the hard yards while away on tour. One trip to Miami produced a couple of memorable moments. One came when we all went go-karting at a local track in Fort Lauderdale. Being the competitive beasts we all are the race was keenly contested and I was sent off by a track marshal for being too aggressive. This was probably just as well since it meant I wasn't even still racing when Valda clipped another kart and managed to flip it over completely. Fortunately, she didn't have a scratch on her but it could have been different and that would have been an interesting conversation with my LTA employers.

Later that day it was Valda again. This time we were in a Miami nightclub (I'm not sure why since I can't stand those places) when we were suddenly called up on stage as a group for karaoke. It caught us completely by surprise since we had no idea what was happening. It transpired that Valda had put our name down to sing 'Wake Me Up Before You Go-Go' by Wham!, a dreadful song that was light years away from my own liking for heavy metal. We were so bad we managed to clear the area of spectators within a minute or so. Knowing only the chorus we tried in vain to follow the lines on the songbook in front of us. That was moderately successful until we reached the song's famous line 'I wanna hit that high' featuring a high note that few could reach. Most of us didn't even try but Clare Wood went for it, missed it by a mile and we all collapsed in hysterics. It was a high note that was also the low point of our brief singing careers and we slunk away off the stage in shame!

On another tour, this time to the Far East in 1990, my lovely future wife Dannie was also with us. She was always great to have along since she provided another face for the girls to be around and to chat with, and she could get them off the subject of tennis into all sorts of feminine talk I simply couldn't provide. We needed to change an air ticket and, long before the days of the internet, she'd gone alone into Tokyo to the airline office. While she was away I noticed that the following week's event in Singapore hadn't got a full entry list and so, unbeknownst to Dannie, I'd entered her into the qualifying there. The rules at that time didn't allow her to withdraw and so the die was cast – she had to play or she'd be fined! It was a complete stitch-up and by the time she came to play her match in the high heat and humidity of Singapore the following week many of the other girls were looking forward to the match enormously, and it attracted something of a crowd. She was drawn to play Paulette Moreno from Hong Kong, well known to us since she was coached by Kevin Livesey, a long-time friend and compatriot of mine. Kevin entered into the spirit of it all and didn't tell Paulette what she was up against in the first round. So when, as they walked to the court, Dannie said that the match really wouldn't take very long in the high heat Paulette (another chatterbox like Dannie) thought she was trying a little psychological warfare. A few minutes later I still believe the turning point came in the match when Dannie misjudged a ball and it dropped in to give Paulette a 30–0 lead in the first game. If that *had* fallen out and it had been 15–15 who knows what might have happened! As it was Paulette went on to win a predictably one-sided contest with the highlight probably the sight of them both happily chatting away with each other at each change of ends while the chair umpire kept looking behind him in bemusement at them both. After the match was over the umpire then went to Dannie and asked, 'Have you been injured for a very long time?' It was a kind thought but it gave us all a laugh. Dannie and Paulette became friends and have stayed so ever since their epic encounter. In the considered opinion of many observers it was the peak of Dannie's professional tennis career!

Australia was always a much-anticipated tour for us all and I loved seeing everybody I'd known from my own playing days there. All the tournament venues were great, but the jewel was Melbourne. We had a great set-up with our own base at Roy and Denise Richards' house in Armadale, one of the suburbs there. Roy was a doctor and so looked after all the ailments when necessary, including a time when Julie Salmon ended up in hospital with appendicitis. Naturally, I would stay with my adopted family Nugget and Jim Howse plus my little Aussie brother Ian and little Aussie sister Jan, in Glen Waverley, but then drive in to collect the various girls at their housing each day. It was a home away from home and we all loved it. For some reason the Aussie trip was one where you would be flying home at the end of it all, see another plane flying in the opposite direction and wish you were on that one to start it all over again.

I worked with most of the young female players in Britain at some stage during my time with the LTA. Often it was on a single-Tour basis but that could involve numerous weeks at a time. Colette Hall and Shirli-Ann Siddall were two that were great friends but separated on different circuits at one time. I was working with Shirli-Ann around Australia and New Zealand while Colette was with Keith Wooldridge, a lovely man who had also been an excellent player in his younger days. We were all to team up in Oklahoma City in America for an event and the girls were delighted to see each other. Keith and I decided to let them go out separately from us since they were almost certainly sick to death of being with their old coaches/chaperones and could do with some girl time. Keith and I went off to find somewhere to eat and wandered into a restaurant, asked for a table for two and sat down. Once our eyes became accustomed to the dark we then realised, to our horror, that it was Valentine's Day and every table was set for two with a lovely candle in the middle. Our fellow diners were all clearly on a date and we were getting a few strange looks. To this day I like to tease Keith about him being my valentine!

It was all a great challenge and I enjoyed my time working with them all, and gave everything to the cause. But it didn't stop my ruder friends outside tennis, who thought I never actually worked at all, enjoying it when I told them of going to the barbers in London one day just before a trip. The hairdresser was cutting away and making conversation asking if I had anything planned in the coming week. I said that my girlfriend was pregnant and that we were spending time together before I had to go away on a work trip. Further questions then established that I was going away for six weeks with my Challenger Squad to Australia. He laughed and said, 'So, to summarise, you're going to Australia with a group of highly talented, and probably good-looking, young female athletes leaving your pregnant girlfriend at home. How the hell did you get a job like that?' I suppose, put like that, he did have a point.

Chapter 13

Coaching the British National Teams

Part of the role I had in my LTA years involved coaching the British Fed Cup and Olympic teams. While it was an important role each had a team captain or manager and so my own involvement was mainly hitting with the teams, organising practice sessions and being a general liaison between team members and the captain. Ann Jones, the former Wimbledon champion, was often captain and a terrific influence. She had been around the Tour for a long time and brought her down-to-earth, common-sense approach to the role. I'd been working with most of the girls on a regular basis and all were well known to me. Getting on pretty well with those around me meant I was able to provide a little gel if tensions ever mounted as they can.

Central to all of this was Monique Javer who had come to British tennis from California in 1990 as she qualified for Britain due to having a British mother. On the face of it having a new number two to strengthen the team was good news but the other girls had seemingly little in common with her. You can't make people get on together and this proved to be difficult. Some felt that she'd come to Britain to access the greater funding that the LTA spent on their players compared with that available for players in America. I just wanted to make it work.

Monique was attached to my group of girls at various events and for a while I worked solely with her. This worked out fine for most of the time and I tried to help her integrate with the others. She had a curious supporter in David Wynn-Morgan who wrote articles for a tennis magazine he published at the time. He regularly attacked the LTA in these and took every opportunity to slate every possible policy or decision involving Monique, another reason why the other players had their backs up.

The British number one at the time was Jo Durie and a more reasonable and nicer person is hard to imagine. Much the same could be said of Sara Gomer, a delightful girl who had the most wonderful touch and power but little self-confidence, and the naturally gregarious Clare Wood. It was these three that went with Monique to Frankfurt for a Fed Cup week in 1992 that was to prove difficult.

From the start there was a frosty atmosphere. Team dinners were a test of diplomacy as we tried hard to steer the topics for discussion away from anything that might become contentious. Practice sessions were carefully planned to get all the players ready for their matches while minimising the chance for internal dramas. I would go through the usual drills I did with Monique, ones that she was familiar with and believed in. Then we would get a player from another team to play practice sets with her. Match days were easier since the non-playing members would sit on the side of the court, being supportive for the common cause. I can't say it was a happy team but we were getting through it.

In the middle of a difficult week came a moment of pure comedy. It was the evening before the team was due to play a match and Monique was to open proceedings with a singles at 10am. This meant, in Monique's mind, that we needed to have an early dinner, get back to the hotel and have an early night ready for her match in the morning. Nothing wrong with that at all and so we all met in the lobby ready for the transportation that would take us to the Italian restaurant selected for the team dinner. Unfortunately, the driver was late and when the minibus finally arrived Monique jumped straight in the front passenger seat leaving Ann, as captain and senior member of the team, to join the rest of us in the back. Then 20 minutes after leaving we were back outside the hotel as the driver had got lost. Monique's hopes for an early dinner were struggling badly and she was getting frustrated as the driver tried to work out which way to go. The atmosphere in the back was becoming tense and, realising we now had an explosive Monique on our hands, Clare tried to ease the mood. As we stopped at red traffic lights she looked out of the window at a furniture store and said, 'What a lovely sofa'. As a way of changing the subject this was painfully transparent and some giggling and knowing looks were starting to be exchanged in the back. This drew some huffs and tuts from the front seat, which only made it worse. Schoolkid humour had now firmly taken over and those in the back were starting to see the comedy in the situation. The lid finally came off as Sara, with a comic's perfect timing, delivered a stage whisper that was meant for those closest to her: 'Has anybody got a gun?' That was it. No one could hold it in any longer and loud guffaws of laughter filled the space. Monique ignored it completely and we all prepared for another difficult social evening. Like the team's minibus we were more than a little bit lost.

Even during such a week we did manage another amusing episode off court. It came when we went to play golf on a free afternoon at a lovely golf club near Frankfurt. A telephone call was made on our behalf so that they were expecting us and we were warmly welcomed when we arrived. But the staff seemed a little confused when we asked to hire clubs, balls and everything else required to play. There were some disappointed faces watching as we teed off from the first tee. They'd thought we were the British golf team not the British tennis team. So when we started swiping away and playing some dreadful golf there were some upset people around I'm sure. To their credit they never said anything and thankfully no club officials were watching when Sara produced her moment of magic a few holes into the round. The practice swings had gone well, she addressed the ball, took a swing and we all looked expectantly up the fairway to see where she'd hit her ball. We all missed the fact that she'd taken a big divot that curled perfectly and settled completely covering her ball, which hadn't moved an inch. I've played a lot of golf and I've never seen another shot like it. It took pure genius!

Somehow, we survived the week and returned to London to lick our wounds. It wasn't a successful time and the results had been pretty much as predicted for a team that was always likely to struggle on clay courts. Back home again everyone went their separate ways but only for a few days because very shortly later nearly the same group were heading off to the Olympics in Barcelona. A training camp had been organised at Bisham Abbey where some clay courts had been laid for teams preparing to play abroad. Much discussion took place behind the scenes as to what we could do to reduce or minimise the problems that existed in the ranks. We soldiered on but team atmosphere and camaraderie were at a premium and it wasn't the happiest of times.

The British team for the Olympics did at least have a different dynamic in that it involved the boys as well. Chris Wilkinson and Andrew Castle were there and so I had some distraction with them – welcome under the circumstances as it was a return to the more familiar atmosphere of the men's locker room for me. Once again, the clay courts proved tough for our players when faced with the skills of the opposition. Curiously, two played each other when Sam Smith beat Sara Gomer in the first round. They were all keen to enjoy the Olympic experience, though, and to see the other stars from different sports. It made a change from the grind of the regular Tour.

Many of the tennis stars, plus the superstars of other sports, choose to get themselves a hotel room rather than enter the holiday camp atmosphere of the Olympic village. They need to prepare properly and putting up with autograph hunters, souvenir team pin collectors, dodgy beds and a roommate when you're used to better isn't going to help you get ready to deliver a gold medal for Queen and Country. There are only a few who have a serious chance to win the big prizes and the rest do the best they can, hope for a miracle that will probably not happen and spout the famous quotation, 'It's not the winning that matters, it's the taking part'. That's fine if you're just happy to be there but rubbish if you're there to win.

Back in Britain the Fed Cup team was invited to a reception at 10 Downing Street to meet Prime Minister, Maggie Thatcher. It was a most interesting evening. Her husband Dennis was doing the meet-and-greet but Maggie joined the party a little later. She circulated and did the room, going from group to group with consummate ease. Everyone was more than a little in awe of her and she led the conversation, telling us about the decoration of the room and the various paintings hanging on the walls. As someone who follows politics a bit I waited for my chance and then asked a question, knowing she was to visit Poland the following day. 'What are you hoping to achieve at your meetings with General Jaruzelski tomorrow?' I managed to ask. Suddenly, the easy tone changed and she fixed me with the steel blue eyes for which she was famous before immediately switching into lecture mode. It was fantastic and I got a slight insight into what it must have been like to face her across the despatch box at Prime Minister's Question Time in the House of Commons. The Iron Lady would have made a hell of a tennis referee!

My time at the LTA provided much travel and many memorable moments but I didn't wish to be there forever. The shuffles and reshuffles, the endless debates on why British tennis was underachieving, the feeling of frustration that our players weren't seen as being as good as other countries' and above all the personal desire to be independent were all factors. Those outside the system expect those within it to be able to conjure up limitless funds for whatever player or vested interest they personally support, and that was neither possible nor the answer. No one has the magic formula in those circumstances. Also, I now had my wife and young daughter in our north London home and I wanted to be with them each night and not in a foreign hotel room on my own. It was time for my next challenge.

Chapter 14

What It's Like to Be a Coach on the Tour

A coach is a teacher, someone who helps another to become better at whatever the chosen subject is. Anybody that fulfils that role is a coach in my book. It's very wide ranging so it includes all the different sexes, ages and fitness levels that make up coaches on the Tour. So the good news is that we all definitely qualify so far!

Anyone watching sport has spent time listening to amateur 'expert' opinion from the stands. I've certainly had the privilege of sitting or standing alongside many outstanding football coach eccentrics in my time. They were all fully qualified in their own minds, held strong opinions and were convinced that they knew more than the coach of their team that was currently being paid to do the job. Furthermore, they were happy to let that coach have the benefit of their opinion. These views, bellowed from a touchline and heard by all within earshot, are usually just seen as part of the atmosphere. But if that same eccentric gets involved with a team that happens to do well then they're regarded as some kind of guru. There are colourful characters like this in every sport and tennis has its share.

There are also the coaches in the TV studios and commentary boxes. They offer their expert opinion on what players have done or should be doing, usually all with the benefit of 20/20 hindsight. Are they correct? Well, we'll never find out because they'll never have to prove that their theory works. I know from experience here because the only matches I've ever lost have been when I've been on court. I still to this day remain proudly undefeated from the sidelines! That's why I have so much respect for anyone who gets out there and has a go but considerably less for those who prefer to be armchair critics and act as self-appointed judges from the outside.

Out on the Tour there are the younger, active coaches who can still hit a mean ball, can double as a hitting partner for warm-up purposes and are able to demonstrate precisely what they're asking their player to do. They might be a former player themselves and still look good in a tracksuit. Speaking with my official's hat on briefly I can also say that these younger coaches are a nuisance when you're roaming the locker rooms looking for a player you don't know very well. It's embarrassing when you ask the coach if they are your missing player only to be told that they're a coach! Don't laugh – I've done it!

As the years go by these younger coaches start to put on a bit of weight, stop moving around the court and instead stay in one corner when they hit or else feed balls out of a basket. Their experience tells them when they need to get other practice partners in for their own player and now they're well on the way to becoming the off-court coach. These coaches will stand and look on sagely as their player hits with another. They become expert at fielding balls and throwing them to their player when needed but being careful to still carry a racket in case they get mistaken for a ballboy. The occasional pearl of wisdom is offered during breaks in play and they are expected to join in the general chit-chat at the start and finish of each practice session or during drinks breaks.

Naturally, a coach can also be someone who has never played the game. They might simply be a trusted friend who is good company for a player and someone who makes them feel happy and relaxed. Don't underestimate this because life can be tough on Tour and players must find their own way to survive and to thrive. If having a mate along helps then go with it. This also applies to spouses, all family members and any number of others who make up the leading players' entourages. Agents, fitness coaches, physios, psychologists and goodness knows who else might be on the payroll if they can make a difference.

But there is a concern for many coaches. Are they important to the player and do they have any kind of job security? The answers are often not very and not much. How can they justify their existence? Family members have a slightly better chance because it's tough for even the most hard-nosed player to sack a parent. But those employed on a professional basis may only be one bad tournament away from the chop. There aren't too many 25-year mortgages being paid by players for a coach. The competition is fierce and players will regularly change coaches if they think they can do better elsewhere.

All coaches work out a schedule with their player and then commit to a period of time that could just be a trial event, one swing of a tour or something else much longer. They will usually stay in the same hotel, eat and socialise regularly with them, watch all practice and matches and offer what feedback they can in terms of planning and tactics and then at postmortems afterwards. They will scout future opponents, act as a source of encouragement during matches and be around in such close proximity that relationships can easily become strained. Frequently, there's an age gap and that may cause social differences. It's like a marriage in some ways. When it works well it's marvellous but if it goes wrong then there's tension not far behind.

Inevitably, some players are more high maintenance than others. An easy-going nature for both player and coach makes it a lot easier but life's just not like that. The player is ultimately the employer and yet most players are looking to be told what to do by a coach who is using their experience to help. If they don't like the advice and

131

won't act on it then hello problems. Some players are very needy when on court in matches. They look to their player box after every point and expect something back in return. So you see coaches jumping up and down and offering support and encouragement, trying to supply energy to their charge. Is it needed? Well, if the player thinks it is then most entourages will meekly obey.

If a player likes noisy support that's what the coach will likely supply except when it's not wanted in which case they must sit quietly. Trouble is then they might be accused of not caring so a bit of earnest clenching of fists might be the way forward, that is until the chair umpire starts looking for signs of coaching which is a whole other issue. The player will certainly get upset if they get coded for coaching when the coach has done nothing more than offer encouragement! Some players expect and want coaching despite it being illegal so then the coach must try to get their message across without drawing the attention of the officials, because they're certainly watching for it, unless it's being conveniently allowed!

And no one, whether the coach or any support group, should be seen to be enjoying themselves too much on the side of the court. At Davis Cup one year I was one of the supporting team members on the side of the court caught smiling by Buster Mottram during one of his matches. He thought we were laughing at him, which wasn't true, but Paul Hutchins, the captain, warned us to be more careful as Buster was getting upset! When a player gets something in their head it's a problem for all, even if it's imagined.

Off court, coaches quickly get to know the other coaches and gossip, views and ideas will be exchanged with anything useful being stored away for possible use later. As a coach I used to keep extensive notes on all the other players. Whoever my own players would be drawn against I'd go to the notes for anything that might prove useful. I'd also update them at every opportunity with new information. Over time these notes became extensive. All players have certain basic characteristics and there will be obvious strengths and weaknesses that can be quickly noted down. General attitude and reaction to adversity was always of interest to me plus patterns of play that they would favour on big points. This was useful but every match is different and much depends on how competing styles match up against each other. The successful execution of any game plan is also crucial. It's all very well to go into a match knowing what you will try to do but what about when it's not working? There may be a rain break to discuss it but usually a player must work it out alone unless a coach gets involved with some illegal advice.

I never worked under the new rules that now allows the passing of advice to players during matches from the sidelines. As ever, it may work for some but will be another source of potential friction between player and coach if the player doesn't buy into the advice they're receiving. More pressure on the coach I reckon.

Finding ways to motivate your player becomes a very personal thing. There's no one size fits all here. Little targets and goal setting in both practice and matches gives a distraction that can really help. And reward and celebrate when these targets are achieved. As an example I was working with Sarah Loosemore, a very good young player from Britain, at the big Miami event in Key Biscayne in 1991. On our way to and from the player hotel each day we would pass a very nice-looking restaurant that caught Sarah's eye called the Rusty Pelican. She would always comment on it so I said we'd go there to celebrate when she qualified. Not *if* she qualified but when. A few days later the goal was achieved and so we went there before resetting goals for the main draw. It was just a bit of fun, nothing serious, but a lovely little positive distraction and a target for her to focus on.

The power of motivation is very strong once it is accepted and bought into. On a personal level as I first started to play full-time my goals were to play at Wimbledon and for the Davis Cup team. Both were great motivations for me and I was thrilled to achieve them. But perhaps then was the time to reset them and aim higher still. Goals should be achievable but realistic too or you risk them getting lost amongst the inevitable setbacks along the way. Achievable short- and medium-term goals don't prohibit still holding a longer-term dream.

On a much more basic and humorous level one lad allegedly received very powerful motivation at a junior event I played overseas many moons ago. He was dating a local girl and it was the hot romance of the tournament. Rumour had it that he was on a promise. She would sleep with him if he won the tournament! Whether it was true or not I don't know but I do know that he tried as hard as he possibly could, won the tournament and the rest is pure conjecture. Whether his coach knew and approved or not we'll never know!

As a coach you try to provide the player with everything you possibly can to support their performance. But there's the problem – it's their performance and not yours. You're dependant on someone else to provide the proof that you're doing a good job. If they win you feel rewarded but if they lose then you're left thinking what else could I have done? It's out of your control. And what about the situation where you travel internationally, stay away from home, prepare your player and then find they're ill or injured and have to withdraw from the event without even playing? You mop up the mess as best you can. You arrange the doctor or physio appointments, make the revised airline bookings, cancel the hotel and head off to the airport thinking what a frustrating waste of time that was!

Life on the Tour for the coaches is one of much travel and much insecurity. They work hard with their players as best they can but then sit on the sidelines to watch matches, often with a feeling of helplessness as they wait for their player to decide the win or loss. They face the same stats as the players. Half will lose in the first round and only one in eight will feature in the fourth round. Dealing with these stats and keeping the player motivated is a constant test for them all. You feel every loss personally, the turnover is great and it's a hard way to earn a living. But, as with all things to do with pro tennis, success is thrilling and the prospect of achieving more provides them with the hook that keeps them on the Tour. As with caddies on the golf tour they're only there in a supportive role but you'd better believe it – the competition within their ranks is enormous.

Chapter 15
Hurlingham

In some senses leaving the LTA in 1995 and joining the magnificent Hurlingham Club in Fulham, London was like leaving the sport altogether. There were vague similarities in that there were lots of tennis courts set in beautiful parkland gardens but any pretence of aspiring to excellence in terms of tennis standard was pure fantasy. Its excellence lay in different areas. With its riverfront acreage alongside the Thames this private members club oozes exclusivity and is an oasis of tranquillity close to the centre of London.

The large main house is surrounded by manicured and spacious grounds where the various sporting activities take place. Its many attractions and upmarket status mean it has a long waiting list. Though tennis was only a part of the whole operation it had a large and busy programme to keep me busy. Managing the tennis side of things demanded an extension of my past experience but I also had to learn new skills that would prove to be useful in the future. The necessity of becoming computer-literate was simply a matter of spending time and putting in a little effort and in future years this paid dividends as refereeing became very reliant on computerisation. But other things, like learning to deal with committees, was something that required a little more thought and experience.

I had to adapt to working with a committee instead of thinking and acting as the individual you are as a tennis player. Most committees have only two or three people who actually make decisions. Their views are usually the only ones that matter since the rest of the committee are likely to fall into line providing the key people agree. That means that the work done prior to meetings, canvassing support from the actual decision-makers, is the best way to ensure that the committee makes the decisions you feel are right. There is a problem to this in that you can spend much time gaining the support of the important people and just when things are going well their term of office finishes and you have to start again with the successors.

As with most private clubs the vast majority of the members were perfectly nice and reasonable and just enjoyed their time at the club. However, there were also the two per cent who took up far too much of the staff's time in dealing with them. I suggested in jest that we introduce a rule that would have dramatically improved the atmosphere around the club. Every year the members should be allowed to take a vote and vote out the two worst-performing staff members. In return the staff members should also vote to remove the two worst club members. This would have got rid of the worst offenders each year and encouraged everyone else to behave themselves and treat each other with respect. I thought it was a great idea and still believe it would work well in most private clubs! But sadly, it was never going to be introduced. So the grumpy element of members remained together with some underperforming staff who had been there too long and seemed unmotivated but were protected by employment law. Their salaries had grown over the years due to annual inflation rises to the point where they couldn't match their salary if they were to move anywhere else. It's a situation faced by many clubs.

Feeling a bit like a chameleon I stayed for a few years at Hurlingham without ever feeling it was a natural fit for me. It would never be a place for life. In the meantime the naughty side of me bought a wonderful 25-year-old Land Rover that was ex-army and with camouflage colours. I loved to park it next to the Mercedes and BMWs, knowing that it looked a disgrace. It used to puff out black smoke from its exhaust and one day drew a cry from a group of our older ladies, in very upper-crust tones, 'Excuse me, excuse me! We're choking back here!' as I started it up one day. I apologised of course but was chuckling away inside at the whole scene and secretly loving every minute!

Dealing with the difficult members was a good rehearsal for future tricky conversations while refereeing. Very early in my time at the club I walked through the front office where the bookings were taking place with a line of members waiting to reserve their favourite court for the following week. 'Good morning,' I said to everyone and no one in particular as I breezed through. About 20 minutes later came a knock at my door and I went to greet an older man dressed in his tennis whites. 'Hello, Mr Jarrett. Could I have a word please?' 'Yes, come on in,' I replied. 'No, I think outside would be more appropriate,' he said, and so I followed him outside where no one could hear, intrigued.

'A few moments ago you came through the office and said, "Good morning".' 'That's right,' I replied, thinking I was on fairly safe ground so far. 'What you should have said was, "Good morning, Sir Charles",' he continued. Now I'm not often lost for words but this was an occasion when I was. I looked at him for signs that he was pulling my leg or joking in some way but there was no such sign. This man was serious. He was pulling me up for not using a title I didn't even know he had.

Naturally, I got my own back by immediately renaming my closest colleagues Sir Oliver and Lady Polly, and they returned the favour by making me Sir Andrew. We would happily call each other by our new nicknames in His Sirship's hearing and I do hope it didn't totally go over his head. A more serious discussion concluded that he'd wanted to make sure that I, as a new member of staff, wouldn't forget who he was. He was correct even if I felt he might have found a better way of introducing himself! It became a test of my professionalism when making the draws for the various members' tournaments while I was there!

Lady Polly was with me the time we interviewed candidates for a front office role. A tall lad with a strong West Midlands accent walked in wearing a suit that didn't fit too well and it looked like it didn't see too many outings. Craig was his name and he was early for his appointment. Polly wasn't ready so I made him a tea and we chatted for a while during which it soon came out that he was a great lad and we had a mutual love for football. Once Polly arrived we went through the formal side of the interview during which the subject of other sports came up and Polly asked if he supported Coventry City. Craig, in his strong West Midlands accent, immediately came back with, 'Cut me in two and I'm all Sky Blue!' I knew there and then he was someone I could work with. He got the job and proved to be a great character and a fantastic team member!

One of my responsibilities at the club was to referee the club championships each year. Being the Referee at Wimbledon a few years later was a doddle each year compared with this gig. I worked hard on the order of play and produced something that considered all the various problems that many members had given me about their own availability to play. The minute this was posted all the calls started … Lydia can't possibly play at that time because she's got her flute lesson then, or Henry's asthma is playing up and he needs to get a new puffer, or Candice doesn't want to play against her because she doesn't like her. Let me tell you, dealing with the agents of leading players years later was far easier!

One year I arranged for official LTA umpires to come to umpire the finals to give the day something special and different from the norm. The girls' Under 18 singles finalists had probably battled through a draw size of only four or so and featured two friends, let's call them Cynthia Barrington-Smythe and Poppy Super-Model. Cynthia and Poppy went out to Court Six with a proper LTA chair umpire and commenced their match. After an hour or so the chair umpire came to see me. 'Andrew, I've lost my players,' she said. 'What do you mean? What's happened?' I replied. 'They got to a set all, went for a toilet break and haven't returned,' she told me. 'OK, wait here and let's see what's happened,' I said, and went to look for them. They weren't in the changing rooms according to Lady Polly and so I went further afield, finding them both having tea together in the main clubhouse about 200 yards away. 'What are you doing?' I asked them. 'We were feeling a bit tired so thought we'd go for tea and finish off later,' they said. 'Didn't you realise you had a chair umpire who was waiting for you on court?' I asked. 'Oh, sorry. Would she like to join us?' came the reply. You couldn't make it up. I told them to finish off without the umpire and let me have the result later and released the bemused chair umpire from this somewhat uncompetitive match!

I tried hard to get the tennis section to join the 20th century. It wasn't an easy task but we did make a little progress on some fronts even though it was now the 21st century. I would have liked Hurlingham to have become the leading club in the country but it seemed content to settle for much less, a quiet backwater of prim and proper respectability without ambition. It was all so gloriously and yet frustratingly British. Still it did allow me to go home every night rather than be on the road in Jazz's early years. I had to accept that if we could only be one century behind the times then we weren't doing too badly at Hurlingham!

When the call of the real tennis world came again my own journey was to continue. This time it was into the world of officiating. I spent my last couple of years at Hurlingham now just doing a little coaching. I'd stopped the management role because I needed the time required to gain experience in refereeing by working at some lower-level events. As it had been with coaching it was time to serve another different apprenticeship in the industry of tennis.

Part Three
The Officiating Years

Chapter 16

A Telephone Call That Started the Refereeing Journey

If you'd told me when I was a player that one day I'd be a tennis official I simply wouldn't have believed you. Me, an official? I certainly didn't feel like one and it would've seemed ridiculous. Like all players I'd suffered my share of terrible decisions, had a good moan about them and saw officials as a necessary evil on a tennis court. That said, I always appreciated the long hours and the dedication that so many showed and would always go to stop by the referee's office at the end of any event I played just to say thank you. So when it happened it was curious how I came to start a very different path to any I'd previously conceived.

I was at my desk at Hurlingham when Chris Gorringe, the Chief Executive at the All England Club, called to ask if I'd ever considered refereeing. I recounted a story from many years before. Fred Hoyles, the predecessor to Alan Mills at Wimbledon, had drawn me aside one day at Wimbledon when I was still playing to ask the same question. As a result he'd convinced me to sign up to what was then called the Referees' Society. It cost me the princely sum of £5 per year and for that I got a set of accounts sent to me once a year that I promptly binned and thought nothing more of. But it must have sown a seed.

It transpired that the All England Club was starting to look at succession planning for the Referees' Office. Alan was many years into his reign there and could not go on forever. His team of three assistants were also nearing the end of their careers and the danger was that the whole team would age together and cause a problem. The club was worried and wanted to start to get plans in place for the future.

Initially, three of us were invited to spend some time in the Referees' Office during The Championships to see how it all worked. The others were experienced officials and referees and they'd worked at the highest level as chair umpires and knew the world of officiating very well. However, the club liked having a former player as Referee in Alan. They'd been comfortable with him in charge since they felt he understood what it was like to be on court competing under pressure. He was also a member of the club, something also valued since it meant that commitment, loyalty and understanding of the club's position was a given as well.

Alan's Assistant Referees were Tony Gathercole, Jean Sexton and Peter Mornard, backed up by Maureen Paremain who acted as Secretary/PA to Alan and his team. They were all great friends and had been together a long time. I felt privileged to be allowed in on my watching brief. I watched the detail that each went into in their own respective areas and tried to understand the complexities involved with running the greatest tennis event in the world. In some ways, though, it was a throwback to another age. Times were changing but much was still done by hand and computerisation was only starting to be introduced.

Progress made since then has been dramatic. But my role then was to watch and learn and so I mucked in and checked lists and did whatever was asked of me. All four were most generous with their time and they were good company who kindly accepted me as the outsider. None were keen to retire and so they could so easily have regarded me as a threat. The other prospective candidates also did something similar in terms of time in the office around their own commitments and after it was all over for another year more discussions took place.

I must have fitted in with Alan's team enough to encourage the club to support me in starting the long multi-year process of gaining further experience and getting the necessary officiating qualifications. While keeping their options open the club were seeing me as a possible long-term successor to Alan. From my side I was flattered that they would consider me, saw the honour and responsibility of the job but above all thought it was something that I could do and do well. I talked to my wife, Dannie, about the whole project and decided to take the chance and go for it.

Initially, it meant attending a basic refereeing course put on by the LTA and run by Sultan Ganji, a well-known figure to me. He had refereed many tournaments that I'd played in over the years and it seemed funny to now be learning new skills from him and not just checking the time of my next match. Sultan was a vastly experienced referee and one who had also travelled widely. He told many a tale when you could get him chatting and his enthusiasm for refereeing and for life was infectious.

Armed with my basic refereeing qualification I then started working at local junior events, learning very quickly along the way that while players were fine to deal with it was the parents, coaches and general hangers-on that usually caused the most problems. I got used to the queries, the complaints and dealing with the occasional outburst of bad behaviour, drawing on my own past experience of what it had been like to be a young player trying to make their way in the sometimes highly charged atmosphere of junior tennis. Competitive tennis is competitive no matter what the level. Some people deal with competition well and others don't. Some think they have the answers when they clearly have little idea. Nearly all think the world is stacked against them and many expect the referee to put things right! It's life, both good and bad.

Two lads played out a badly behaved match in Milton Keynes in my earliest refereeing days. There was no chair umpire and I ended up watching it closely from the sidelines to discourage further problems, going on court a couple of times because of dodgy line calls. When it finally finished and they walked up to the net to shake hands I was glad it was over. But then the winner decided against the traditional shake of hands, instead pushing the loser away with enough force to send him staggering back. I quickly went on court again to separate the two of them and sent each to their coach or parents.

Then came my introduction to the world of writing reports in these situations. The loser was out because he lost. The winner was also now out because I defaulted him from the tournament. This meant the player due to play the winner in the next round now had a walkover into the following round. All concerned needed to be spoken to, to explain my decision, and then the telephone calls made and reports filed to make sure that everything was suitably documented. You must make these kinds of decisions very quickly and you'd better get them right because there are plenty ready to challenge and offer an alternative opinion.

I was also being sent out to watch experienced referees at work at various low-level professional events and this proved to be very useful. I worked the busy qualifying and start of the main draws, seeing and helping with all the issues that arise at the start of a tournament week. Events usually become straightforward once the sign-ins have taken place, the entries have been decided, the draws have been made and the first rounds have been played. Seeing how vastly different characters handled the same rules and particularly the way they each dealt with the players was much more interesting to me than reading and learning rule books.

On this programme I shadowed Alan Mills, Tom Kinloch, Carl Baldwin and Sultan Ganji. Some were very strong on the computer technology side, others had good people skills, but I also saw weakness on rules issues. I was very keen to become 'perfect' on rules and would read and analyse the rules to tedium. I was very aware of a fact that had quickly become apparent to me. Players don't know the rules and nor do coaches. Here was I, after so many years as a professional player and coach, having to read and understand the rules for the first time. It made me a very inquisitive assistant to my experienced referees as I quizzed them about every aspect of the rules and how they did things. I learned a lot and was so grateful to them all.

Partly because of my backing from the All England Club, partly because LTA Officiating might have been intrigued at the idea of a former player getting involved and partly because I did (most of the time at least) know what I was doing, I was put forward for the next examination level for refereeing. This was the White Badge course administered by the International Tennis Federation, which was, for me, in Luxembourg. I was surprisingly nervous about this since I had everything to lose and little to gain. I was expected to pass, had Wimbledon backing and desperately needed to avoid screwing it up.

When I got there I immediately teamed up with Angie Woolcock, a lovely Aussie girl who I knew from the circuit and who was herself being promoted by the WTA. She was under the same pressure to do well and so we formed a common bond, studied together and supported each other through the three-day experience. It was a relief to pass and we always remembered our shared time when we subsequently met up. For Angie it was to be a truly shocking story. She quickly progressed through the ranks of the WTA, becoming a very capable official to match the fabulous human being she always was. But then the unthinkable happened and she became ill with the debilitating illness of motor neurone disease. When she subsequently died I cried along with the rest of the tennis world. What a dreadful loss to her husband, family and all her many friends.

The events in Luxembourg gave me a badge and the opportunity to upgrade the events I was working at to the lowest level of professional tennis, ITF futures and circuit events. I was on the way.

Chapter 17
Starting to Referee International Events

My new White Badge in those days meant that I could work some events that today would not be allowed. Standards change and supposedly improve and you would now require a full international badge. I hadn't reached that stage yet.

I worked some small women's $10,000 events including one in Frinton, a sleepy little town on the Essex coast of England. I'd played there in the past and knew it was a members' club where they had good grass courts but little in terms of entertainment or social life outside of club activities. Julie Piper from the LTA was the designated tournament director, Barbara Lloyd the chief of umpires and there were some British chair umpires that I knew, though not well. All would be intrigued to see how the new boy would do.

As it transpired it all worked out well but one of the best things about the week was working with Tony Little. He was a stick-thin, chain-smoking Londoner with a wonderful sense of humour and was one of the chair umpires for the week. He was always entertaining and could appreciate life's varieties to the point where the tennis officiating world always regarded him with more than a little nervousness. During the week I was able to witness a couple of Tony classics. First, he was umpiring a match involving a Dutch girl, Suzanne Van Hartingsveldt, who was getting a bit fed up with some of Tony's calls. At 4-3, second set she walked towards the chair to change ends, looked up at Tony and gave him a long mouthful of Dutch. Quick as a flash Tony responded, 'Code violation, audible obscenity. Warning, Miss Van Hartingsveldt'. 'What did I say? You don't understand Dutch!' she said. To which came maybe the best (though possibly wrong!) response I've ever heard. 'I don't know, darling, but you sure as hell weren't inviting me out for a beer!' They both then had a good laugh about it as she towelled down and got ready to continue. It was marvellous.

Later in the week Tony was chairing a women's singles semi-final involving two long-forgotten players playing an unmemorable match. A small crowd of disinterested spectators were watching in complete silence, some possibly asleep. Finally, out of nowhere came a great point. Both players conspired for one point only to produce tennis from the top drawer in the middle of a match of complete mediocrity. Tony announced the score then turned around in his chair to address the small silent handful. 'Come on,' he said, 'it doesn't get any better than that!' Sometime later, Tony met his officiating end after another injudicious comment that didn't find such forgiving ears. The harsh world of political correctness brought its views to the discussion and tennis lost a great character. I missed him around the tennis world and we were the poorer for his departure.

After a few international events based in Britain I unexpectedly got a call from the ITF asking if I was available at very short notice to work three small men's events in January 2003 in India. Now any up-and-coming official is keen to add greater experience to their portfolio in the (likely mistaken) belief that if you work and do a good job you will be offered more work in the future and you can progress your career. Later, I was to realise that there is little advance thinking in terms of career planning and that it was far more likely that they'd been left in the shit by a late withdrawal and were desperately trying to find any replacement to fill the gap at all. Certainly, I was keen to get on in the refereeing world and so I happily accepted the offer which was so early in the new year it nearly interrupted New Year's Eve with my young family. I'm glad I did because it turned out to be the most rewarding refereeing I ever did.

It started inauspiciously as I arrived at Heathrow only to find myself denied boarding as I didn't have a visa for India. I'd played in India many years before without the need for such a trifling nuisance but hadn't realised it had changed. Not an impressive start, Jarrett! Twenty-four hours later, more than a few quid lighter and now with a passport containing an impressive-looking stamp I boarded my flight for Delhi and then a subsequent connection to Lucknow. There I was met and taken to my hotel in readiness for the start of the event the following day. It was a men's futures event with the minimum level of $10,000 prize money – not much when you realise that is the total and it's going to be split between 32 singles players for a start. No one gets wealthy at these events.

When I arrived at the rather 'Last Days of The Raj'-type club I was delighted to meet up with Ali Katebi. Ali is an Iranian and a very good chair umpire who had been designated for the three-week circuit. Little did we know at that early stage that he and I were to become what we have since recognised as 'Indian brothers' as it was the two of us working together who somehow managed to keep the whole chaotic show on the road. I'd read through the fact sheet on the flight and so when I met the local tournament director I checked some basic details about the first event. 'I can see the four courts here,' I started while gesturing to those I could see surrounding the clubhouse, 'but where is the fifth court mentioned on the fact sheet?' 'Oh no, we only have four,' he replied. 'Ah, OK, and I notice that we're due to start at 10am each day since we have a 64 qualifying, so what time is darkness?' 'Well, it's usually a bit too wet in the morning to start at 10am so it's more like 11am and then it gets dark at 5.30pm most nights,' came the reply. I was doing some mental arithmetic and quickly realised that we had no chance to play the qualifying in the two days allocated for it. In the event it turned out to be Tuesday night before we finished the qualifying, and that was without any rain!

Meanwhile, I had asked for an officials meeting 30 minutes before the start of play. At the given time there were only two people present, Ali and I. Ten minutes before play was due to commence two more chair umpires arrived followed bang on start time by a third. Now we could at least start the matches even though I'd never met these guys before! Then as the matches were on court warming up prior to starting I could see some rather odd-looking people making their own way on to the courts and taking up positions vaguely on lines. Apparently, I had linesmen as well even though they were dressed in a very strange assortment of clothes and one didn't have any shoes on at all!

I settled back to watch some of the next few minutes of play and it wasn't long before I realised that here was enough entertainment to keep me amused for a week. Only trouble was it was at the chaotic end of acceptable and I was meant to be getting it to look a little like professional tennis for the ragbag of players that had travelled to play these events from various countries. Ali was soon frustrated by it all and at the end of his first set he called all the line umpires on his court up to his umpire's chair at the net. 'Please. Just go away!' he said. 'Just go somewhere else!' With that he proceeded to umpire the rest of the match on his own since that was far preferable. Somehow or other we muddled our way through the week and by the Friday it was time to leave Ali to finish the Lucknow event while I went back to New Delhi to start the second. Lucknow had been held on grass, New Delhi was to be on hard courts and the final week would be up in Assam, where the tea comes from, on clay courts. Now it probably wouldn't happen at any level in the world but then it was India, and pro tennis at its lowest level, and so it was OK!

New Delhi provided some riches in that we suddenly had lots of courts to use and it was also the home of the All India Tennis Association. That meant it had offices there and facilities that seemed good in theory but in practice things just didn't quite work out as they should. One downside was that it had rooms on site which meant they could save on my hotel room by housing me there on site. I expect that the young lads that arrived for National Training might have found it to be OK but I was a pampered bloke that had given up my own home in Britain for a few weeks to be put in a small basic room that had the necessities but little more. Apparently, necessities didn't include heating and it was absolutely freezing. I spent an uncomfortable night wearing all the clothes I had with me and in the morning (my birthday as well!) I decided that no way was I going to spend a second night in that room so I checked myself into a very comfortable hotel a short distance away. I explained to the organisers that they could either pay for my room or else I would charge the ITF, or if they wouldn't pay then I was going to pay for it myself. Whatever happened I wasn't staying in their guest rooms again. They paid.

There was a lovely ending to this story in that at the end of that day I went to my new comfortable hotel and checked in at reception. I never like to advertise things like birthdays outside of my immediate family and so it had been a standard day at the office, albeit a rather exotic Indian one. As the delightful girl on the reception desk looked through my passport as she was checking me in she suddenly looked up, gave me a beaming smile and said, 'Can I wish you a very happy birthday, Mr Jarrett?' It was a lovely moment and very much appreciated after all that had happened earlier that day.

The final week of this mini-circuit took place in a remote part of India up between Bangladesh and China in a city called Jorhat. As soon as we landed it was apparent that mobile phone signals were interrupted, supposedly due to security. There was a big police and army presence and the excuse was that these borderlands with China were in need of some muscle to deter the rather large neighbour from indulging in any unpleasantness.

It was tea country up there and Ali and I found we were housed in a tea plantation, a rambling old property surrounded by fields in the middle of nowhere and without any other guests whatsoever. We had a cook and a cleaner to look after us and we each had a room that would have comfortably held a medium-sized wedding reception. Right in the middle of the room was a bed covered by a large mosquito net but very little else apart from a small dressing table. We felt both grand and vaguely ridiculous at the same time!

Meanwhile, back at the tennis club we had a sorry tale from a Russian player who had gone through a terrible experience in getting to the qualifying sign-in. His plane had been cancelled and so he'd taken a small plane to another airport about six hours' drive away from Jorhat. Arriving there without any local currency he'd taken a taxi through the night across a mountain-pass road with death-defying drops and a driver who apparently welcomed meeting his maker at every turn. When he'd got to the hotel it was closed for the night and so the taxi driver had waited with him for it to open so that he could get his money. Then the hotel refused to let him check in and so he'd had to wait all morning until his room was ready. Funny how that doesn't seem to happen to Murray or Djokovic, isn't it? It's not always an easy life for young players and you can understand why their first points, enough prize money to eat and reach the next tournament and an improved ranking are huge in their lives.

The Jorhat tournament promoter was very proud of his event. It was the first professional tennis tournament ever held in his city and the courts had been relaid especially. He also took me out after dark to show off the new floodlights that had been constructed. Out came his light meter to show how they met professional standards and were aligned correctly so each court had an even distribution of light. Unfortunately, it was still all dependent on the local electricity grid, which went down on a regular basis. So it was no great surprise on the first day when we used the new lights to finish off a long match that had reached darkness on another court that they all went off due to a power cut and so were rendered useless. Oh well, it was a nice try and caused us all a wry smile!

Jorhat amused and challenged me. First, there was little or no internet. It was before the days of wireless and so the old familiar dial-up noise went over and over again as it tried to connect without success. I had to take a car ride downtown every evening along dirt roads since there were no paved roads in Jorhat at that time. The city centre was lit up after dark by strings of single bulbs suspended from the shop fronts and market stalls that lined the roads. There was an internet café of sorts there and I would spend an hour or so trying to get the results back to London. International phone calls were also something to be treasured since the phone lines rarely worked. That meant that getting any updated entry lists or withdrawals was difficult to say the least. But you know what? It was fun. We made the best of everything and, by and large, the players appreciated the fact that you were doing the best you could with what we had.

It's important to be honest and to keep players in touch with regular updates. Players like being spoken to as regular human beings without any unnecessary dressing. Keep things simple; don't exaggerate or try to be clever. And cut out the pomposity. If you try to play the high-and-mighty official who's there to impose then you get the same reaction that I myself would have given. Call people by name, treat them decently and most people will react in a positive way most of the time.

The tournament director had clearly read the rule book and knew that medical backup was needed. But even I was impressed by the set-up he had there. It looked like something out of the American hit comedy series M*A*S*H. It was a tent alongside one of the courts and inside was a long table behind which were seated two nurses in full nurse uniform and little red crosses decorating the front of the tent. During one of the qualifying matches one of the players requested a trainer on court. I was standing in front of him and saw the scene before he did. I had to warn him that the medical treatment he was about to get was probably a little different to anything he'd seen before in tennis. A little old lady, in full nurse uniform, came on to court clutching a little medical-supply bag in one hand. I tried not to laugh as he explained his problem and she listened attentively before giving him an aspirin. It was so far removed from anything remotely athletic but done in such a kindly, gentle way that you couldn't possibly take offence or get upset. Even the players just saw it as another part of 'Incredible India'.

On the day of the finals there was a crowd to watch. I wasn't sure where they'd all come from because it had been relatively sparse during the week but the little stand was full and the men's singles was nearing its completion. The tournament director came into my office to say, 'Andrew, the presentation ceremony will take place after the match ends and we have some local dancers who will perform as part of it. It would be wonderful if you, as the ITF supervisor, were to join in with them'. I was horrified. I am the epitome of 'dad dancing' and wanted no part of this but it was impossible to escape. It would have been too rude to have refused. And so it was that I came to join the exotic Indian dancers in front of a few hundred people as they wiggled around to the noise made by the various strange instruments their mates were playing at the same time. Thank goodness no one captured it for posterity!

The whole India trip was wild and bore little resemblance to top-level professional tennis but it was also a wonderful experience. I wouldn't have missed it and it was, in many ways, the most challenging and enjoyable refereeing I ever did. The rule book might as well have been thrown away. Ali and I ran the events as closely as we could to what was expected but it was mixed with some Indian magic and was certainly somewhere that helped me learn the trade of becoming a referee.

Greece was another slightly unexpected place to be refereeing low-level pro events. I went out to the lovely Greek island of Syros and also to Kalamata in 2004 for another couple of men's events there. Syros would have been even better but for the cold wind that blew across the island. It was Easter time and so the full effect of the hot Greek sun was yet to be felt. My wife Dannie earned her keep there by trotting out to take care of the hardy band of chair umpires who worked all day with barely any rest. She would take hot coffees to them and check that they weren't suffering from hypothermia. This event was amazing in that we had three of us working there who were to officiate in Wimbledon finals only a few years later. Eva Asderaki, herself Greek, was already clearly destined for better things and she was able to help those of us from other countries to learn some of the more obvious Greek swear words to listen out for from the local players. James Keothavong from Britain was also learning his trade and would later go on to Grand Slam finals and become one of the best umpires in the world.

The Syros event was also memorable for the time when the tournament director, a larger-than-life character, produced some tennis balls that weren't legal. They weren't on the official list of balls but he must have got a deal on them so I expect they were either free or very cheap. Sadly, they deteriorated quickly to become a very poor ball indeed. I'd previously called off in Athens on the way to Syros to pay a visit to the Athens Olympic tennis site. They were holding a test event there and I could see first hand how unprepared the site was for a major event. It's come as no surprise to hear that it's now largely overgrown and abandoned. What a waste. But I knew they might be a source of balls to replace the disastrous ones we had on site. In the meantime we had to play on since we were on an island and they couldn't arrive quickly. There wasn't time to wait until they did. So we became a very rare event – one that played with ball changes at seven and then nine games in a men's $10,000 event. The tournament director was furious and barely spoke to me afterwards. Too bad.

Another event linked to these in Greece was a similar-sized one in Cyprus. However, Cyprus had a local hero in Marcos Baghdatis who played just to support the event in his home country even though his standing in the tennis world was way beyond this level. They had the dream final there as Marcos came through to play Konstantinos Economidis, the exotically named leading Greek player at the time. The little stadium court there was pretty full and it made for a great local tennis occasion. Marcos won, to the delight of the locals, but the highlight for me was seeing a young child becoming a distraction in the stands. I first heard the disturbance and worried that we might have to have the child removed. I needn't have worried. It turned out to be a relative of Marcos who was calling out to him. Then came the best bit. Rather than get upset about it Marcos, and Konstantinos, would call and talk back and it was all played in a thoroughly agreeable, understanding, South European, relaxed fashion. It was marvellous and a credit to both players.

Before leaving some of the early events I have to mention Ireland and the Ladies' Irish Open held at Castleknock. I refereed there for a few years and got to meet and work with Des Allen, the CEO of Irish tennis, and his lovely assistant Aileen. Between them they seemed to run Irish tennis on a shoestring but it was delightful for all that. A handful of volunteers helped out in different roles and somehow Ireland played its part very well amongst the tennis nations of the world.

Castleknock itself was the friendliest of clubs. Smiling faces and very adequate facilities greeted the players who were all made to feel welcome. The courts themselves were of the dreadful synthetic grass variety, an absolutely shocking surface on which to play quality tennis but from a refereeing point of view they were a godsend. When it began to drizzle or even rain quite heavily nobody would dream of trying to come off court. Certainly, the locals were used to these conditions and so the other international players were almost shamed into doing the same. It took a torrential downpour to stop play.

Leading up to the event was an ITF junior tournament, also in Ireland but some hours away from Dublin. On the afternoon of the sign-in for the qualifying I received a most unusual phone call. It came from a Croatian girl who was en route but had no chance of making the deadline for the sign-in. 'Please sign me in by phone. I'm on the way and will be there as soon as I can,' she implored. I politely explained that wasn't allowed and that she would have to hope that the tournament would take pity on her case and offer her a wild card, knowing that was highly unlikely to happen. 'But please,' she continued, 'my sponsor won't understand and I have to play the event with you. It's the only reason I've played the junior event and I've been delayed but am definitely coming. I'll be there as soon as I can.' Once again I turned her down and then came the final plea: 'Andrew, please, you must understand. I will do anything to get into the draw. Anything at all'. At this point I got a bit worried so tried to inject some humour by saying, 'I'm sure you don't mean that', only to be interrupted quickly by, 'Yes, I do mean anything at all!' I was now concerned enough to end the call as quickly as I could and related the story to Des Allen. I asked him and Aileen to be there at the time we anticipated the girl's arrival on site in order to be present and to witness whatever might then be said. I also took the precaution of phoning Dannie to tell her what had happened and that I had also informed Des and Aileen. As it turned out the precautions weren't needed and nothing more was said when the girl arrived. She didn't get a wild card, didn't play the event and had to satisfy herself with entry to the doubles for which there was no problem.

In many ways these small events are far more enjoyable than the big ones. There's little or no money to warp the senses and those playing are fuelled by either a genuine love of the sport and a desire to be the best they can be or else they have ulterior motives such as the wish to travel. There are quite a few what I call tennis tourists out there. They will use the facilities of professional tennis to see the world and to gain some life experience before moving on to something a little more profitable later. No harm in that and it does produce some interesting characters along the way. As a referee you get to deal directly with the players since the coaches, agents and general hangers-on have no umbilical cord feeding them so they tend not to exist at this level.

Back in England there were various ITF futures events in places such as Wrexham, Bath, Glasgow, Edinburgh, Bournemouth,

Sheffield, Swansea, Sunderland and Newcastle. I used to enjoy the north-east of England events in particular. It's a part of the country that I love to visit. The people are so friendly and have a great sense of humour and love of life. One local lad, Adam Barraclough, was well known to me through connections with the Rushby family in Derbyshire and I also knew of his great love for Sunderland FC, his local football team. He thought nothing of travelling the length and breadth of the country to follow the Black Cats. He'd signed in for the qualifying and he called me to find out when his match was. While I was talking I noticed there was something strange about the call; it didn't sound local. So I asked him where he was and was surprised when he replied that he was in Derby. 'Why are you in Derby?' I asked. 'I'm here to support a mate of mine who got arrested and his case is heard today in court.' This wasn't the answer I expected. 'What did he do?' 'Well,' he replied, 'a few weeks ago I was with him at Derby for the match with Sunderland and he was given a couple of warnings by the Derby stewards about standing up during the match. He was then given a third and final warning but then there was a chant, "Stand up if you hate the Mags"' (the Mags meaning Magpies or Newcastle, the hated local rivals of Sunderland). 'Well, of course he had to, didn't he?' Being a football fan I could just imagine this situation and understand the powerful logic of this tribal argument. I only hoped that the judge was also a fan!

Chapter 18
The Officiating World

If you've decided that you're unlikely to make it as a pro player, can't see a way into the coaching world, don't have the financial muscle to set up a new tour and still want to get involved with professional tennis how about becoming an official? After all most countries are crying out for those willing to take the plunge into this particular area of the sport.

First off, it's probably worth explaining that tennis officials are themselves split into different disciplines. There are line umpires who call the lines, chair umpires who manage the matches and who can overrule the line umpires, chief umpires who organise the teams of line umpires and supervisors/referees who oversee it all, making the draws, deciding the orders of play, fining the bad boys and girls and managing the whole tennis side of an event.

The officiating world in professional tennis is little understood. Basically, no one really cares about it except for the officials themselves whose very lives it, in some cases, takes over. Meanwhile, the rest of the tennis world doesn't understand what goes on, has little respect for the men and women who actually make the calls and would really rather they all went away completely, except for the fact that officials are needed to allow the sport to take place since professional players can't always be trusted not to take advantage if left to themselves!

As long as they get calls right officials usually stay out of trouble. When that happens they're ignored and the media writes about the game and not about the player (usually after he or she has lost) complaining about bad umpiring. You'll never see an opposing view put forward either because officials are not allowed to comment. So since they are unchallenged only the player's view will get airtime.

In recent years the advent of electronic line calling (ELC) has meant that we now know that, on those calls challenged (which are only the close ones by definition), the officials are right two thirds of the time. So the players only get it correct in one out of three situations when there is a good chance they'd have grumbled at the official for ruling against them. If ELC had been around in the days of McEnroe then it would have changed many of the abusive conversations he had. 'You cannot be serious' may have been followed by, 'I certainly am, and since we can all see you were wrong by the length of your d**k you'll have to admit that I was right, despite it being a very, very close call'! Well, perhaps not quite like that but you get the idea.

As ELC has developed it's now being used to call all the lines at many major events. It means that you only need a chair umpire and no line umpires at tournaments using this system. With no line decisions to make there are no challenges any more and so the responsibilities of the chair umpire have reduced accordingly. Some fans will miss the confrontations but it's progress and controversy will just move to the shot clock and code of conduct judgments. Players will always find reasons to get upset!

ELC or not the officials still have to pass the judgment of the players since both the men's and women's Tours have their own officiating departments. Ultimately, these are employed by the players themselves and so it's in the interests of the officials to have a good relationship with the players if they want to work. Serena Williams took exception to Eva Asderaki, who was probably the finest female chair umpire in the world at the time, over various on-court issues. She decided that she didn't want Eva in the chair for her matches and the WTA allowed this by keeping them apart. Since Serena was regularly involved in finals it meant that the players, the tournaments, the spectators and the TV audience were prevented from seeing the best official in charge of the most important match of the week. The tennis hierarchy gave in to the player. That's just wrong on so many counts. It didn't matter that players are regularly heard on worldwide television using language that if used by any official would have guaranteed they never worked again. That's double standards.

The Aussie Open in 2022 saw an amusing example. One men's semi-final featured Daniil Medvedev from Russia against Stefanos Tsitsipas from Greece. At one point the Russian went mad with the chair umpire claiming that the Greek was being coached by his dad. Funnily enough it was all Greek to virtually everyone in the stadium. So the Spanish chair umpire contacted the Swiss supervisor who arranged for a non-working Greek chair umpire (the same Eva Asderaki) to go and sit near enough to hear what was being said. The Greek heard the Greek, told the Swiss, who told the Spaniard, who issued the code violation for coaching. Now that's joined-up officiating using multiple resources. Having been coached Tsitsipas then proceeded to lose quickly soon afterwards so it makes you wonder how good the coaching was in the first place! The Greeks knew who was responsible for them being caught so I'm guessing that their next meeting with Eva behind the scenes might have been a bit awkward.

Everyone wants a quiet life and because the media will create a story when there isn't one it's far easier to keep the players quiet by merely granting their demand even when it's wrong and not in the sport's interest. The Grand Slams and the Davis and Fed Cups operate outside of the Tours and, surprise, surprise, this means different officiating. The Slams are independent and so can run their own affairs but the ITF, who are linked to the Slams, regard them as being a part of their empire and try to influence through their officiating department. This particular empire also administers the world grading system of officials, albeit with some limited support of the Tours. This is useful for the Tours since they don't have the considerable hassle involved in organising officiating schools around the world but they end up with a steady supply of new officials trained, suitably graded and ready to be abused around the world.

So to summarise, for those who haven't lost the will to live already, there are three different officiating organisations that run officiating in professional tennis. They all pay lip service to getting on but then go their own separate ways as they fight hard to protect their own patches. As a former player I don't get this approach. It's a terrible legacy of when tennis went open and the Tours set up in competition to the federation-led circuit administered by the ITF. As a young player I dreamed of playing in the finals of the big events around the world. It was my dream and it's possible. But if you're a young official you can dream of being the chair umpire in the big finals but as you climb the slippery pole you come to realise that the professional tennis world is carved up into those with ATP, WTA or ITF influence and you will only work the finals of the events to which you have signed your allegiance to with only rare exceptions. The repercussions of this are great. Everyone loses but they don't necessarily realise it. The officials themselves have their personal horizons cut by two thirds and the spectators, the tournaments and the players are subjected to secondary officials at the top events and not the best in the world as they must surely expect and deserve.

The atmosphere behind the scenes, with officials jostling for position to be awarded the plum matches, is not always healthy. Those in charge of their own empire are fiercely protective of their positions and all regard their own group as being the best. Working officials make officiating selections and frequently select themselves for the main roles and the ones they wish to have in what is a blatant conflict of interest. They're not working for the common good of the sport. Some are close to retirement age and have no desire to change the system, while underneath them young officials get fed up with the lack of opportunity due to the three cartels that operate and so leave to pursue something else.

Even within the sport most don't realise this situation exists. It can lead to amusing moments, though. Like the time a male player showed his ignorance of the system when he had a right go at a female chair umpire at a Grand Slam event. 'You're a disgrace to the ATP!' he raged, not realising he was revealing his own lack of understanding. The chair umpire in question was contracted to the WTA, working at an ITF-linked event and had nothing at all to do with the ATP.

The officials themselves are a very diverse bunch. They come from a wide variety of backgrounds and bring many surprising skills that only become apparent on closer examination. John Parry, for example, is a retired Parachute Regiment instructor (that's special forces) with a zillion great stories to tell of his dealings with some of the toughest fighting men in the world. Some young smart-arse tennis player isn't going to make much impression on him. So many of the international officials are excellent and dedicated to their work with few exceptions. There aren't many traffic wardens or groupies who just want to get a great seat close up to watch their tennis heroes play!

One problem that exists is that of attracting younger officials into the sport. Age discrimination laws mean that it's tough to exclude older officials even when a younger image is preferred. The United States is foremost in this. Because they've now worked 147 years at the US Open they have greater experience than the youngster who's starting out and hasn't been there yet. It doesn't matter that the bloke with 147 years of experience has declining faculties because to exclude him would be to discriminate against those people. Of course, it's not as bad as that but you get my point. The US Open has people looking over the selections for chair umpires checking these things. They produced a racist document with a complete breakdown of the racial profile of every chair umpire. They wanted to ensure that each grouping had fair representation on the show courts and were split fairly on men's and women's matches. There was little concern on their part as to whether an official was suitable for a particular match. 2018 saw the insistence of appointing a female chair umpire for the men's final and a male umpire for the women's final. It didn't matter what the best thing to do was as long as it ticked the politically correct box.

I always wanted the best officials to do the top matches. I didn't see black, white, Asian, Hispanic, gay, straight, abled, disabled, etc. I just saw officials. I didn't care whether they came from the ATP, the WTA, the ITF or were independent. They were appointed solely on merit. If that makes me sexist or racist then I plead guilty as charged. To do anything different is just politically correct nonsense in my opinion!

A big issue is women chairing men's matches and to a much lesser extent the other way around. Historically, there were few women officials in comparison to men and so it was rare for the top men to see a woman umpiring their matches. Now it happens on a regular basis so it's less of a surprise. But if we're honest there are some male players out there who can be difficult, will react to anything and perhaps come from less-enlightened backgrounds. So now you have to be clever. Putting anything other than the top female officials on matches involving such players, particularly ones on courts without ELC, is asking for a problem. The US Open did it with Fabio Fognini in 2017 when he was defaulted from the doubles event and given a major offence charge after his first-round singles. What Fabio did was wrong. He used particularly offensive words when addressing the female umpire and he paid a high price. But you know what? He wasn't the only one who got it wrong because it was a poor chair assignment. It wasn't fair to that chair umpire to be put in the firing line either. A problem pre-empted is one that never happens.

Fortunately, there are many great officials both in the work they do and as people. They do their work quietly under the radar for the most part. If they do a perfect job no one will notice them. If they get it wrong then it's exposed by cameras and commented on by the world. It's tough and they are undervalued. It's a pity the system they operate under is broken and nothing like one you would put together if you started afresh. The fact that the leading official within the sport's governing body, the ITF, was investigated in a five-month inquiry by a leading independent QC, was found guilty of 'abuse of power' and given a 12-month suspension in 2022 does little to reassure the outside world that the system is anything but grossly flawed. The fact that the same official was then reintroduced (after the initial fuss had died down) back into a position of influence showed a depressing lack of understanding and willingness to address the fundamental flaws in the system. It was a real kick in the teeth for that most important word for officiating, integrity. But there's little desire amongst those in charge to make the much-needed changes.

I saw it all when working at the ITF, as Chief of Officiating. A completely new independent officiating organisation to service the needs of all professional tennis is needed. It could supply the officials to all pro events around the world and also manage their training and development process. Funded by all the major organisations and administered by suitably qualified people it would take the party politics out of tennis officiating. It would work for the betterment of the sport and not themselves. Is it likely to happen anytime soon? I'm not holding my breath!

Chapter 19

Working as a Tennis Civil Servant

It's fair to say that nobody much likes governing bodies. Whatever the colour of the government there are plenty of people on the outside who think they know how the country should be run and are happy to offer an opinion. The same is true of sporting governing bodies and I worked for two of them, the Lawn Tennis Association and the International Tennis Federation. Broadly speaking, the LTA run tennis in Britain while being affiliated to the ITF who (supposedly) run tennis around the world. Both are neighbours in south-west London in Roehampton, which is also the site for the Wimbledon qualifying. Convenient, isn't it?!

The LTA is fortunate to have a significant amount to spend when administering the sport in Britain. This income is the envy of just about every other national federation in the world. But having money to spend and producing success are two different things and the LTA has found that over successive decades. Even when the occasional world-class player has emerged they have been reluctant to give the LTA much credit for it. The fact is that tennis is an individual sport and the sooner a player realises this, and doesn't rely on outsiders, then the more likely they are to achieve their goals.

Scott Lloyd, son of one of my old doubles partners David, is the current CEO at the LTA and appears to be quietly overseeing some positive change. Though facing many challenges British tennis is enjoying improvement with notable international successes raising confidence and expectation levels. Belief is a huge motivator and there are encouraging signs that the underperforming juggernaut is finally steering a better path. But for many years it wasn't looking rosy and survival, rather than progress, was the impression given.

The consistent winners of the past several decades were those employed in senior positions as the LTA set about producing world-class players. Those charged with heading up the organisation plus some high-profile coaches in National Training reaped the rewards with high salaries. But coaches are dependent on the players they work with even more than the players are dependent on the coaches. If Pep Guardiola was appointed manager of Scunthorpe United and took them to the Premier League then I'd be far more impressed than if he won three successive titles with a mega-millions club. That's why I was always more impressed with Brian Clough's success than Alex Ferguson's.

Player development has always been important for the LTA and so they appointed people with demonstrated success overseas. The feeling given was that British coaches lacked international experience and were therefore not as good. The overseas coaches came and worked hard with the young British talent that was probably not world-class potential in the first place, won the lottery and then departed, leaving British tennis no better off. The rest of the world scratched their heads in amazement and wondered how they could grab themselves a ticket on the LTA gravy train. However, the appointment of the Scot Leon Smith has been a welcome and refreshing change and his determined, common-sense, can-do approach sets a great example to all the players. The much more positive environment that now permeates through British tennis is partly a result of his influence. Let's hope worthy British coaches continue to get their chance because they need encouragement to believe they can also be the best in the business too.

For many years middle-ranking staff at the LTA had to make regular readjustments every time a new regime came into being. An initial consultation process would take place followed by the announcement of a new five-year plan that looked remarkably similar to previous ones with priorities that reminded those old enough that the big wheel had come full circle once again. New people would arrive, the existing people would shuffle around to accommodate them, some would leave, the initial honeymoon period would end, the pressure for success would mount, the scapegoat would leave or be fired and the cycle would repeat again.

Meanwhile, the numbers employed at the LTA steadily grew and a state-of-the-art facility was built at Roehampton to house them all. Experts in every possible discipline were hired including those needed to ensure that all the relevant guidelines on best practice could be followed to the letter. But this magnificent structure also included beautiful indoor and outdoor courts together with all the backup facilities such as gyms, treatment rooms, etc. as the LTA left no stone unturned in the pursuit of excellence. It's a great facility to have but it needs to be maintained at a large cost. The nation's top players can only use it sporadically since they will be competing overseas much of the time while the younger developing players will naturally spend most of their time growing up in their regions. The offices are full but there remains the challenge of maximising the usage of the beautiful asset.

Despite everything they do most are reluctant to give the LTA much credit. I sometimes think that if nine of the top ten players in the world were British there would be those who would simply claim it was a disgrace that it wasn't all ten! It's a thankless task. Andy Murray came through to superstardom and people believed it was because he was based in Spain and got out of the system. A small crop of Scottish lads came through together at about the time the NTC (National Tennis Centre) was finished in Roehampton and suddenly the focus of British tennis was north of the border and not south-west London! Supporting those that are willing to help themselves is the goal but how you do that is always open to debate. As in national government as soon as decisions are made those outside will criticise, and it has always been that way.

When I worked at the LTA it was during my coaching period and so I was away from the headquarters for most of the time working with players. That suited me fine as I've never been one for office life and all the politics that often come with it. I see those who dedicate decades making the same commute to the same office doing the same work and applaud them. It would drive me crazy. The regular salary was reassuring but it came with strings. Maybe the excitement of being a player not knowing whether I was going to win the tournament or crash and burn in the first round was missing!

Many years after my time at the LTA I joined another governing body in the ITF in 2008 to head their officiating department. That sounds rather grand but at the time the department only contained two people including me. Luckily, my only colleague was very good and we recruited another soon after to make up a close-knit team of three. It was an appointment that I'd considered for several days before accepting since I knew it was likely to be a political minefield. It's the federation of all the national associations around the world. Every country has its own version of the LTA and they all affiliate to the International Tennis Federation. The problem is that each is its own little empire running independently from any other including the international organisation which tries to link them together. The ITF is financed with income from sponsorship and its management of the embattled Davis and Fed Cup (now renamed) competitions. These events were subject to much debate about their futures before being substantially changed and now seem belittled. As a former Davis Cup player that's disappointing. Their linkage with the Grand Slams gives the ITF a little more credibility but the reality is that they lost control of the professional game years ago to the ATP and WTA Tours and struggle to sustain their authority now.

My role at the ITF involved the management of all the qualified officials in the world and gave me a great opportunity to get to know them better. We organised schools for officiating around the world and would occasionally teach at them together with other officials contracted to the ITF. I was also closely involved with the appointment of officials to the Davis and Fed Cup ties worldwide, something I opposed on a conflict-of-interest basis since I too was a working official. I made a point of never selecting myself for the major ties to avoid the obvious charge of self-interest. I wanted better fees for all officials but budgets were tight and some felt that they were too expensive anyway. The monetary constraints also affected the many genuine, hard-working and committed lower-ranking staff members at the ITF. Unfortunately for them, there are many young, talented people keen to work in sport administration and so they can be easily replaced when they realise that it is difficult to progress within the organisation and decide to move on.

Seeing all this at close quarters challenged my sense of fair play. I refused to travel business class on principle even when allowed to do so. My own expenses reflected what I would have spent if I was spending my own money. That's only fair. I wanted to restructure things to give the opportunity to raise the low fees paid to officials when they took on the significant responsibility of running events. I wanted to promote their cause and felt that I knew how to go about it. But progress was glacial and the obstacles in the way weren't moving. After resigning once and being persuaded to return I finally ended the personal frustration of not being able to achieve more and left for good. I still applauded the goals and the ideals of the ITF, and felt guilty about leaving my excellent immediate working colleagues, but the progress I wanted wasn't happening.

One of the most frustrating things about government, whether national or sporting, is the waste of resources. When it's not their own money some are more prepared to spend it than if it's coming from their own pocket. Brought up with old-fashioned principles of 'waste not, want not' it was difficult to see the wastage I too frequently witnessed. Any business that involves travelling and staying overseas on a regular basis is going to face large costs but please ensure that those sent away 'on business' are doing something useful and are not there just for decoration!

The thorny issue of officials' pay was finally challenged in 2015 after a decade or more of little or no improvement. They had become paupers in the land of the jet set, sometimes sharing the hotels but never the income levels of others working in pro tennis. The fact that officials continued to do the job at all surprised me but any involvement with professional sport is attractive. Those deciding the levels of remuneration for tennis officials were themselves on contracts that insulated them from the realities of such poor pay. They didn't feel the same urgency for change and were under pressure to keep costs down by their own bosses. They didn't choose to make waves. Meanwhile, the small groups of contracted officials within each major group of the ATP, WTA and ITF were more focussed on protecting their own teams rather than improving conditions for all. It was a case of 'Why can't we get business-class travel for our group?' rather than 'How can we encourage a general rise in fees for all officials?' So the chance of getting a groundswell of opinion to support the cause was minimal. There was much dark muttering amongst the rank and file but little action.

One charismatic, independent and very brave chair umpire dared to put his head above the parapet with a letter addressed to his fellow leading officials and the issues were at least being debated out in the open even though few wished to jeopardise their own personal positions. The Australian Open and Wimbledon announced significant rises for the leading officials and suddenly the rest of the tennis world was forced to recognise that it couldn't go on any longer. They had to improve the conditions for the officials. So it did get better and tennis officials were raised up from subsistence levels to that of being merely poorly paid. Would it have happened without a forcing of the hand? No, of course not!

With electronic line calling taking over from line umpires it may be that the role of chair umpires is changing to that of managing the match, calling the score and liaising with the IT experts who set up the systems. With less bodies involved on court those that remain may be valued more highly. They take on significant responsibility and deserve more than just the honour of sitting there. After all, they're the first target for any complaints. As progress continues the officials' voices need to be heard and considered by the senior tennis civil servants at the world's federations. Because not every event can afford the expensive set-up costs of ELC and these events still need to be officiated.

Governing bodies can be great to work for. I loved the feeling of being able to contribute to the growth and development of the sport. If motivation and morale within the organisation is high you can put up with the criticism from outside, much of which is ill-informed. In working with players for the LTA and with officials for the ITF I felt that I played a part. But for governments to be loved they must be perfect and that's a big ask. The ATP and WTA also attract considerable negative comment from their own members from time to time so it's probably beyond reasonable expectation for any of tennis' versions of the civil service to ever become popular.

Chapter 20
Davis Cup Tales

Working as a referee at Davis Cup ties is quite different to working at regular tournaments. Once the formalities of the draw are completed you liaise closely with the team captains on all issues to do with their players. During the matches you sit immediately behind the chair umpire and become part of the team of on-court officials. Over the years there were many memorable moments and situations. Here is just a small selection.

Luxembourg v Hungary (Luxembourg, May 2002)

It was my first Davis Cup tie, an old mate Balász Taróczy was the Hungarian captain and Gilles Müller was playing for Luxembourg early in his very long career. The doubles match was on court and had been playing for over four hours in front of a small but very enthusiastic crowd. At 8-9 down in the fifth set Gilles, who was just about to serve to save the match, came to me with sheer desperation in his eyes to say, 'Andrew, I need to go to the toilet and I need to go now!' As Luxembourg had already used up their allowed number of toilet breaks I explained that he would need to go on his own time and would be crazy to go now since it would likely involve code violations and potentially losing the match. He said he had no choice and so ran off the court with a line umpire in hot pursuit. We started the clock and duly issued a warning followed by the required point penalty as the seconds passed. Now the pressure was really on since the next stage was game penalty and that would mean match over. I don't know who was the most relieved when Gilles came running in to take up his position to serve at 0-15 – the Luxembourg captain, me as the referee or Gilles because he'd finally had his much-needed pee!

South Africa v Portugal (Durban, July 2003)

Playing in a team is a pleasant distraction from the rigours of the individual Tour. It's a chance to enjoy team spirit and to indulge in some of the pranks that lads away together always enjoy. So late one night when a knock came on my door and I opened it to find two lovely young South African women asking me if I had ordered them to my room I was immediately suspicious! I told them I thought they must have the wrong room then tried to see where they went next. Next day I went to both changing rooms making a joke of it, saying, 'Come on lads, which of you lot ordered those two girls on my behalf? It was very kind of you!' Much better to bring it out in the open and to laugh about it than to have the possibility of it being a genuine attempt to bribe me. Besides, it was a chance to show the players that I'm human, can share some humour with them and not just be the faceless official that is only out to spoil their day.

When the tennis did get started it featured a strange situation. Wesley Moodie, the big-serving South African, was leading Leonardo Tavares by two sets to one and it was 6-6 in games and 6-6 in the fourth-set tiebreak when a few drops of light rain started to fall as the players changed ends. As it was a hard court there was little tolerance to damp conditions and so I desperately hoped that we could squeeze in a couple more points to finish the match or at least the set. The players started to test the surface and we moved on to 7-7. In the next point Moodie came into the net, Tavares hit a passing shot down the far sideline and the line umpire called out with no overrule from the chair umpire. The Portugese went crazy complaining that the ball had been in and as the argument raged the rain turned torrential and we ran for cover. Twenty minutes later I cancelled play for the day as there was no prospect of returning to the court even though it was now match point, on serve, to Moodie. Back at the hotel the TV was showing the highlights and it ended with a very clear view of the final shot showing the ball as being in. It had been a bad call!

Overnight, I imagined what the players would be thinking. Moodie would be thinking, where should I hit this next serve? Tavares would be wondering, where is he going to serve? While all I could think was, I hope the serve isn't a fault that's not called and the match ends on an 'ace' and another bad call! What happened? After the usual intros and warm-up we restarted at match point. Moodie missed his first serve, stayed back on the second but came into the net and put away a winning volley to cue the celebrations enjoyed by all winning teams at the end of a victorious rubber. It was a strange one and no one could recall it happening before.

Ukraine v Norway (Kiev, March 2005)

This tie came just a few months after the Orange Revolution that overturned the Ukrainian presidential election and so emotions were running high. This was in stark contrast to the low, low temperatures of Kiev in the winter. A constant blast of freezing air came into the indoor tennis arena when the doors needed to be left open during the construction of stands to allow machinery access. Consequently, the practice days took place in freezing conditions and I had some cold and unhappy players. But our hosts were very warm and welcoming and were delighted when I decided that we'd be scoring in Ukrainian and English instead of the Russian and English that had been the case in the years up to then. At this time there was no hint that this beautiful city would become the centre of world attention in 2022.

In the evenings we were hosted at dinners where regular vodka toasts were proposed and it would have been too rude to refuse. We drank to the health of presidents, to the sport, to good friendship and goodness knows what else. Then at the end of the week my wife and I had one final evening where we went out on our own, taking the opportunity to have a quiet night away from the vodka. On leaving the restaurant we decided to walk across the road to see the magnificent ice sculptures that had been in position since the start of the winter and suddenly we felt chilled to the bone by the bitter cold. It was then we realised why the locals loved their vodka; we had no internal insulation. Put that one down to a life experience courtesy of tennis!

Germany v Thailand (Düsseldorf, September 2006)

Thailand featured the identical twin Ratiwatana brothers in their team who played doubles. The days leading up to the tie had given me plenty of opportunity to try to find a way of separating the two but by the time Saturday came round and the doubles match was due on court I was still no wiser. I'd hoped that they'd have some minute difference in clothing that provided the answer but as they warmed up I realised that I still had no idea. As the players started to warm up their serves I made my way to the foot of the umpire's chair, looked up at Andi Egli, the vastly experienced Swiss umpire, and asked him if he'd solved the puzzle. Andi not only confirmed he had no clue either but also told me that the Thai captain had admitted that he also had no way of telling them apart. I don't think the same brother served all match but we'll never know for sure now!

Belarus v Sweden
(Minsk, February 2007)

Sweden closed out a long fourth match and now led the tie 3-1 with one dead rubber left to play. These matches are notoriously difficult to get players to take seriously and this was no exception. After the required ten minutes to nominate the team had passed I went into the Swedish dressing room to find Mats Wilander, the non-playing captain, surrounded by the rest of the team all knocking back a celebratory beer or three. 'Who's going to play?' I asked Mats. 'Dunno, they're all drunk. Can I play?' he asked with a grin. It would've been great if he'd been able to given his reputation amongst fans worldwide but sadly the rules didn't allow it. So a few minutes later a rather wobbly Thomas Johansson walked on to court to play a less than competitive match against Vladimir Voltchkov. It was a very relaxed encounter before he was able to rejoin his celebrating colleagues shortly after. One point in particular lives in the memory. It was a cross-court, one-handed backhand slice marathon with Voltchkov that they both enjoyed until one did eventually make a mistake. Neither tried any variation but the quality of these backhands was testament to the ability of them both and was a wonderful exhibition to any youngster. Good fun and big smiles greeted the end of the point from all concerned.

It had been my first visit to Minsk and it also gave another hint of bribery. On getting the assignment I asked my peers what to expect. One told me that I'd be met at the air bridge when the plane landed, be taken through customs and immigration with minimum fuss to the public side where my bodyguards would be introduced. Then it was a police escort to the hotel and later on I'd meet a young lady who was to be my translator/personal assistant for the week. I was intrigued! Sure enough it all happened just as forecast at the airport and soon I was on my way to the hotel with two huge man-mountains dressed in the ill-fitting suits of the Soviet era and a police car ahead with flashing lights clearing traffic out of the way. It was brilliant and I felt like I was in a TV programme!

Next day I was doing the usual site checks when the tie organiser, a young, casually dressed man, came into my office and said, 'Andrew, I'd like to introduce you to Olga. She will be your translator and assistant at any time day or night throughout your stay in Minsk'. I looked to the door and in walked a short skirt and high boots containing the lovely Olga. It even made me briefly forget the problem of trying to get an internet connection! Well, I spent the next 48 hours wondering what exactly was on her job description. She came around the site with me translating for me and generally helping out until my wife arrived a couple of days later, at which point the two of them immediately became best pals and went off shopping and sightseeing together! Olga was not averse to the possibility of an overseas husband and a life abroad, though. She dated one of the Swedish players and started a relationship that my wife was counselling her about as she had some misgivings as to his intentions. I was fairly sure about his likely intentions myself but that didn't stop the two girls from debating the pros and cons of the arrangement! This went on for some months afterwards with Olga even coming to work in the UK to further her dreams. A year after the Minsk tie I worked another tie involving Sweden, this time in Israel, and more on this follows shortly.

Serbia v Georgia (Belgrade, April 2007)

This was the most one-sided contest in Davis Cup I've been involved with. Novak Djokovic had just won his first Masters Series event in Miami and was returning to Serbia to a hero's welcome. He was backed up by Janko Tipsarevic, Ilija Bozoljac and Nenad Zimonjic in a team that was clearly going to be too strong for a weak Georgia side that had only Irakli Labadze as any kind of recognised Tour-level player. Then when the Georgians arrived Labadze was sporting a sling on his recently broken arm and announced he was only in Serbia to party! This left a three-man team that was completely out of its depth.

After the second day Serbia were leading 3-0 on a poor indoor clay court that ripped up every time someone changed direction on it. Fortunately, not much movement was required and so we had the result confirmed in double quick time, fortunately with no injuries. This meant that the Serbs could head off to their spiritual home of Novi Sad for a long night of celebrations for Novak while the Georgians made for the centre of Belgrade to party hard themselves.

Next morning we were due to start the two dead rubbers at 12 noon. At 11am I hadn't seen anyone at all at the time of the team nomination change deadline. Not a soul from either team, player or official. Spectators started to arrive and the officials trooped in as planned but it was less than 45 minutes before the start of play before Janko Tipsarevic arrived looking so rough he could barely walk in his trademark wrap-around sunglasses. Within a few further minutes I had Ilija Bozoljac and one of the Georgians appear and it seemed that these were the poor souls who had drawn the short straw to play. No one had practised of course.

Twenty minutes after the start Georgia had won their first set of the tie 6-4 and Bozoljac went for a toilet break after playing like death warmed up. I sent a line umpire and then waited a very long time for them to return to the court. When they got back I asked the official what had happened. He replied that Bozoljac hadn't gone to the toilet at all but had leaned over the basin before throwing up long and hard. He'd then washed up and made his way back to court where he proceeded to win 7-6 in the third and final set. It was some effort even though the Georgian was so poor I felt that I would still have had a chance against him if I'd played. Naturally, his teammates found the whole thing very funny watching him suffer though.

Czech Republic v Switzerland (Prague, September 2007)

This was the best Davis Cup tie I was ever involved in. 15,000 people packed into the Sazka Arena (later renamed the O2 Arena) in Prague to see their top-notch Czech team of Tomas Berdych and Radek Stepanek take on Roger Federer and Stan Wawrinka from Switzerland. The opening day saw Federer and Berdych win to leave the tie at 1-1. The doubles on the next day was a classic, with Roger showing why he's probably the world's best doubles player (if only he'd play) teaming with Yves Allegro and coming within a whisker of beating Berdych and Stepanek before losing. This set up the clash of the number ones, Berdych and Federer, in the first Sunday match.

Berdych played brilliantly on a court that had been specially set up for him and Radek. He played all the tennis in the first set and Roger was hanging on by a thread. But Federer won it on a tiebreak. The same thing happened in the second set and so despite being second best throughout Roger was somehow two sets up. It was almost unbelievable except that Roger is the master of grasping opportunity when it arrives and this was a perfect example.

Now two sets down Berdych slammed his racket into the signage on the net, breaking it off, before sitting down for the set break. James Keothavong, as the chair umpire, turned to me to confirm it should be a code violation to be correctly given after a few seconds to allow Berdych to calm down. Roger was pre-emptive, though, growling in his chair, just loud enough for us to hear, 'What's a guy got to do around here to get a code?' It showed he was totally tuned in to the situation. Earlier James had overruled on a service line call that was directly in line with the Czech team bench who had all stood up to protest the call. Roger just snarled, 'Sit down' at which point the Czech team all obeyed and shut up. The great man had spoken and no one was going to dispute his word even if they had been quite happy to have a moan at the chair umpire. The third set of the match was a routine solitary break and Federer had levelled up the tie at 2-2.

This then meant a fifth rubber between Stepanek and Wawrinka, which was another epic with Radek prevailing at the end of a tense third set that saw him dealing with cramp as well as a fired-up opponent. He barely made it over the finish line in a match that would surely have gone Stan's way if he'd managed to win the third set. All in all it was a wonderful tie. I'm not easily moved by the tennis I watch but this was a marvellous advert for the Davis Cup.

Israel v Sweden
(Ramat Hasharon, February 2008)

Olga had made contact and said that, by chance, she had a friend in Tel Aviv and she was visiting at the same time as the tie! She asked if she could meet me there. Of course, it was a thinly veiled chance to meet her Swedish tennis player there but I had no objection and so I arranged that she would be my guest at the official dinner on the Wednesday evening before the tie. We met in the hotel reception ten minutes before the start so we could walk in together. When I went to the meeting point I waited only a couple of minutes before she came up to me with a huge hug and kiss. She looked stunning with every man turning to take in the vision as every woman shot dagger looks in her direction and checked to make sure their own man wasn't looking at her! My stock with both teams went up enormously but I was quickly reminded of my age when the Swedish general secretary, who had previously met my wife and daughter, came up mistaking Olga for my daughter! Oh well, it was fun while it lasted! Dannie rather liked that bit when she heard from us both as she was still in contact with Olga and could picture the scene.

Serbia v USA
(Belgrade, March 2010)

My friend Dennis chuckled when he heard I was going to Belgrade to referee this high-profile tie. 'Last time the Americans went to Belgrade they only saw it from 2,000 feet as they were bombing it. It should be lively' was his reassuring observation! I had refereed several of Serbia's ties in the past involving Novak Djokovic and his highly motivated teammates and they had proved to be very enjoyable and inspiring in equal measure. But now this team had matured to genuine Davis Cup contenders and the visit of the USA, led by their captain Patrick McEnroe, was always going to be tough. It was held at the Belgrade Arena with 15,000 fanatical fans inside on a specially laid clay court to maximise their chance of success against the giants John Isner and Sam Querrey, backed by the doubles experts the Bryan brothers. It was to prove to be a tie when I made not one but two judgments that were technically against the rules of tennis in Davis Cup.

The first match saw Viktor Troicki against John Isner in a long, emotional match. Towards the end the Serbian captain called for his team trainer to attend to Troicki. I went on court as their trainer examined his leg. 'What's the problem,' I asked while looking at what, to me, was a clear enough case of cramp as his leg muscles were twitching. The trainer told me it was only a leg strain. I didn't believe him so called for the independent doctor who is there for precisely reasons like this. The doctor was Serbian, spoke briefly to the trainer, coach and player and then confirmed a leg strain to me. Under the rules a medical timeout treatment for cramp is not allowed but if it's a strain it's OK. We as officials are dependent on the medics to provide the medical expertise in such situations and so, after a further query re cramp, I reluctantly allowed the treatment. The Americans went nuts just as I would have done if it had been me in their position and I was loudly berated by both Doug Spreen, the American trainer, and McEnroe for allowing such seemingly blatant abuse. I rode it out explaining that I had no choice but after the match finished I made a point of meeting with the Serbian captain, Bogdan Obradovi , to tell him I wasn't happy and wouldn't allow it again if the situation were repeated.

Just a few hours later in the second match of the first day Djokovic was playing Querrey and once again the Serbs called the trainer in what was a carbon-copy repeat of the previous match's situation. Only this time it was Djokovic with the injury and now there was no chance of the independent doctor telling me anything other than what the Serbs wanted me to hear. I took a deep breath and denied the treatment to the fury of the Serbs and, of course, following much angry gesticulating, by the crowd who let me know what they thought. I just hoped that the Serbs weren't fully au fait with the rules as this was one decision I was going to take on my own. The match continued and then we had another cracker.

The chair umpire got down to make a ball-mark inspection and on returning to the chair he forgot to reconnect the Trinity net machine that calls net cords. It's easily done in the haste to be ready quickly. As Querrey threw the ball up to serve he realised but it was too late to stop the serve. I suppose it was inevitable what would happen next. The ball hit the net cord, the chair umpire missed the call and Djokovic returned the ball into the net. Everyone in the stadium had heard the net cord except the chair umpire who told the Serbs he hadn't heard it. At this point Nicki Pilic, the Serbian coach, saw the disconnected Trinity machine and the argument took on another significant element. I was called to the court to rule. When I spoke to the chair umpire he told me what had happened, that he'd panicked, that he had in fact heard the net cord but had failed to call it and then felt he needed to claim that nothing had been heard. It was a real mess. I had brief seconds to consider. I ruled it as a net cord and that the point be replayed. In terms of the rules the loss of Trinity meant that the responsibility for calling net cords was with the chair umpire who hadn't made the call and so therefore the point should have been Querrey's. However, everyone had heard the call, including the chair umpire though we couldn't admit it now, and so I reckoned I could sell it on that basis. Morally it was correct but legally it was wrong based on what the chair umpire had told the Serbs. Now it was McEnroe's turn to go nuts and he let me have his opinion for several subsequent changeovers as the match continued.

Czech Republic v Italy (Ostrava, February 2012)

This had very little that was memorable about the tie itself but everything to do with the fact that it was held in Ostrava, which is a bit of a Czech industrial eyesore. In fairness, Leeds and Stoke are probably worse though that may be my football bias coming through! Nonetheless, it would be true to say that this place will never feature on the holiday bucket list of the rich and famous.

The tie was held in February and it was freezing, and I do mean freezing. The temperatures had plunged and we were getting numbers of -15 to -18°C almost every day. I was on a big walking fitness kick at the time in preparation for a big Pennine Way walk later in the year and I was putting miles into the legs regularly with ten miles a day being the target.

One morning I left the hotel very early to walk my ten miles, which typically would take me two and a half hours, and it was -17°C. Suitably dressed in boots, hat, scarves, heavy coat and further layers underneath I was prepared and ready and looking like Scott of the Antarctic. I tramped around the awful city trying and failing to find anything that was scenic amongst the derelict urban wasteland. So bad was it that I took my camera and snapped away happily to later make up a PowerPoint presentation in a mock tourist office promotional style just for a giggle.

When I got back security stopped me at the entrance to the hotel. They challenged me in Czech and so I tried to reply. Only problem was my mouth had completely frozen and I was completely unintelligible. I couldn't believe it. Looking in the window I could see my reflection and suddenly realised why they'd stopped me. My hat was white with frost and the back of my coat also had a layer of frost across where my body heat had frozen against the material. I looked just like I'd been sleeping rough and was coming in for a free breakfast! Fortunately, the reception staff recognised me (probably as that lunatic who'd gone out earlier walking in such ridiculous temperatures) and came to my rescue.

What happened in the tennis? Can't really remember but I think the home team won.

Canada v Spain
(Vancouver, February 2013)

This was an intriguing tie as it pitched a Canadian team with Milos Raonic on home courts against Spain who had a fabulous Davis Cup record but also a team shorn of their leading players. It just goes to show that Davis Cup is all about getting your best players on court. I knew how my first Davis Cup tie as a player had felt and so I had an interest in all debutants who were playing this wonderful competition for the first time. As I went to the Spanish dressing room to collect Marcel Granollers ready to play I remembered that it was his first experience despite being a regular Tour player. As I walked with a very nervous looking Marcel and his captain Alex Corretja I simply turned to Marcel, smiled and said, 'Welcome to Davis Cup. In all the excitement of the next few hours don't forget to enjoy it'. Both men seemed to appreciate the words. With that we joined the Canadians and made our way away from the peace and quiet of the changing rooms to the cauldron of noise waiting on the match court.

The same tie saw the best single individual moment of captaincy on court that I've ever witnessed and it came from Alex Corretja. It came towards the end of that same second match on the first day. Canada were leading 1-0 courtesy of Raonic and Corretja's player Marcel Granollers was losing to a totally inspired Frank Dancevic who was playing the match of his life to lead 6-1 6-2. Score-wise he was killing Granollers and it was based on an attack-minded, risky strategy that was working well. But Granollers is a grinder and one who can gradually turn a match given any chance. The third set became very tight early on with long games going advantage, deuce, advantage and the crowd was getting very excited. Then Dancevic got a break and started to close in on the finishing line. Those close to the court could sense the tension knowing that if Granollers could somehow find a way to win the third set the match could go the distance. Granollers was trying like hell, Dancevic kept risking and while it was working it was also starting to become just a little ragged with occasional errors and doubt creeping into his mind. Corretja sensed the time was right to get into Granollers' head. At the 4-1 changeover the crowd continued to go nuts and so Corretja knelt down in front of his player, took a large towel and placed it over both of their heads. He then spoke to him, almost nose to nose, trying to give him the belief that he could still win this match. It didn't change the course of the match, Dancevic winning shortly afterwards, but it was so powerful, so personal, and it reinforced my own view that Corretja (such a classy man throughout the tie) was one of the best captains you could wish to have at Davis Cup.

Poland v Australia (Warsaw Sept 2013)

This tie saw Pat Rafter, the top bloke Aussie captain, leading a team that included a mix of some old-school Aussies including himself, Lleyton Hewitt, hitting partner Peter Luczak and coaches Tony Roche and Josh Eagle with the new generation of Bernie Tomic, Nick Kyrgios and Marinko Matosevic. It made for an interesting contrast in attitudes and Pat had his hands full. He made some amusing comments intended to gently tease Luczak, who had Polish heritage and was acting as his translator. Luczak then brilliantly 'translated' saying, in Polish, that Rafter came from Queensland so no one could understand him anyway but he thought Rafter had said that he liked Polish chicks! The room loved it and we English speakers had no idea why. By the time it was translated back to Pat it was too late for any further comeback on the grinning Luczak.

USA v Slovak Republic (Chicago, September 2014)

This tie was held in Chicago. At least that's what they told me. As far as I was concerned I was met at Chicago O'Hare airport (presumably named after the famous Derby forward of the 70s!) and driven to a nondescript hotel on the edge of a nondescript trading estate a short drive from a bog-standard stadium where the tie was set up. Two teams were to face off in an area unused to holding major tennis events and the biggest names were John Isner and Sam Querrey, good players both but neither have excited the American public. The only famous faces on show were the charismatic US Davis Cup captain at that time Jim Courier and the mercurial former player Miloslav Mecir.

Very little happened throughout the tie of note as the US claimed their win. The only highlight was a lowlight for me at the draw when I managed to cause a pretty funny screw-up. (If you're going to fuck it up then do it in spectacular style I always reckon!) The team captains have to give the names of their singles players for the first day literally moments before the draw, which is held on the previous day. This particular event, like most around the world, featured the two teams on either side of the table where the name would be drawn that would decide the order of the two matches for the following day.

All I had to do was place the four singles names (two from each team) into the pot from where a local VIP would draw the name. Only problem was I'd been spending time getting the draw assistants prepared at the side who would put up the names as I read out the match order. To make life easier for these assistants I'd set up the expected names for them so that they could readily select the correct names. Then came the shock from the Slovak captain who nominated the unheralded Norbert Gombos ahead of the much-higher-rated Lukas Lacko, a real surprise. I hastily went to the assistants table to ensure they had the change, completely forgetting the all-important names that were now in the pot on the main table.

Moments later, at my cue, and after having announced the names of the nominations for the singles, the dignitary reached into the pot and drew out the name of Lukas Lacko who wasn't even playing the following day. My heart sank as I knew instantly what had happened. They say it's how you recover in moments like this and I quickly announced what had happened, took responsibility for the mistake but then said that this meant the number two player from the Slovak Republic had been drawn and so Norbert Gombos would play the number one US player John Isner in the first match. No one complained and that's what went up on the draw board and the draw was done. It was a mortifying moment, though.

Afterwards, I went out quickly to find the two captains to apologise and explain. Both were great about it and Courier laughed and said, 'I thought I'd seen it all but that's the first time I've seen that happen!' Since then we always go out of our way to greet and say hi to each other. He's a good guy.

Argentina v Brazil (Buenos Aires, March 2015)

Thanks for that one, I thought as I saw the assignment. The two heavyweights of South America lined up against each other in a Latin American dogfight on the red dirt of Buenos Aires. With huge rivalry between the two nations this was never going to be a walk in the park. In fact it turned out to be a car park as the usual venue for home ties in Buenos Aires, the Parque Roca, was being renovated so they used a strange place, Tecnópolis, that was more of an exhibition centre and constructed as an 8,000-seater temporary clay court especially for the tie. It was strange in that we had the usual office and changing facilities remote from the court so it meant organising a convoy of golf carts every time we wanted to go to/from the match court. In the world of officiating this means something else that could possibly go wrong and so an added concern.

You always find out things on match day that didn't necessarily seem apparent in the days leading up to the tie. This tie's little surprise came when it transpired that there had been no attempt at segregating the 500 travelling Brazilian fans from the 7,500 Argentine fans. The Brazilian fans were in little pockets dotted around the court so it was impossible to see with any certainty who was causing what noise or disturbance during matches. Realising that this meant that any use of the partisan crowd rule was impossible, due to the practicalities of identifying who was doing what, I knew I was in for a lively tie.

Fairly quickly, it became apparent that the baiting of the visitors was going to centre around the disastrous World Cup football match that Brazil had lost to Germany at home. Both countries like their tennis but love their football and so it was a matter of pride and honour lost for the Brazilians to be humiliated 1–7 by the Germans. Change of ends in the Davis Cup tie was regularly punctuated by 'Uno, Dos, Tres, Cuatro, Cinco, Seis … SIETE' as the Argentines reminded the Brazilians of the score. As a wind-up it worked beautifully because the football-loving Brazilian tennis players were most definitely upset by the baiting and started to bite. One or two came to me to complain but what could I or anyone do about it? It wasn't disturbing the play itself since they'd quieten down by then and while certainly gently teasing it was scarcely abusive stuff. As a football fan, well used to the taunting on the terraces, it was fairly benign stuff and actually, truth be told, quite funny!

Plenty of other things were going on to keep me well occupied during the four (yes, four!) days it took to complete the tie. It went the extra day because of the longest singles match played in Davis Cup history as Leonardo Mayer beat João Souza 15–13 in the final set of a match that went six hours and 43 minutes. It was an epic and ended with both players well past their limits of endurance, suffering cramps and surviving on sheer willpower alone. The efforts of Mayer kept the hosts in the tie since they were 1–2 down after the doubles but it meant we only had time for one set of the final deciding rubber between Federico Delbonis and Thomaz Bellucci before darkness intervened and allowed us all to go back to the hotel to escape the madness overnight.

On the final, extra, day we returned to complete the tie. I'd found out that the 500 visiting Brazilian supporters had been on a charter tour and would not be attending. Also it was a weekday and so the majority of home fans would be back at work. I started to contemplate a quieter day with a tiny crowd despite the importance of the occasion and state of the tie. Wrong! I hadn't counted on free admission being announced and soon there was a long stream of fans who had never watched tennis before and so had no idea how to behave. All they knew was it was important, it was against the local rivals and it was free of charge. For two hours prior to the start I watched a steady stream of fans walking past our offices and on to the stadium where another boisterous crowd quickly made its presence felt. Delbonis handled the occasion well, won the match in four sets and Damien Dumusois gave a performance in the umpire's chair that, when added to his efforts over the entire tie, cemented my view that he deserved a men's singles final at Wimbledon in due course since he was at the top of his trade. (He subsequently umpired Federer's win over Cilic at SW19 in 2017.)

Here's one from the Americas

As referee at Davis Cup I sometimes needed to exercise discretion when I witnessed things that happened. There was the time when a leading player dominated his team to the point that his own captain was terrified of upsetting him. Practice times were arranged so that the player wouldn't get upset and even when they were on court together it was clear there was little respect from the player to the man who was nominally the one in charge. Leading two sets to love he went off for a toilet break and the captain joined him at the next urinal. While peeing the captain tried to be encouraging: 'OK, great play. Let's get off to a good start and get on top of this guy with an early break in this set'. The player shut him down not even looking at him, saying, 'I've only come in here to get away from all that shit'. With that he turned, walked away and returned to court to complete a routine three-set win to clinch the tie. Cue the usual celebrations in front of an ecstatic crowd who had no idea of the tension within the ranks of their own team.

This one's from a former Soviet Union-influenced country

It featured a top visiting player who had not one but two attentive and very beautiful ladies around him for the tie. When I arrived to check in at the hotel they were draped all over him like jewellery on a sofa by the entrance. They would even go on court during practice and field the occasional ball for him while certainly not dressed in 'suitable tennis attire'! When you get high-earning players away together in a well-bonded team atmosphere boys will often be boys and excesses may not always be too far behind. Team managements are then faced with trying to keep the focus on winning the tie while often condoning off-court events and trying to keep them out of the media's attention. It has always been this way and good luck trying to stop it!

And somewhere at another tie deep in Eastern Europe

The morning of the first day I was doing my usual checks around the venue and saw what seemed to be the assembling of a Miss World show. About a dozen attractive young women were preparing for their role as escorts to the VIPs and were all dressed identically in short black cocktail dresses. I did my best to be professional and not to stop and admire them and moved on. Twenty minutes later my two male chair umpires arrived, came to the office and asked if there was anything they could do to help. I told them to go to the presidents' box, get themselves a coffee and just look around and see if there was anything worth reporting. Forty minutes later they returned saying, 'Thank you, Andrew. That's the best job anyone's ever given us during a Davis Cup tie!'

Soon after this the teams arrived and jaws dropped as they saw the girls on the way to the locker room. One of the lads looked at each in turn, turned to one of his team's support staff and said, 'I want that one', pointing to his favourite. He hadn't even spoken to her. Later that day I heard the girl when she was told that the player had asked if he could have her phone number as he'd like to take her out. Unbelievably, she smiled sweetly, said, 'that would be nice' and passed over the required information. No, no, I wanted to cry out. Don't do that. He's not after a nice dinner and an exchange of sweet conversation. But then I thought again. Nor is she! Times really haven't changed that much.

The match started and by the second evening there was still an exciting final day in prospect to decide the tie. We were at dinner when the ITF rep looked at his phone, turned to me and said, 'Andrew, our evening is about to change'. Apparently, cleaners had been into the away dressing room and had found graffiti all over the walls, mirrors and lockers. Drawings of male genitalia and references to someone identified by only initials were there and the hosts were outraged since they thought it was derogatory to one of their players who sometimes struggled to keep his weight under control. It had already escalated quickly to the federation presidential level with emails flying back and forth. We had to act quickly. I asked that no more be said or done and that we should meet in the visitor's locker room early the following morning. I told the hosts I thought they were wrong in their assumption of the likely target and that nothing should be said to the press.

At 8am the next day we gathered to see the art exhibition. Sure enough the culprit had been busy and a veritable collection of the lad's knowledge of the male anatomy was on display. The visiting team management was embarrassed and keen to make amends. I got their assurance that it was, as I'd thought, references to another player with the same initials from their own team and that it was an internal prank between team members.

I made arrangements for two meetings to take place, one between the two captains and the other between the two presidents. At each the visitor assured the host that it wasn't aimed at the home team's player and was just the actions of a misguided youth. They also confirmed that the visiting team undertook to clean up the mess themselves and would leave the locker room in the state that it was found. Once this was done it remained an internal problem and would be dealt with as a team discipline issue.

Now I do like a good 'Who did it' mystery on TV but I never did find out for sure who the artist was. But as it happened during the doubles match I was able to eliminate two of them from the frame, plus the captain of course, as they had excellent alibis!

Davis Cup is such a high-pressure environment to play tennis in. Emotions run high and it inspires some players to heights that wouldn't normally be possible while others are intimidated and underperform. As a player I saw it from one side but as a referee I was able to witness this drama from a completely different perspective. I saw some wonderful captains but also others who appeared out of their depth. I saw teams with great team spirit but others who were a group of individuals that came together just for that tie. One thing was very clear, though. No matter what nation was involved the passion to win for the country was huge. Players love to play for their country and that won't change. But now the home and away element has gone from Davis Cup together with the best-of-five-set format that made it so special. And the result is it doesn't make the pulse race quite as much as it used to.

Chapter 21
The VIP Speech

Just occasionally, when refereeing a Davis Cup tie, you might be asked to make the speech on behalf of the ITF. Usually, they'll have some 'VIP' who you've often never heard of that flies in to deliver two simple speeches, one at the dinner and one at the draw. Sometimes they elect to save a bit of dosh by getting the referee to make the speech and they give you the script to deliver so that you do the right thing! It goes through the motions of thanking the hosts, promoting Davis Cup and then praising the players for turning up and playing the event. Nothing wrong in that you might think but it does lack any kind of honesty, imagination or humour. I used to gently tease how I might one day give the following speech instead!

Honoured guests, ladies and gentlemen,

Welcome to this Davis Cup by BNP Paribas tie between _____ and _____.

First, I'd like to start by saying a big thank you to all those here on the top table. The support you offer by your mere presence means that all those waiters, waitresses, chambermaids, cooks and others who derive their employment and an opportunity to earn a living from your patronage are able to feed their families. You have their great appreciation and we too appreciate your attendance without actually really doing anything very much at all. The fact that you choose to travel in first or business class and stay in five-star luxury, at somebody else's expense, contributes greatly to the economy. We are indeed very grateful.

Next to those who supply the tennis technical expertise, the players and their support groups who actually put on the show. I'd like you to know that we so appreciate what you do and that we will do what we can, not only with words saying how good you are but also with the least we think we can get away with financially to keep you all on board with the gig. After all, if it were not for you guys we couldn't justify coming together to enjoy the very fine dinner and excellent wine we have here tonight!

And finally, thank you to those of you at the distant tables behind the pillar, that is if you can hear me. You are the people who actually put it all together and it is your great privilege to be allowed to work this marvellous event. Please remember that the paltry amount you get paid is more than made up for by the sheer pride and joy you can feel at being allowed to contribute to your country's Davis Cup effort. I'm sure you realise that there are many others who would be pleased to take your place so don't bother asking for a pay rise because the budget just won't stretch that far.

So with the thanks to everyone now complete can I now propose a toast to the gravy train and how we can stay on it as long as possible.

Thank you, ladies and gentlemen!

It would have made a welcome change from the usual formality of the official dinners. The players are usually there in team uniforms under sufferance and leave as soon as possible and the only speeches that are listened to are those of the two captains. That's unless there's a debutant who is required to make a speech by tradition and this is always well received. Their teammates love seeing them put on the spot and you do get a small insight into the characters of the player. Some inevitably struggle with embarrassment while others might produce a performance full of passion, humility and humour. But it was a fun initiation ceremony of sorts as another player was welcomed into the Davis Cup community.

Chapter 22
On-Court Situations

B
eing a referee has its moments. You're based in your temporary office surrounded by everything connected with the event and then suddenly the walkie-talkie summons you with 'referee (or supervisor) to court please'. It may be from the event control centre or direct from a chair umpire. Either way something has happened and you're about to deal with it. The first time it happens it's a little scary but over time you realise that it doesn't matter whether it's tough or trivial, you're on show and it will be a test of your knowledge, your judgment and, most importantly, how you're going to sell it.

It may be from a distant outside court with only two players and no umpire but it also might be on a Centre Court with 15,000 spectators plus millions more watching and listening to your every word. The chair umpires these days are very good so most situations are dealt with routinely but it does leave the unexpected. You may have to make a ruling on a logo size, perhaps supervise a medical situation, decide on a suspension for bad light or the state of the court or answer a question from a player who wants to speak to you. This can sometimes bring comedy.

'Supervisor to Court Six' came through when I was working at the Australian Open in Melbourne one year. It was on my patch of courts so I checked the order of play as I hurried to court to work out who it might be. Fernando González was playing so he seemed a likely customer and when I reached the chair umpire sure enough it was he who wanted a word at the next changeover. I approached the player and said, 'What's the problem, Gonzo?' 'It's the ice,' came the reply. 'You need more?' said I, assuming it had run out but also wondering why it hadn't been sorted by the court services people. 'It's too cold' wasn't quite the answer I was expecting! After some more confused conversation I eventually worked out that it was a language barrier problem and what he really meant was he wanted some normal-temperature drinks as his water was too cold. OK, that's an easy one!

A fairly common one is to listen to a moan about the quality of the line umpires or sometimes the chair umpire. It must be horrible for the chair umpire who calls the referee knowing that they're then going to have to listen to a catalogue of claims from the player telling you how badly the umpire is doing. Most of the time this is just a test of your people skills and ability to listen calmly before explaining that just because they don't like the calls they're not going to get the umpire changed. So after a bit of a rant the match continues but you do stick around to watch and make your own judgment as to what's happening. You also will likely make a note not to assign that player and umpire together for a while until they've had a chance to kiss and make up.

Another time I was working at the US Open when I ran foul of an officious security guard. She was big and very ferocious and came muscling on court when I was sorting out a logo problem with Rennae Stubbs, Cara Black, Caroline Wozniacki and Sabine Lisicki before a ladies' doubles match. She didn't believe I was allowed on the court and so came on to remove me! Even the players jumped to my defence, which might have stopped me being forcibly ejected, not to mention bruised, there and then. This lady was not to be messed with and was in security for a good reason. Once the girls moved to resume play I went to the side of the court. But the guard continued to stand on the court unaware so I called across asking her to leave the court since the players were ready. 'You don't tell me what to do; I tell you what to do!' she shouted back at me aggressively. I probably shouldn't have but couldn't resist replying, 'Sorry, I didn't realise we were married!' and smiled back. Sadly, it was a bit wasted on her as it went straight over her head but some of the crowd enjoyed it – probably more than me!

Another favourite of mine happened at the Aussie Open in Melbourne featuring a popular and charismatic ATP trainer at that time. These guys work hard and are often the unseen heroes of the circuit patching up, as they do, players and sending them back out into battle. This time the trainer was called to court to deal with one of the qualifiers from Kazakhstan and I dutifully trotted on after him to take a look. What followed was a classic featuring the vastly experienced trainer who has seen it all but still manages to always see the fun in life.

Trainer: 'What's the problem?'

Player: 'It's my stomach.'

Trainer: 'What's wrong with your stomach?'

Player: 'It hurts.'

Trainer: 'OK, I take a look.'

He then examines him.

Trainer: 'I'll give it some massage and then the doctor can give you a Panadol.'

Player: 'What? I don't have the flu!'

Trainer: 'You have pain. It treats pain. That's why it is called a painkiller!'

Player: 'Huh. Can I have some hot cream?'

Trainer: 'If I put hot cream there and you sweat it will run down to your balls and then you run like a rabbit!'

At this point I had to turn away as I was laughing so much!

Later on in the event I met up with the same trainer on another outside court for a call. He had to deal with one of the Russian players. For this bear in mind that medicals can only be taken for a new injury or for a pre-existing one that has got worse.

Trainer: 'What's the problem?'

Player: 'It's my knee.'

Trainer: 'What's wrong with your knee?'

Player: 'It hurts.'

Trainer: 'When did it start?'

Player: 'Three years ago!'

Trainer: (with a big Gallic shrug and considerable scorn) 'Phew! I give you a pill. No treatment!'

Back in the office one day I enjoyed one of his rants about the doubles players cluttering up the draw, causing overcrowding in the locker rooms and player lounges. It was the mixed doubles sign-up and all the doubles players were manoeuvring to find a partner ranked highly enough to get in with to add to their prize money. 'What is this mixed doubles?' started my favourite trainer. 'It's unbelievable. Some of them don't even know each other. Maybe we should have "zoo doubles" and they could sign up with a dog!'

Over to the Far East now and vastly experienced chair umpire Cedric Mourier who probably thought he'd seen it all on a tennis court until one day when he was in charge of a match between pantomime villain Fabio Fognini and Viktor Troicki on an outside court in Beijing at the China Open. This was a high-risk match for officiating since Troicki was also prone to the occasional lapse in discipline including a magnificent rant at Wimbledon only a few months earlier. But nothing could have prepared Cedric for when Fognini complained about a 'shitty court'. When he looked across sure enough there were some suspicious mounds in the corner and the player had noticed the smell. Cedric called for court services to do a bit of cleaning. By the time they got there, though, our proactive, leading ATP umpire had taken a towel, done some mopping up and sorted out the turd problem himself to reduce the delay in play. ATP supervisor Thomas Karlberg had assumed it was bird shit but no, it transpired that a ballkid had felt unwell with a stomach ache, had got severely caught out and just dumped on the court! Unbelievable! The inquest afterwards wondered if he'd worn underwear, how it had managed to make its way down his trouser leg at all and perhaps most of all why he hadn't simply left the court first before dropping his load. It was China and so we never found out the full story but then it was even better to leave some of this amazing tale to the imagination.

Back to Melbourne again where the Aussie Open was in full swing. I had just finished a long day out on HiSense Arena (since renamed) and was walking back to the main area when word came through on the walkies that a spectator had collapsed on Rod Laver Arena, the main stadium court. This type of situation is often tricky since it doesn't involve anyone on the court and technically play could continue but there's usually disturbance around the stands and a judgment call is taken whether to stop play or not. Just occasionally, it's very serious and it wouldn't be right to be continuing while someone was potentially in a life-threatening situation. A couple of minutes later and the next call stopped me in my tracks. The spectator turned out to be Nigel Sears, my long-time mate and old school pal from Millfield days, who was coaching Ana Ivanovic. He's also Andy Murray's father-in-law and Andy was playing at the time so I knew that his group would all be occupied elsewhere. I went in to see the tournament director to volunteer to give him some support at the hospital since I was probably the person who knew Nigel best.

The match he was watching involving Ana Ivanovic had stopped and the players had been taken off court during the interruption. I went up into the stands and Nigel looked in a bad way as he was carried out on a stretcher. By the time he had reached the ambulance he was at least speaking and I was able to see and pass that news on to Ana to reassure her before leaving for the hospital myself. Once at the hospital I waited while they conducted various tests and was then ushered into the emergency room when they felt it was OK to do so. Inside, I found Nigel sitting up looking fine though a little embarrassed at what had happened. Once we'd established he was OK we then slipped quickly into our normal mode, which is two

16-year-olds just messing around. I was able to pass on the message from his son Scott who had seen it all on live TV back in Britain and it was a classic. 'Tell him his abs looked good on TV,' he'd said and Searsy laughed, appreciating the humour that we were all starting to see in the situation.

I don't think the nurse in the emergency room was used to laughing and the abuse we gave each other. I accused him and coaches in general of stooping to anything at all to try to put off their opponents, even faking a heart attack. All he wanted was regular updates on how Ana's match was going since she had restarted and it was live on the TV in the room next door. Coming back from getting a score update I spotted his immaculate, brand-new trainers under his bed and couldn't resist asking him, 'Nige, they're going to keep you in overnight here. If you don't make it through the night can I have your trainers cos they look like they might be my size?!' The nurse was starting to appreciate our relationship by now and we all laughed together. A potentially terrible situation had turned out all right. Little did I know then that I was to be involved in a similar situation myself only a couple of years later!

One on-court situation had nothing to do with tennis but is probably my favourite-ever moment on Centre Court. I'd been approached by Fergus Murphy, a leading chair umpire, to see if I could help two of his best friends, a couple from Ireland. The man was intending to propose to his girlfriend and wondered if it would be possible on Court One, where they had tickets, after play finished. I thought Court One would be OK but Centre would be far better. We decided to set it up without asking permission from the club since that risked the answer 'No'. I mentioned it to a couple of people and a plan was hatched. Towards the end of the day Cilian and Caroline came into the Referee's Office on the pretext of being shown around. As soon as the Centre Court programme finished we waited until the stands had emptied and I offered them the chance to take a look at the most famous court in the world. Of course, they accepted. We walked down to the courtside and behind the umpire's chair where, pre-planned, I asked the ground staff if it would be possible for our couple to step on to the grass where the net had been left in place instead of removing it as is normal at the end of the day. Out into the middle of the court went Cilian and Caroline and he went down on one knee. The question was asked, she said yes and they embraced each other in the middle of the deserted court. Well, not quite deserted as there were many people there with cameras, suitably tipped off, all recording the moment and also the one immediately following when the ground staff turned the water sprinklers on them! Well, we couldn't have them getting too carried away because I'm sure there's a rule against that sort of thing on Centre Court!

As the Referee it was time to play a more grown-up part. AELTC

Rafa, Roger, Gerry and I helped by a young lad for the coin toss at my first Wimbledon gentlemen's singles final in 2006. All were nervous for different reasons. AELTC

Checking, checking and then a bit more checking from behind Centre Court. AELTC

You learn to grow a thick skin because it's usually the Referee's fault!
Evening Standard

By the net post with James Keothavong for a presentation, this time for Serena Williams. AELTC

Sitting quietly and appreciating the sheer majesty that is Centre Court. AELTC

The air of excitement in the stadium prior to finals is wonderful. This is prior to the 2013 final when Andy beat Novak to end the 77-year drought for British men's singles winners at Wimbledon. AELTC

Like a chameleon there were times when a stern look was required. AELTC

As a Grand Slam supervisor at the Australian Open. You get to field some stray balls, direct spectators to the nearest toilet and just occasionally sort out the odd problem on court!

The Referee's Office team on my last morning in 2019, plus a very special guest in Black Rod, my friend and former colleague Sarah Clarke.

A trio of Referees with my predecessor Alan Mills and successor Gerry Armstrong.

She instantly became my favourite Duchess!

It's all over and who better than Dannie and Jazz to share the moment with me.

Ready for the next part of our shared journey together.

Chapter 23

A Hostile Reception in Israel

It was the banner that read, 'Welcome to Is-ra-hell' at the side of the court that first alerted me to the fact that this was going to be a tougher than usual Fed and Davis Cup double assignment. Maria Sharapova and her Russian colleagues plus an entourage of 50 odd hangers-on were the visitors and the local lads had come out in force to ogle her legs, ask her to marry them and generally have a good time. As their usual staple diet of sport was football and basketball there was going to be some provocation!

During the first match in Ramat Hasharon in February 2008 the crowd managed to get to Dinara Safina so that despite winning the first set 6-0 against local heroine Shahar Peer she ended up a distant second. The crowd had raised Peer but also got to Safina and were now ready to devour Sharapova. The chair umpires and I worked hard with interventions both on and off court informing the crowd of the need for quiet at certain crucial times but odd excited spectators always made it a nervous moment of expectation as the Russians threw the ball up ready to serve. In the split second before contact you waited for an explosion of noise designed to put off and intimidate.

Safina didn't cope but Sharapova did. She destroyed the hapless Tzipi Obziler despite a brief flurry of resistance at the end and the match was tied 1-1. So one-sided was it that the couple of occasions where the crowd started to imitate Sharapova's grunts were not the right time to use the partisan crowd rule. It wasn't going to do anything other than incite the crowd to worse. Afterwards, the Russians didn't agree and lodged a protest at the weak officiating. While they had a point it would have carried more weight if Safina hadn't folded at the pressure. They were worried because they expected 2-0 but were looking at 1-1 and the tie was still alive.

On the next day the two number ones did battle and once again Sharapova did the business. She was hard as nails mentally, ignored the hostility and won very comfortably. From her point of view it was a job well done.

The crowd had one more chance to influence and when Obziler went 3-0 up in the first set against top-tenner Anna Chakvetadze (Safina had been dropped for this one!) a shock seemed possible. The crowd were still on the edge of being out of control and I did use the partisan crowd rule in a vain attempt to rein them in though it made little difference. But Chakvetadze is a formidable competitor and gradually turned it back her way to hold a set and a big lead in the second. The match seemed to be close to finishing except for a hint of a recovery that caused the crowd to rise again and then for Anna to completely lose it mentally. She pumped her fists and snarled at the crowd after every winning point causing a huge reaction of noise, jeers and constant whistles. I told Tarpishchev, the Russian captain, that he needed to calm her down. This eventually happened and we reached the finishing post a few minutes later with Russia winning 3-1.

The following week I stayed on at the same venue to referee the Davis Cup tie between Israel and Sweden. The Swedes had arrived early enough to witness the crowd at its worst against Russia's women and were understandably worried. I decided to take the unusual step of requesting a meeting with the entire team over lunch in the Swedish locker room on the Monday immediately after the Fed Cup tie. I explained to Mats Wilander, the Swedish captain, that it might be useful in order to discuss the crowd and how we might get the best playing conditions the following weekend. Mats agreed and so it was that I addressed the players. I explained that I thought that the crowd would be better for their tie because they weren't as pretty as the girls and that they wouldn't get the same number of horny lads there for the wrong reasons. Also those who had been at the Fed Cup tie would have greater experience of what was expected at tennis matches in terms of crowd participation. But I also warned it was going to be a tough crowd, one of the worst they would come across, and that they had their own part to play. I asked them all to make no reaction to anything at all. Whatever happened they should keep quiet and calm and work with the chair umpires and I to identify any individuals who we could first warn and then throw out if they didn't stop what they were doing. If they didn't do this and reacted angrily we were all going to have a long weekend!

The Swedish lads were brilliant. They took on board what I had to say in good spirit, played their part to the full and with Jonas Björkman showing all his experience and leadership they came away with the win. Nothing rattled them and they were focussed and never distracted by the crowd. They gave an object lesson in how to deal with hostile spectators.

Chapter 24

The Challenge of China

Throughout the years I played and coached China was simply not on the tennis radar. There were no international tournaments and so when it became part of the tennis scene I wanted to visit at the earliest opportunity. That came for me when Beijing hosted the Olympics in 2008 and I went there to work as a supervisor, patrolling courts to sort out any problems that occurred there. Over the coming years I was to return many times, all at the same centre in Beijing, to be referee for the China Open.

The major attractions of the Great Wall, the Forbidden City and the Summer Palace were ticked off in the early visits as was the obligatory Peking duck meal and the test of bargaining skills at the Silk Market where traders hawked their stocks of counterfeit goods. Prices were by negotiation and dropped quickly from 'you're having a laugh' to a mere fraction of what the genuine article would sell for on Fifth Avenue or the Champs-Élysées. I wasn't much interested in the goods but loved the challenge of the negotiation on the price.

One visit was a day trip from Hong Kong over the border to Shenzhen with my wife and our dear friend Paulette Moreno (she of the Singapore match fame with Dannie!). The two girls would look at the goods and select what they were interested in and then I would handle the negotiations. All tactics were employed including a claim of poverty because my *two* wives were a nightmare, they cost me so much money and how could I possibly afford both? It was all good-natured, involved much laughing and smiling and we ended up with full bags on the way back to Hong Kong so presumably the traders were happy too.

China had decided to build a tennis empire from the ground up. The Chinese Communist Party saw the success of the Russians in winning gold medals at the Olympics and with tennis then rejoining the Olympics at Seoul in 1988 the race was on to become a tennis superpower. This meant that state-of-the-art facilities were constructed, international events were brought in and player production factories opened up across the country. This meant huge opportunity for the Tours to expand into this new market and to take advantage of the seemingly limitless funding that was suddenly available.

It's naive to think that sport and politics can be separated in somewhere like China. Nothing there happens without the support and approval of the government so the advance of tennis clearly coincided with this new initiative from the Chinese Communist Party. It took tennis from being virtually non-existent to the third most popular sport in their vast country. Tennis, and particularly the WTA, saw the chance to introduce new events with major prize money and huge growth was achieved at a time when tennis faced challenges from other sports and leisure interests elsewhere. It was great for the bottom line.

China seemingly targeted the ladies' doubles event as a quick way to achieve success internationally. Spectacular success came in the form of gold medals at the Athens Olympics in 2004 for Li Ting and Sun Tiantian and this win no doubt helped to encourage those promoting the general programme. Further success came with Zheng Jie, Yan Zi, Zhang Shuai and Peng Shuai all winning Grand Slam doubles titles while Li Na made the ultimate breakthrough with her singles win at the French Open in 2011 followed by an Australian Open in 2014. She hit the big time but also caused waves in China by playing a leading role in breaking away from the contract formula used by the state to keep their players competing for China rather than themselves. Keeping politics well to the fore of Chinese tennis is also Hsieh Su-wei, another Grand Slam doubles winner, but she comes from Taiwan which is another contentious problem for the politicians of the world. Su-wei just plays tennis, and very well, but the political problem follows her around and that's not her fault. Peng Shuai stirred things up late in 2021 by allegedly accusing Vice Premier Zhang Gaoli of coercing her to have sex at his home, causing the WTA, the IOC and even the UN to express concern when she seemingly disappeared. Politics in sport: I wish they weren't connected but I'm afraid it's obvious that they are.

Early visits to China for me were interesting because they were so different to the norm I was used to. Vast construction projects across Beijing produced forests of high-rise apartments, shopping centres on a scale rarely seen plus the infrastructure to meet the demands of the millions who flocked to live and work in this mega city. Multi-lane highways linked the ever-growing suburbs to the city and the air was filled with planes that could take you to more cities that you'd never heard of all containing yet more millions of people.

The factories in and around Beijing all helped to contribute to some well-documented smog problems. The Tours were used to having conversations about heat rules but here we were being asked what, if any, policy was in place when smog became an issue. The reality was that there was no formal policy but data was continually gathered and the medics were aware of any players who had breathing problems. From our practical point of view all we could do was to make sure that the floodlights were turned on all day whenever the smog was bad. At least this brightened up the court from the dull, overcast sky that the pollution caused. We were only there for a short time but I feel so sorry for those who live with these conditions on a regular basis.

The traditional, beautiful, ancient China of legend was systematically marginalised and confined to small pockets of history by the overwhelming brutality of concrete. As years went by I continued to visit and came to recognise and better understand how the Chinese population now lived. Chasing the material benefits and dreams that this development brought was all very well but at what cost? Control, discipline and a lack of humour and individuality there made me come to dread my visits in later years. The censorship was almost comical but no one was laughing. News reports simply went blank when anything controversial was covered and you could forget looking up anything on Google because it just didn't work. It was banned, controlled and you must obey, or else.

It all produced a population that was very difficult to work with and quite different to the rest of the world. You always had the feeling that those selected to work alongside the foreigners imported to run their international events were there because they were considered 'safe'. As for the foreigners themselves I knew we were only there because we were needed to fulfil the regulations. We would be replaced by locals just as soon as they could be trained up with the necessary qualifications to keep it all Chinese.

Confused conversations were the norm. Ask anyone who has travelled there. Many locals you come across, including in the workplace, speak a little English, nod enthusiastically and agree to do something but have not understood what you said at all. Later on you realise that whatever it was that was agreed has simply not happened so you patiently go back and repeat the process and then it happens again! It drives you mad!

It led to all sorts of situations, some funny and others just frustrating. For example, the toilets servicing the players on the outside courts in Beijing were situated in the four corners of the block of courts we used there. Site checks had ensured that all were operational and ready for the start. Then toilet breaks in matches were proving a problem because the toilets had been mysteriously locked causing the players to go back to the locker rooms several minutes away. This wasn't great and it needed sorting so after a few of the now famous confused conversations we got them all unlocked again. Then players started to complain that the toilets smelled terribly. This was often a problem anyway but this time it was because people were smoking in there, something that was prohibited in the area. More confused conversations then took place trying to get this new problem sorted. By the middle of the week we had guards in place to ensure that the toilets were both unlocked and also smoke-free. Throwing a few more people at a problem in China is easy because there are plenty around even though you may need to wake them up first. Then, finally, just as we thought we were all sorted on the toilet front another player complained that the toilet was locked but when he knocked on the door the guard emerged putting out his cigarette! The event finished the next day so that problem never got solved but merely rolled on to the following year.

The hierarchy system there meant that orders were given and followed regimentally. So if a foreign official like me came in and wasn't the immediate boss of the person being asked to do something then it probably wouldn't happen. You couldn't go direct to the staff member because they needed to hear it from their boss. Talk about time-wasting and frustrating! One day we needed the lights turned on in the main stadium following a player request as it was a dull day. So the order was given and then we waited, expecting it to happen immediately. But no such luck. The person whose job it was to flick the switch needed to hear it from someone who wasn't on site and he wasn't answering his phone. It was a tough sell trying to explain that one to the player!

Maybe it was all summed up back in the rather nice hotel room that Dannie and I had for one of the events. In the en-suite bathroom there was a very exotic toilet. It glowed blue when you approached it (a bit eerie this in the middle of the night!), had a heated seat, flushed itself and closed its lid down again once the business of the occasion had been completed. It was both impressive but also, for me, came to symbolise China. It was technologically advanced, in many ways very impressive but despite all that it remained fundamentally a shitty experience.

Chapter 25

The Nuts and Bolts of the Job

What does a referee do? I was often asked because many get it confused with being a chair umpire, thinking that I (as a referee) would sit in the highchair and get abused by players. I would tell them that I was too old and blind to go anywhere near the umpire's chair and that my role meant that I got abused by players (and their entourages) off court instead.

At most events you can fairly easily split the running of a tournament into two areas. If you're responsible for everything that happens away from the courts then you're probably the tournament director. If you're in charge of everything that happens with the actual tennis on court then you're probably the tournament referee. The two people work closely together of course and the bigger the event the more people will also be involved. In the case of Grand Slams that cast list runs into many thousands.

The highest-profile parts of the referee role are ensuring the correct players are entered according to the selection system used, making the draws, putting together the order of play for each day, taking rain and roof decisions as and when required and fining the players who need to be relieved of a little of their prize money. These little jobs do require contact and liaison with virtually everyone else on site in some way or another and so communication becomes a vital, and sometimes difficult, part of the job. The need to ensure that decisions are instantly put out to the world means that the IT support unit is crucial to the success of the whole operation. The singles events at major events are made up of players who are directly entered by both Tours, the ATP and WTA, according to ranking. The leading players don't enter, they are automatically entered, and it is their responsibility to withdraw if they need to for illness or injury reasons. As professional players they are expected to play the leading events and will be hurt in terms of the ranking system if they don't. The money's not too bad either so they generally do!

In addition to direct entries there are qualifiers: these are successful players who come through preliminary rounds. Entry for this is, again, by world ranking. If your ranking isn't high enough to warrant direct entry into the main draw or the qualifying events then you will need to be awarded a wild card. These can be given to anyone and are regarded by some as presents to the unworthy to fill the remaining places in the draw. Wild cards are used to take care of top players who have fallen in the rankings due to injury, up-and-coming young players who are seen as the future and leading 'home' players who will give local interest to the event. In practice they are always contentious since they are subjective decisions and so open to opinion. There have been some strange wild cards awarded over the years but the tournament director is able to have almost full discretion, provided they don't get caught doing something naughty like selling them of course! There are often applications from all sorts who reckon that it's worth giving it a go on the basis that 'they can only say no'. Well, that's true I suppose but they're normally wasting their time. Mostly, the application comes from the agent who is under pressure to do their best for their player. If the player says jump they jump. If the player says apply for a wild card they apply for a wild card.

There have been many entertaining applications over the years but my favourite came from a window cleaner in Wimbledon. He applied saying that he'd had a dream in which he'd won Wimbledon and wanted to make that dream a reality as it would be a wonderful story. He'd been playing a bit recently and his serve had improved so this would be a factor on the grass at Wimbledon. He hadn't actually played any tournaments before but this would only add to the appeal of the story when he finally lifted the famous trophy. He wasn't successful in his application so we'll never know whether this deprived The Championships of its greatest-ever story.

Making the draw is usually the referee's first real opportunity to really screw up in public. There are many further chances later on but this one might be live in front of the assembled press or sometimes televised depending on the event. The entry lists are checked, rechecked and then checked again. They are then further checked by the Tours and the ITF representatives and all the details are entered into the system ready for the draw presentation. These days it's perfectly possible to simply press a button and a randomly produced draw will be instantly prepared by the computer. But some events still prefer to create a show of the ceremony and maintain some tradition by selecting numbered chips from a bag for the draw.

Often it will be a local dignitary or VIP who selects the chips with the different numbers and they'll pass them to the referee who then reads the number and announces the name. The IT support unit simultaneously enters the data and so it can be shown live on screen at the same time as the announcement is made. It looks slick and it is … provided the names and numbers are correct! I would practise the names beforehand since many are difficult and not necessarily well known even to those of us within the game. The secret lies in not getting tongue-tied by them. Did I always get them correct? Definitely not. There's no doubt that many of their mothers would be truly appalled at my efforts but I worked on the theory that only the native-speaking journalists in front of me would realise that I'd just completely butchered Michał Przysiezny's name since if I said it confidently enough few in the room would know better.

If an event decides to just keep the process simple and doesn't need to make a fuss then a computer-generated draw is made. Once the correct data is entered a player or Tour manager (representing the players) will be asked to be the one to make the final click of the mouse and the draw will instantly appear on screen. Is it completely random as it should be? Well, the computer geniuses who write the software programmes assure that it is and who am I to argue? That doesn't stop the visual check immediately afterwards once the paper copy is produced to make sure the seeds are in the correct spaces and that it all looks correct before it's signed off and released to the world.

Once you have a draw you can make an order of play and this is always open for discussion and difference of opinion. With most events you just get on and do it. But at the major events it involves wide input after which something goes out with the referee's name at the bottom of it that has certainly been checked over and debated by many. I sometimes say that provided every player plays at 2pm on the Centre Court every day there will be no arguments regarding the order of play. If they can also win their matches every day then you've got happy bunnies everywhere. It's really that easy!

The tournament director, the ATP and WTA Tours, the ITF advisor and the media all have their say at the Grand Slams and all will have their own opinion as to where priorities lie. There are so many considerations including some obvious and some not so obvious. In principle the best players will play on the best courts. No surprise there but then many players have a higher opinion of their status than the rest of the world. Some may have contracts linked to playing on the main stadium court since appearances there will likely attract more media coverage and hence TV time for advertisers. Ever noticed the little advertising patches on the arms of players? Some of those might be for one match only and the deal may also include the ludicrous caps worn in the player boxes by coaches and the hangers-on. Yes, seriously.

Bracket matches will be played at similar times. This means that if the winner of A and B is due to play the winner of C and D in the second round then their first-round matches will be played at a similar time to avoid one winning player having greater rest time and so gaining a perceived advantage for the second-round match. A player playing late one day will not usually be scheduled early the following day. Since the order of play for the following day is often released before the end of play you can be left dependent on matches not running late. If this were only singles then it would be much easier but it can involve doubles and mixed matches as well. Particularly precious players don't want to play first or last match of the day, will put in their request and then complain loudly when it doesn't happen.

Doubles involvement certainly causes difficulty with scheduling. Singles will be played before doubles and doubles before mixed except for extremely rare circumstances. So a player's singles schedule will frequently be dictated by their opponent's doubles involvement. It's a relief for those involved with scheduling to see multi-event players lose so that these complications are reduced.

There will also be requests coming in from various sources. Media sometimes ask for particular matches not to be scheduled at the same time as a major counter-attraction in the world somewhere else. For example, notice would likely be taken of the matches scheduled at the football World Cup to avoid unnecessary clashes. Players may advise that they're carrying an injury or maybe they have a medical scan appointment at a local hospital. That would probably influence the schedule to try to accommodate the request if possible but illness and injury requests will only be granted if it's felt that there is no significant disadvantage to their opponent out of fairness to them too. Coaches sometimes work with multiple players and so scheduling will try to avoid their players playing at the same time if possible. If several players from the same country are competing on the same day then it makes sense to spread them through the day so that spectators who want to follow that particular nation's players have a chance to see them all.

So there are many considerations and it's not always possible to take care of them all. Most people concentrate on the leading players who get the most publicity but I can assure you that the least-known player in the field is really only interested in his or her match schedule and if it doesn't suit them they will be unhappy. That's when you need a referee because then they do at least have someone to shout at!

Excellent computer software now helps with scheduling. Much time and effort has gone into its development over many years to reach the point we're at now and, of course, it's an ongoing effort. The earliest attempts at computerisation eliminated the human errors like scheduling a player for both singles and doubles at the same time or perhaps putting on the same match twice. Now that might sound basic but it's perfectly possible when you're dealing with hundreds of players. It also makes you look a complete incompetent, which is usually not helpful even if it gives the locker rooms a good laugh at your expense! In recent years state-of-the-art scheduling systems have been installed that work very well. They might vary a little at the major events but all are very visual with giant screens that offer everything connected to the refereeing process at a glance: draws, orders of play, current scores, interviews, live coverage of all courts and the ability to pass on-screen messages to all in the restricted areas regarding changes to schedule and possible weather information. It's very hi-tech and very useful. It would be unthinkable to return to the old days of working it all out with paper, pencil and a very well-used eraser.

Troubleshooting problems is the last resort. You must be organised, have everything prepared and ready and try to think of everything that could possibly go wrong. Then you'll be surprised by something completely different. Like the day that 'Pimplegate' suddenly erupted in 2013. The leading players of both Adidas and Nike were looking suspiciously at each other across the changing room fearing that the other lot had got an advantage. Rules dictate the number and length of pimples under the sole of the tennis shoes and also where they can reach up the sides. After discussions and much analysis of various shoe models came the job of carefully policing the offending models to the point of removing pimples with nail clippers so that they complied. Surfaces can perform differently depending on weather conditions and court usage and that means that you might even require different soles to cater for this. It's a competitive world at the top of professional tennis and this spat shows the detail to which the leading players and their entourages will go to get any sort of advantage.

A more unusual situation might be a report from medical staff of an outbreak of a virus that could affect players, staff, ballkids or indeed anyone on site. Procedures are in place for such occasions. Fortunately, they are rare but there have been cases involving individual players, groups of players and ballkids over the years. While the loss of a handful of staff might be grossly inconvenient somehow the show goes on. But if it ever were to affect a particular player who has to be withdrawn from an event for the safety of the remaining players then that would be far more contentious. If the player does so voluntarily then it's fine but if not then all sorts of legalities can quickly be encountered. Public health concerns now seem to override everything and the Covid-19 pandemic has certainly brought this whole issue into great focus.

A common situation for every referee is deciding when it's too dark to continue play. This may also involve whether to stop play to close a roof due to imminent adverse weather as many events now have a moving roof providing this option. Doubles tends to be more amicable but singles matches often involve a player who wants to stop and the other who wants to continue. You use your experience and common sense to decide when it's the correct time to finish. What's important in these situations is to stay completely impartial and to judge based on the facts. What's the weather forecast? What time is dusk? How thick is the current cloud cover and is it likely to improve or worsen? These are all very relevant and you decide if it's realistically possible to reach a better point before stopping play. You decide what is the correct decision and don't allow the wishes of one player to take precedence over the other. There's no exact science to these decisions and that's why some leeway has to exist for the wonderful coverall statement in the rules that 'the referee's decision is final'.

Over the years I learned that one man you needed to make good contact with at any outdoor event was the groundsman. After the tournament director he was the first person that I went to see to ensure that we could work closely together. It's because he knows his courts far better than anyone else. Groundsmen can be a breed apart and I love them. One of the best was Maurice, the main man at Newcastle. I loved going there, listening to his stories and I quickly learned to trust everything he told me. He knew when the courts would be fit for play after rain and also which courts would be ready before certain others. As the referee you are meant to be the source of all knowledge including when it's going to stop raining (yes, really!) and therefore when a player will be back on court. I could guess but a quick chat with Maurice and his like meant I could speak with much more confidence when giving answers. He also made me laugh. Impeccably polite whenever in the company of all women he would then lapse into barrack-room language the second the lady had left his earshot. He was old school like that. One of the more printable stories about him came when he saw one of the rough, tough English chair umpires from the north-east of England up in the chair on a bitterly cold Newcastle day. Everyone else was in multiple layers against the cold while Brian sat stoically up there in his polo shirt refusing to acknowledge that anything was remotely uncomfortable. Maurice looked, shook his head, turned away and remarked to his junior sidekick in his strong Geordie accent, 'He thinks he's a fooking polar bear!'

You can't do the job without these wonderful, committed people around you. They are pure gold and the best of them are guaranteed to brighten any day at any tournament. It's a big team event behind the running of professional tennis events and they all have their vital role to play.

The best referees will be used to making decisions constantly throughout the day. It's not an exact science and the factors involved in the decision-making will change constantly. Matches run quickly or slowly requiring court changes, the weather plays it's part by suddenly causing play to cease due to rain with rescheduling required, orders of play need to be made and then remade as situations change and all this against the backdrop of constant player queries and requests.

Good people and organisational skills are a given as is the ability to give calm leadership when required. Sometimes you must persuade and, if necessary, enforce decisions on the reluctant. You are responsible for protecting the sport's image and reputation against those who would abuse it and you are expected to be able to solve every problem. Is it easy? No. Is it a challenge and hugely rewarding when the show is over and the event has been successfully completed? Most definitely yes.

Chapter 26

What It's Like to Be an Official on the Tour

A ll the major tennis events are officiated by a travelling band of international chair umpires who are well known to the players. They're used to working together on the ATP and WTA Tours around the world and for Grand Slams they're joined by an ITF group who also work the major team competitions. Because they may work up to 30 weeks a year it means they rack up plenty of air miles. All international officials are graded, first by the passing of exams and later by ongoing evaluations provided by their peers and by tournament directors in the case of the supervisors and referees. This whole process is little known to the public, goes on constantly behind the scenes and is very comprehensive.

Because the cost of these international officials is very high efforts are made by the tournaments to keep the expenses down as much as possible. A minimum number will be engaged from overseas, those on site will be worked hard and as many locals as possible from the same locality or country will make up the numbers required to run the event effectively. The advent of electronic line calling has already made a dramatic change to the numbers of line umpires needed and this will only continue. But for now international chair umpires will still be needed not least because each one should be from a different country to that of the players competing to ensure impartiality.

The days of line umpires at the top level are certainly numbered. Electronic line calling has now been accepted. It means that the vast numbers required to service 16 match courts with up to nine line umpires plus one chair umpire are almost gone. These officials need rest time with spare teams being rotated in at regular intervals. This means that a day's work for these on-court officials involves reporting well before the start of play, being assigned into their teams for the day and then working sessions calling lines on court all day until released by their immediate boss, the chief umpire. In their rest time they have a suitable restricted area where they can eat, drink and spend time mixing with the other officials.

For many it's a good opportunity to travel, to make new friends and to see some top-class tennis at very close hand in the major cities and on the major show courts of the world. The age range is considerable as are the ways of filling in the hours of time spent in the rest areas. Books, games and sometimes school or university studies are all popular particularly when long hours of rain cause everyone to wonder how long it'll be before the referee finally gets around to cancelling play for the day!

Away from the courts there's the chance to see a new city or perhaps try out the restaurants. But be careful of going out late to a club or having that last drink in the bar at the officials' hotel. Someone will see you and there's always the 12-hour alcohol rule that applies before the start of play the following day. The officials' code of conduct covers many things designed to ensure that officials don't get involved with anything likely to bring the game into disrepute. It also requires officials not to offer opinions, on court, off court, in the media or in casual chat, that could be overheard in a crowd.

If there's a major incident on court you'll certainly hear from the players in their post-match interviews plus the TV commentators and possibly the coaches, agents and anyone else who wants to join in on social media. But you won't hear from the officials on court. You never get to hear their side of the story. The best you might get is an authorised statement from a referee, a tournament director or possibly the Tour's head of officiating. Those actually involved have all been 'cancelled' to give it the modern expression!

Over the years officials have been trained and encouraged to be thoughtful, restrained and undemonstrative on court. They shouldn't be the show but merely the quiet voice of authority when required. In previous eras some officials used to be seen as characters in their own right and if you went to watch a match where they were sitting in the chair you'd be assured of entertainment by simply watching and listening to them. But the breed of chair umpires today is much more professional even though they must all be mentally strong to even contemplate taking on the responsibility that comes with dealing with high-profile disputes in the full glare of the media. It's no easy task and it's one that can seem thankless at times.

Some chair umpires have been in the public eye now for several years. Because they regularly work the major matches and they're introduced by television commentators they do become well known to tennis fans around the world. When they walk around the grounds on site at an event they're easily spotted because they will be in the uniform of that event with sponsor logos and the colours identifying which event they're working. All quietly accept and deal with it trying not to draw attention to themselves. But it is at least a little recognition for the work they do. Nobody in life can be perfect but sports officials are expected to be as close as possible. If they get it right nothing is said but when they get it wrong plenty are all too ready to point it out!

The chair umpires walk a fine line in many respects when it comes to their relationships with the players, also covered by the officials' code. They inevitably have, and need to build, a good relationship with players because it helps when it comes to managing matches. Players are more likely to trust officials they know than those they don't. It's natural. But it can also work the other way. If situations occur on court and there's a dispute it can sour that relationship and cause problems in the future. So officials know the players but must be careful not to get too close or be seen to be friends since that runs the risk of ending in tears with accusations of bias.

Referees and supervisors work together with the chair umpires to help manage on-court situations. If the team of officials work well together then matches are managed with dramas kept to a minimum. Off-court contact with players is usually dealt with by the referees and supervisors. They can move around the locker rooms and the player restaurants to liaise with any player who needs a quiet word about any issue. This helps to keep chair umpires out of the firing line if there's been a disagreement and the show can go on.

It's inevitable that there'll be arguments from time to time. Highly competitive players battling it out for big prizes with borderline decisions or judgments being made will inevitably cause disagreements. So players get mad and officials get used to getting it in the neck. They can't answer back because it's not allowed so they grow a thick skin, realise its usually not personal and tolerate a certain level of grumbling. It's not pleasant but that's just the way it is. Anything beyond the level of acceptable and further action should be taken against the player. But it does mean that international officials need to have the self-discipline to resist landing a punch to the jaw or giving an expletive-laden mouthful back when it happens. You are allowed to think it, though!

The goal of all officials is to do a quiet, effective job, getting the calls and the application of the rules right. If they achieve this the tennis does the talking and controversy surrounding some officiating issue doesn't become the story. Good in theory but there's a lot of paddling going on beneath the surface to get it right. The officials themselves try to perform well and get good grades in their evaluations. If that happens they can boost their chances of securing invitations for future events. There's always great competition and interest in the acceptances for the major events. Every event has its own budget for officials which affects decisions and that's understandable. What is less clear is when tennis politics get in the way with officials of lesser ability being selected above clearly better ones. That one I could never understand or support.

And what of a personal life for officials and, come to that, all those travelling regularly on the tennis Tour? Well, it's not easy is the honest answer. The necessity of being away from home for many weeks a year is a problem when it comes to maintaining a relationship. The glamour and excitement of being off around the world can be very seductive but the realities are soon found to be quite different. Only the full-time, contracted officials have any kind of financial stability and then it's at a level that doesn't reflect the responsibility they take on. The rest are living on little more than expenses and so are reliant on second jobs or independent wealth to keep going. Paying rent or mortgages is tough and having dependants makes it even tougher for the majority. Then there's the strain on relationships of being away a lot of the time. Perhaps it's no surprise that proximity means that some find partners amongst the other officials but the code of conduct prohibits liaisons with players so that's regarded as forbidden fruit!

Dannie came with me when possible and, for me, that was such a support. It was unusual for a partner to travel with an official but for us it worked even though it came at considerable expense. I was lucky that she enjoyed travelling and she was able to spend time around the courts without getting too bored. Most events allowed us to have the evenings together and they could be fun but when matches were scheduled late into the evening time together could be limited. Some events were better suited for her to come to while others provided the chance to see parts of the world together that we would never normally have contemplated visiting.

The international nature of officiating on the Tour is a wonderful thing. Every week sees a different group of colleagues thrown together to form a close-knit team. All are reliant on each other to perform effectively as they're on the same team. Off court the chance to learn from each other and to share thoughts and ideas not just about tennis but, more importantly, about where they came from is a great bonus. It makes for a wonderfully international contact list with people from around the globe that, in time, become friends. Hearing about their countries, cultures, religions and current affairs from different points of view helps give a very global outlook. The united nations of officials is a great university of life.

Part Four
It's Only a Game

Chapter 27

Everyone's Royal but Some Are More Royal than Others

Professional sport involves huge amounts of money and that in turn attracts large numbers of extras. Players at the highest level are in most cases rightly well rewarded for their efforts and for the entertainment they provide but many more surround them. And the more successful their superstar the more the hangers-on will see as being their 'fair share'.

It's almost inevitable that there are times when the coaches, trainers, agents, parents, spouses, lovers, advisors and any number of other extras complain about their lives. There are also officials (including referees!), journalists and the army of VIPs who represent all the different national associations and player organisations to think of. Then include the politicians and the celebrities who all want a free ticket to the tennis and you quickly see there's plenty of material for the feature writers to work with.

At all Grand Slams arrangements need to be made for well over 600 players. This means they need to be transported from their hotels each day and to/from the airport when needed. They will be housed in a hotel somewhere at considerable cost and so they receive a generous daily allowance to offset the expense. They will need to be fed from time to time and so most tastes are catered for. This is all free, of course. Oh yes, and all the above-mentioned people will expect exactly the same! And some will make a lot of noise if the standard doesn't meet with their approval.

All this involves an enormous amount of detailed planning. How many guest passes should a player receive? How much food allocation should they get? Who should be allowed to travel in the official car service? How should practice time be fairly allocated on all courts, particularly the main stadium courts in Melbourne, Paris and New York but all The Championships grass courts in the case of Wimbledon?

To be fair and reasonable every event makes rules as best they can according to their own circumstances. But if a player feels hard done by instant reaction on social media is likely to compare it unfavourably to other events. Welcome to reality. The ATP finals, when it was held at the O2 Arena in London, had eight singles players. Each one was given their own personal changing room to prepare in. How can vast events with many hundreds of players compete unless more than 600 individual spaces are prepared, with every little luxury, on site for each of the players?

All players will ideally practise under match conditions and so the leading players want to be on the stadium courts where their matches are likely to be scheduled. This means that the middle- and lesser-ranking players don't get the same privilege and straight away there is perceived bias against them. The atmosphere is different with the surrounding stands presenting variances in the wind from more open outside courts. It may also be that the court surface is marginally slower or faster than the others and this is vital in the minds of the players who, quite rightly, want everything to be perfect for them with no advantage to their opponent. Major events try to balance these demands and requirements as best they can.

One way to allocate players is by way of reward for seeding

position or for past performance. A past champion may receive special favours as opposed to the local wild card entry. This privileged player may get greater numbers of guest passes, coach access to the car service, longer and better practice time on the show courts and all this without the appearance of bias. If it is a rule and applied equally it's a defence against the criticism that the stars get more privilege than the others, which of course they do. But human nature means that most will always take their due and look for just that little bit more. If an irate player then voices their upset on Twitter the press run the story because that's their job and the event can be made to look uncaring.

The scenario above gets played out with a thousand different variations at every Grand Slam. They all have huge pressure on tickets compared with most other tournaments in the world. If a local wild card player has grandparents, parents and a handful of friends, not to mention his/her partner, then they would all get in easily without fuss virtually everywhere. But the majors are different. Everyone wants to be there, everyone is important and so the pressure on facilities is huge. The option is to say yes to all the requests but then the player areas would be even more crowded than they are at present and players would quickly complain about the lack of space available. Welcome to the world of trying to satisfy those who can never be satisfied.

This also gets played out in other areas as well. The president of the Uranus Tennis Association, who can just about tell the difference between tennis and squash but not necessarily much more, needs good seats on the Centre Court because he wants to watch Roger play. Sadly, the international guest box is already full with people from other national associations around the world and so an underpaid and very stressed employee from the event staff will have to give him the bad news. Because the Uranus Tennis Association is important and the president is a well-connected man this particular demand isn't going to disappear and so the grapevine is called into action to try to swing the necessary tickets. Frankly, the president probably doesn't really care whether he watches or not since he doesn't like tennis very much anyway but his girlfriend (PS Don't mention it to the wife), who he's taking with him, will be very disappointed and we wouldn't want that would we?

Tennis players at the Tour level have seen regular large increases in their prize money in modern times to the point where the leading players are multimillionaires, even those without major titles. If you look at a graph showing how much the top 100 earn then you see the expected increase from 100 as the line steadily rises up to the household names at the top. At this point it goes almost vertical. And this is before off-court endorsement income which can dwarf prize money depending on which player you talk about. Are they worth it? Well, can anyone justify the large amounts paid to captains of industry compared with the average worker or the entertainment superstars who consistently take eye-watering amounts home? The answer lies in 'market forces' and it isn't going to change anytime soon.

The public will pay a ransom to watch the top stars but very little to watch very capable performers (of whatever discipline). Tickets to see Messi and Paris Saint-Germain will be expensive and tough to get while the excellent professionals of Burton Albion struggle to get a worthwhile attendance. Tickets for the Slams can be like gold dust but you can walk into any number of pro tennis events in Britain for little or nothing and be amongst only a handful of spectators. The lesser players don't like to admit this but they are very dependent on the top stars bringing bums on seats to the events they play. Tournament directors around the world are desperate to get the leading players to play and then worry in case they lose early as it affects the on-site spectator attendance and the all-important TV audience numbers and the sponsorship this brings. This means that the top players are able to negotiate very attractive guarantees to play at events. They don't necessarily have to meet performance targets either.

Some years ago a former world number one was contracted to play in Auckland, New Zealand just after Christmas. He arrived a few days early, went on a fishing trip (organised by the tournament) and only arrived at the tournament the day before he was due to play his first round. On the day of his match he warmed up briefly with his wife and then went out to lose to a local wild card player in straight sets. He was paid a lot of money to go on that fishing holiday. The amounts asked for and paid to other leading players are a not so very well guarded secret and leave any nation's average annual wage a long way behind. Naturally, negotiations will likely include first-class airfares for various 'essential' companions depending on the size of the player's entourage.

Meanwhile, the Tours try to contract players to support their events. If you put up a suitable amount of money then in theory you get a certain number of players who are designated to the event depending on their ranking. It's all fine in theory but it regularly runs into problems when illness and injury take their toll. By the end of the season in 2017 Djokovic, Murray, Del Potro, Raonic, Wawrinka, Berdych, Kyrgios and Nishikori were all injured and needed extended time off from the Tour. Serena Williams was on maternity leave and Azarenka was fighting for custody of her son. Not good news for the events who would have liked them in their draws. More time off! is the cry. A larger extended period to allow time for players to rest, recharge batteries and recover from the physical nature of professional tennis. All good in theory but of course we all know what happens in any 'break' – the money men come in and exhibitions are arranged where players can play a little hit-and-giggle tennis for yet more money.

So the tennis royalty commands and the rest of the tennis world falls in line and tries to get itself a little piece of the action along the way. It leads to the situation where the supporting cast of journeyman players, the entourages, the helpers, the volunteers and the officials are like beggars at the banquet. They're there to make up the numbers needed to run an event but let no one be in any doubt who's making the serious money. But for many of these extras it's enough to be close to greatness in the hope that a little stardust (and cash) may fall their way.

Also spare a thought for the doubles players. There are many out there making no attempt to play singles. They may have tried in the past before finding that their game suits the doubles court better. There's enough money in the sport to encourage them to keep going and indeed the more successful of them do make a very good living. They also have coaches, spouses and others that add to the numbers making up the tennis family. Like ghosts they inhabit the same tennis world even though they are rarely recognised. Oh yes, and finally the qualifiers. These players are sometimes regarded as kind of second-class citizens where they travel, practise, train and then play at weekends only. They will play, lose and then disappear only to re-emerge the following week to repeat the process once again at the next stop on the Tour. They are a drain on the tournament directors because they eat their food, make demands on the hotel accommodation and want things like towels and practice balls. No wonder they sometimes get asked the question, 'Are you a player or are you a qualifier?' from tournament helpers not blessed with the necessary tact and diplomacy to deal with them!

One way to distinguish between tennis royalty and royalty of the, well, royal kind is by the security they have. If a couple of students dressed up in a uniform come past leading someone dressed in a tracksuit then it's a good bet that you've just spotted a tennis player. You may not know who it is but the supersized racket bag that looks like it contains their life's possessions may give a clue. However, if you're minding your own business and suddenly there's a bit of a kerfuffle and a couple of suits come past shouting 'make way' followed by someone else it may well be royalty of the royal kind. These are sometimes to be seen on their way to and from their seats or the corporate hospitality areas. They're part of the scene. The photographers and the media love them as do the events because they add a touch of sparkle to proceedings. Everyone loves to spot someone famous, and Wimbledon is fortunate to have Kate, the Princess of Wales, as its patron. She loves her tennis which is great news for all the many royal watchers for the coming years, particularly if she brings her husband with her as well!

Chapter 28

Gamesmanship Rules

There's always a lot of noise around professional tennis as the sport discusses what the game should look like in the future. Commentators can't have dead airtime, journos are under pressure to fill space in the newspapers and everyone needs conversation during the rain breaks so what gets discussed? There's the time taken between points and match formats for starters. TV's desire to maximise ad breaks at every opportunity together with the world now seemingly having the attention span of a two-year-old mean that match formats are reducing. TV audiences and spectators mustn't get bored. Running contrary to this is the view that the sport has existed for many years and that messing around with rules only confuses everyone so leave it alone. If it's not broken don't fix it. Like with Test match cricket this old timer view is doomed.

John McEnroe seemed to have problems tying his shoelaces since they came undone whenever he needed to slow things down, Novak Djokovic would regularly bounce the ball an astonishing number of times, Rafa Nadal would fiddle and fidget, towelling down would take place (sometimes even after an ace!) by many pros and coaches would write reams about the importance of having set rituals before every point. It meant that over time the game got slower. That means that people get outraged and want to legislate against everything.

It used to be that Wimbledon started at 2pm each day; four matches were played on each court and they still finished. For years we started at 11.30am and finally this became 11am after over a decade of lobbying from me and others. Even with this earlier start it's still possible to struggle to get through the day's play on time before darkness and that's without rain delays. The best players in the world deserve to play in the best conditions possible and there's no question that the light conditions in the late morning are much better than when dusk approaches.

In times gone by players would go straight to court at the completion of the previous match, have a brief warm-up and then play without all the breaks we now see for injuries and going to the toilet. They didn't even sit down at the change of ends, only pausing briefly for a quick towel-down and a swig of drink before continuing to play. Now any excuse to slow things down is taken and the breaks are a pain. Are they all necessary? Almost certainly not. So how have we got to where we are now?

The advent of the medical people coming into the sport and the mantra of safety first at all times hasn't helped. Now I'm from the old school, and a grumpy old git to go with it, so it may be no surprise to find that if I had my way we wouldn't have these medical timeouts at all. If a player isn't fit to play then they should shake hands, retire and walk off. Perhaps as a concession I could say that if a trainer/physio comes on it should carry some form of score penalty, maybe a point or a game, against the player calling the assistance. That would soon stop the unnecessary calls. The same should apply to toilet breaks. Let players go whenever they like but again only with a score penalty. That allows for emergencies and stops the play-acting. It would speed up the game enormously.

When I played I had a set formula for dealing with any opponent I thought was trying to disturb my rhythm of serving. If I looked up and found that the receiver wasn't ready and was holding their hand up to stop me and I suspected it was simply to piss me off then I would turn, throw the balls to the ballkid and collect more from the other corner before returning to the line to start my routine again. It soon stopped those with bad intent. Now we have rules that the chair umpires can apply but still there is the suspicion that they're abused by those wishing to stall.

Some players are quick. Federer and Roddick are two of the major names known for getting on with it but there are plenty of others. When Federer played Tiafoe at the US Open in 2017 one was taking an average of 12 seconds between points and the other only ten. It was almost too quick because the spectators didn't have time to fully appreciate the quality of the tennis and to react before the next point was played. There is a natural rhythm to a match and different players and different matches have different rhythms. I wouldn't want to alter that as it's part of the sport's attraction. When you have players regimented into playing all the same, showing no emotion and taking the same amount of time as each other there's a danger we have killed off individuality. Be careful what you wish for. A couple of slow players between points doesn't mean we have a sport-wide problem. Players can regulate themselves to some degree and more rules and regulations sometime end up with unintended consequences. Imagine the outcry when a great match played over several hours reaches 6-5, 40-30, final set and the final point doesn't get played because of a time penalty being given to the receiver. Now we're not talking about the great match, just about the stupidity of a rule that deprives everyone of the finish the match deserved. The first rule in any rule book should be to apply common sense and a false ending like that would be ridiculous. The public watching around the court and on TV want to see great sport but professional tennis players just want to win matches and will seek to use and exploit any rules to their advantage if they can.

Grunting or noise made by players during play has also been a frequent topic. It has always happened. Every player will make a noise when great effort is being put in. You can't expect silence on court when someone's busting a gut to first get to and then hit a tennis ball at full stretch. So when does it become a problem?

Answer: when it's done deliberately to put off the opponent. That must lie in the judgment of the chair umpire. There are so many variations or possibilities connected to this. You can't list them in a rule book because it would just get silly. Use common sense and judgment and trust the officials. But no, we've had tabloids demanding 'Gruntometers' and the like just because a Sharapova or an Azarenka is loud. Problem is Nadal is also loud but has a lower male pitch and so is less noticeable to the ears than Maria. So don't measure the noise or else you quickly get into problems of policing noise with the equivalence of a traffic cop standing with a radar gun and giving out tickets to those caught doing 33mph in a 30mph zone. Imagine that at match point in a Grand Slam final!

I did hear of a player deciding to take matters into their own hands one day. They decided to make an issue of the fact that their opponent was one of the noisy ones. As soon as the grunting started at the far end they would 'moo' loudly every time they hit a forehand and 'baa' loudly every time they hit a backhand! Of course, the supervisor was quickly called to court. Perhaps not surprisingly the chair umpire was told to issue code violations if this were to recur and the situation died a speedy death. However, the player had made his point and the noisy offender at the other end had been shamed sufficiently to restrain himself. Marvellous. I just wish I'd seen and heard this battle of the farmyard for myself!

One I did witness came many years ago at Roland-Garros where Monica Seles (a famous early grunter) was up against Gloria Pizzichini (a very tasty-sounding but also loud Italian). It was played in the open concrete bowl Court Two with a relatively sparse crowd. This exaggerated the acoustic effect of the grunting. At one end Monica was going 'Ah, Eh' on every shot while at the other Gloria was going 'Eh, Ah'! Because of the echo it was difficult to work out who made what noise because it all became one. What entertainment, though! Who cares about tennis when you can enjoy little situations like that? The small crowd was laughing at them both and perhaps that could be the answer – shame them into silence.

Chapter 29

Now Just Play Nicely Boys and Girls!

Whenever equal prize money or comparisons between the sexes takes place anger and strong opinions are never far behind. Media articles regularly use the hot topics of the day like sexism or racism to provoke controversy because that sells newspapers. People love it when a personality gets upset or when a good argument takes place. So here's a very tongue-in-cheek suggestion: remove the sexism completely by simply rewarding the best. Hold a single event open to all to discover who's the best human being on the planet. Anything else could be a sideshow, an exhibition of talent displayed by brilliant athletes who have many wonderful attributes but who choose to play in a limited class. All would be free to enter this open event and the winner would be seen to be the best human being. That way Roger Federer, Serena Williams, Naomi Osaka, Novak Djokovic, Ashleigh Barty, Rafa Nadal, Dylan Alcott, Diede de Groot and all the others would have an equal opportunity to beat everyone else and claim the title.

There could be other events for whoever else wanted to play in them, of course. These could be separate events restricted to men, women, veterans, juniors, transgender, wheelchair players, the deaf, the blind and hey, even Nottingham Forest fans! These events would all be secondary to the main event, which would be to decide the best human being. What about prize money? Well, of course the major lion's share would go to this main event. Every other event that is restricted, for whatever reason, would receive substantially less. Is the above sexist? I don't think so. Unusual and outlandish yes but it's not sexist.

The whole issue of equal prize money is now pretty much historical. All the various arguments have been aired far too often and most people are trapped firmly into one side or the other. Rightly or wrongly it is equal prize money now and that's just the way it is at all the Grand Slams and major events hosting both sexes. Tennis can hold its head high in the court of moral public opinion but it may still have a little further to run as the issue refuses to completely disappear.

In the past there were some amusing views amongst all the fierce debate. When events were moving to equal prize money, having resisted outside pressure for a long time, there was a view offered at the time that went, 'Let's go to the WTA and say, "Thank you for the kind offer from Amelie Mauresmo for the women to play five sets. We're prepared to offer equal prize money on one condition"'. They would say, 'What's that?' 'That the women only play one set!' would be the brutal answer. Ouch!

Another came from one of the mixed Tour events in Europe where the men and women played alongside each other in the same week. The daily discussion was taking place regarding the order of play for the following day. The ATP Tour manager had got his matches nicely lined up in place just where they fitted perfectly when the WTA Tour manager came in and rearranged them all over the place and not to his liking. He cracked. 'I don't mind the women having equal prize money,' he started. 'They can even have more prize money. I don't care. Just let them go play somewhere else!' he finished in what was a magnificent meltdown.

But still the debate continues from time to time. Why? Because the men are now the ones to make a case for equal prize money. The demand was and remains equal pay for equal work. Let's examine this at Grand Slam level. The women are required to play best of three sets in both singles and doubles. The men have to play best of five sets. Because of this the average length of men's matches is considerably longer than women's matches. It also means that the women are more likely to play doubles as well as singles while the men will often only enter the singles. This means the average earnings at these major events for main draw singles players is higher for women than it is for men. The only place where there is equality is in the mixed doubles where the man usually plays a more dominant role. So even here perhaps it's not totally equal. The men could claim there is still inequality in tennis but now because it's the women who get the better deal!

If it were the women who had to play longer for the same money it would be seen as being sexist with a lot of coverage being given to the issue. Does that mean that because it's the other way around it's OK? There's been a lot of silence on the subject so far but maybe that will change in the future.

Having gained equal prize money the women also understandably want equal exposure on the leading courts. Until recently you could argue that there was statistical evidence to show that Wimbledon is sexist. More men's matches were historically scheduled on the top two courts than women's. But the fact that other women's matches were added was ignored. Men's matches have historically (in the main) been more popular to the paying spectators. Why is this? Because generally the stadiums are noticeably not as full for women's matches as they are for the men's. Because the grey market prices (set by demand and supply) for Wimbledon debenture tickets to the ladies' days in the second week were much less than for their equivalent men's days. (A revised order of play for the second week altered this from 2022.) Because TV audience figures are usually better for the men's than for the women's matches. Because a BBC poll of the top ten Wimbledon moments of all time, with 30,000 voters, showed that all the leading memories were of male matches not female. Despite these all being statistically true as many women's matches are played on the show courts as men's.

In the meantime must we conclude that the 30,000 people who responded to the BBC were mistaken? Were those who attend the FA Cup final at Wembley simply unavailable for the Ladies' FA Cup final and should they all give tickets for the women's Ashes v Australia rather than the men's to their families at Christmas? Should people be denied their ability to make this kind of choice? It's a dangerous route to take. Media attempts to level up the playing field by giving equal attention to women's sport have made some inroads. The Women's Euros football in 2022 had the hugely successful 'Lionesses' produce the perfect result for England but this is unlikely to translate into similar attendances for women's and men's Premier League football anytime soon.

The Australian Open and US Open regularly schedule more women's matches on their main stadium courts than men's. This is because they have evening sessions and want to ensure that the day session finishes in time for the evening session to start. Is this sexist? No one mutters anything about it because this time it is the men who are affected! So what's to be done? I expect at some point the men's matches will be reduced to best of three sets at the Grand Slams to match the women so that all will be seen to be 'fair'. Tennis will then be seen to be politically correct but, in my view, the paying public will be the poorer for it.

Thankfully, not all the arguments concerning sexism in tennis are restricted to the serious. One of my favourites came when Richard Krajicek, a former Wimbledon champion no less, went into his press conference one day and claimed that '80 per cent of all the women pro players were lazy, fat pigs'. There was bedlam as the feminists all rallied to condemn him to instant pariah status. All the usual suspects claimed some more column inches as they defended women's tennis and those plying their trade at its forefront. Twenty-four hours later and Krajicek returned to the same press conference room clearly a chastened figure following the criticism. Very solemnly, he said that he was very sorry, had reconsidered his position and wished to make a further statement. He said that he had been mistaken and that only 75 per cent of the women were lazy, fat pigs. It was very funny! Several years later in the PC culture we have today I doubt anyone would dare to show that kind of sense of humour.

It's a pity we can't just enjoy the work of the leading players, whether male or female, without having to pin tags or isms on it. Let them play. Let's have fun watching it without turning it into a battleground with winners and losers. For whatever reason spectators will have their preferences and favourites. It's always been the case and events must showcase these talents or risk seeing a declining fan base in the future.

Now, solutions are much more interesting than shouting about problems. So here's what should happen:

It's inevitable, in my view, that equality and political correctness will prevail at the Grand Slams. Both sexes must be treated equally. But TV companies don't want long matches at early stages (and nor do referees!), but there has to be a differential between the majors and the rest of the tour events. So reduce the format of the early rounds to best of 3 tiebreak sets with a 7 point tie break for the first 2 sets and a 10 point tiebreak for the final set. Keep exactly the same format for the doubles events to make them better understood and to raise their importance too. Then play BOTH mens and ladies' events as the best of 5 sets from the quarter-finals onwards. The women are perfectly capable of doing this and we retain the special nature of these major events.

And, while we're at it let's finally solve the problem of Davis Cup and Fed Cup (or Billie Jean's trophy if you prefer the latest name for it). The ITF killed the Davis Cup in 2019 when they changed the format from the tried, tested and much loved event for a pot of gold.

Instead, have two world groups with 8 nations in each, A and B, with promotion and relegation between the two each year. These would be played over a single week, each at a different venue. Beneath these world groups would be regional qualifying groups to decide promotion to the World Group B. There would need to be potential play off dates built into the schedule at this stage to accommodate the geographical split of those promoted and relegated. Aside from these playoffs everything else could be decided in a single week.

What do you call it? Davis Cup, because at least it keeps the famous name alive. Few outside tennis know what Fed Cup or BJK Cup is anyway. And this new event would be for both sexes. Each team would nominate 3 men and 3 women. One men's singles, one ladies' singles, one men's doubles, one ladies' doubles, and a mixed (if required) would be played for each match between nations, all played on the same day. If there were time pressures, then the two singles and two doubles matches could even be played simultaneously on adjacent courts. Imagine the tv opportunities this uniqueness would provide. For consistency, each singles match would be played over 5 sets and each doubles over 3 sets. Each World Group of 8 nations would mean each nation playing just 3 matches in a single week, something that is perfectly possible. And we would have a mixed team event that everyone could finally understand, with the women included in playing Davis Cup for the first time!

And while we're on a roll let's solve the late matches problem. No one appreciates finishing in the middle of the night. It does mean the events, and particularly the Australian and US Opens taking a financial hit. No separate night sessions. Just have day sessions with a feature match on each of the major show courts given a not before 7pm time. Even a 5 hour match now finishes by midnight.

OK, I think that's it for now. Sexism solved, plus two other major problems, all on one side of A4 paper. That'll do for now. You're welcome! All that needs to happen is for the various tennis bodies to come together and agree to it now. Will that happen? Not a chance!

Chapter 30

The Olympics

I've never been more supportive than 'suspicious' of the whole Olympic thing. At a time when professionalism was fully entrenched into sport the idea that the Olympics could maintain its virginity from a moral point of view was completely naive. The IOC leads from the front in terms of its dubious system for awarding the games to each 'winning' city. The handful of unelected IOC members travel the world at someone else's expense, being courted as if it were a state visit. Votes are allegedly bought and promised with each candidate city doing its best to influence the decision. Would that ever include bribery and corruption? Surely not!

Once awarded to a city the Olympics then make sure of their strict control of all the commercial rights. The multinationals who queue up to line the coffers of the IOC have their own agenda of course and the mass attention of the world's media means that they'll get their name on the TV screens and in the newspapers of the world at the expense of their competitors. It's business pure and simple.

Meanwhile, the athletes are told that it's the dream to win an Olympic gold medal. They dedicate hours, days, months, years and decades to perfecting their art in the pursuit of a lump of metal with some gold plating around it. The tiny few will then manage to turn this into a little dosh by developing their names and making some money from becoming a C-list celebrity. The rest bathe in the glorious knowledge of having been an Olympian while trying to pay their water bill at home.

And how about the citizens of each 'winning' city? They are given a 'once in a lifetime' chance to volunteer their time and expertise to work long hours for absolutely no pay whatsoever! This includes professionals like doctors and dentists who are recruited to look after the Olympic family. This 'family' includes not just the athletes from every country but also all their team officials and support staff. Some of these undoubtedly see the opportunity of getting a health check or their teeth fixed at the same time.

The big bucks from the Olympics go to the small inner sanctum while the people who actually make it happen get nothing whatsoever. Many years ago slave labour was abolished and I'm told that if I set up any kind of business I'm expected to pay any employees that work for me. But if you're the Olympics you can get around it all by calling it 'volunteering'. It's not slave labour and it's genius!

I went to a handful of different Olympics and I can't say I was impressed. First up was Seoul in 1988 where I was the coach to the Great Britain tennis team. Like many others I was intrigued to see how tennis would be integrated into the Olympic family. Many of the tennis players saw it as a chance to mix with the other sports and to attend as many of the other activities as possible. In short it was a holiday interspersed with the need to fulfil a brief commitment on the tennis court. Miloslav Mecir of the Czech Republic won the gold medal beating the American Tim Mayotte in the final. Mečíř took it seriously but then the Eastern European countries have always had strong Olympic connections.

I stayed in an apartment with some of the other coaches from different sports. It seemed strange to be part of a team involving people I didn't know representing sports I had little interest in. I didn't realise there were so many sports I really didn't care about but these are the same sports who need the Olympics more than tennis. Many countries only fund Olympic sports and so these are prioritised. It was a major reason why tennis wished to join the Olympic fold. It wished to develop the sport into more countries worldwide using government funding from those countries.

Four years after Seoul I was in Barcelona, again as coach with a team that was always likely to struggle on the slow Spanish clay courts. Andrew Castle, best known now for being the outstanding broadcaster and journalist that he is, was part of the team and he was determined to enjoy his Olympic experience. He relished being in the athletes' village and seeing all the young lads and lasses from around the world proudly walking around in their team tracksuits. But when the draw was made I groaned as Andrew, a very capable player on faster surfaces, drew Sergi Bruguera, the Spanish clay-court specialist, in the first round. While optimism is usually around prior to any match there was not much to be optimistic about with this encounter. It was a case of damage limitation. Deep into the match and with Andrew trailing by about a couple of light years he looked across at me and angrily gestured, 'What can I do?' My first thought was that he should take out Bruguera's kneecaps when no one was looking. But the kneecaps stayed in place and Andrew soon joined me off court.

Elsewhere, the players did seem to be taking the Olympics marginally more seriously though few will remember that Marc Rosset of Switzerland won gold beating Spaniard Jordi Arrese. That would have been a most unlikely Grand Slam final. As for me I found out what was happening at the Olympics each evening when I phoned home to speak to my wife, Dannie. She was watching on telly and so knew far more about the day's events than I did even though I was there. For me it was just another tennis event and not an overly important one. Tennis has its four Grand Slam events held at different times each year so there's little room for the Olympics to be rather awkwardly fitted into the schedule every fourth year. It doesn't fit easily.

After Seoul and Barcelona I was happy to miss Atlanta, Sydney and Athens but then came a problem when it was time for Beijing. I'd just started the job with the ITF running their officiating department and was expected to be there. No escaping this one then. I went and witnessed the oddity of player selection first hand. Only two from each nation based on ranking and only if they'd played Davis or Fed Cup to qualify. Once all the excellent number threes from leading nations had been excluded to accommodate some very dodgy Timbuktu number ones we had a final list on site. Then there were some last-minute dropouts, which meant that in the end we had to accept a couple of unranked doubles players just to make up the numbers. You just have to shake your head and move on!

My own memories of Beijing centre on two issues. As my wife will confirm I'm no fussy gourmet but the food supplied was truly the worst I can remember on any site. As staff you had the choice of Chinese or western food served in a cardboard box. On day one we opted for the western and it was hard to work out what it was let alone eat it. On day two we opted for Chinese and just laughed when we opened the box while trying to avoid the odour coming out of it. On day three things improved when the Spanish team took pity on us and brought us back some cold McDonald's, which they'd chosen to have instead of the player restaurant food supplied on site. We were very grateful.

The other Beijing memory concerns one night when play overran due to rain and we finished at 3.30am in the morning. It was a ladies' doubles featuring the Russians who then came into the office with their many hangers-on to complain for an hour about the following day's order of play. By that time the transport service had stopped and we had to walk about a mile to the far side of another stadium to take a bus to the hotel. We got back as the sun was rising for the following day, had a brief sleep, breakfast and then turned around ready for a new day at the tennis venue. It was great to get back to the Beijing airport once it was all over.

That was it as far as I was concerned with the Olympics. London

2012 was next and it provided yet another fine reason to resign from the ITF since it then meant I didn't have to be a part of it in any way. I saw the excitement of others as the games approached but couldn't share it. I saw how people applied for hugely expensive tickets without even knowing what tickets they would get. Unbelievable. Still, if you can get away with it I suppose you can't blame the organisers if the public will put up with it. I saw the irresistible force that is the IOC through London 2012 meet the immovable object that is the All England Club. It was a bumpy ride. Endless groups of newly appointed London 2012 people came visiting through our office during The Championships on a fact-finding day out. I've no idea what they all did but they all seemed to be enjoying themselves – so I suppose that was nice.

In the lead-up to the games the British media was full of the need to plan your Olympic journey carefully during the period of the games. So I did. I booked an air ticket to Panama on the day before it started and I returned just after it was all over. So London 2012 was definitely my favourite Olympics. I spent it in the Panama sun playing golf, swimming and socialising with friends and loving every minute. It was an easy choice; after I'd looked down the list of all the sports at the Olympics I quickly realised that if it was a straight choice to be made there wasn't a single day at any London 2012 sport that would be more interesting to me than going to see Derby County's Under 23 team playing at Loughborough University. It wasn't even close.

I've spent a lot of time in Queensland, Australia and have a great fondness for the lovely city of Brisbane. I've seen it grow from the delightful country town it used to be back in the late 70s to the modern city with multiple tower blocks set along the river that it is now. When it was awarded the Olympics for 2032 it did give me an idea regarding the possibilities for 'demonstration' sports there. After all, each Olympic host city gets the opportunity to showcase a sport and Brisbane could introduce a real Aussie cracker. It's that famous old Queensland pastime of cane toad racing which could be resurrected and brought to the attention of the world! And while we're at it how about the mascot? Aussies love to tease visitors, and particularly Poms, with stories about the drop bears who fall out of trees to attack unsuspecting tourists! What a wonderful mascot the drop bear would make for Brisbane 2032. I reckon that could be the catalyst to ignite my interest in the Olympics!

Chapter 31

'Aussie, Aussie, Aussie!' Tennis Fans

Football fans are rightly known for contributing enormously to the whole scene in so many ways, both good and bad, but just occasionally tennis fans make themselves heard as well. I love it when a crowd gets into a match and then seeing how players deal with it. Those who can enjoy the experience and accept the glorious imperfections that come with it all can draw inspiration and play their best. Others get distracted and upset and will use it as an excuse. In my various roles I've seen a lot of tennis and it's great when there's added interest from a bit of crowd participation. Here are some of the moments I've enjoyed.

Aussie Open 2006

The fans at the Aussie Open give a unique atmosphere to the outside courts in the early days of this wonderful Grand Slam. Melbourne's multicultural society and sport-loving people mean that the locals come out in large numbers, some dressed in their national colours to support the 'local'.

Best of all in this era were the Swedes. Knowledgeable about the sport they were loud, positive to their hero without being negative to the opponent and often had a large repertoire of songs to celebrate winning points. My favourite – 'That's the way, huh, huh, huh, huh, I like it, huh, huh, huh, huh.' Followed by complete silence for the next point.

The Cypriots supporting Marcos Baghdatis copied the football-loving following I once saw in Cypriot football. Again loud chanting between points, lots of gaiety, laughter and a wonderful celebration at the end. Marcos walked towards them arms outstretched in front of him, his fingers quivering; and then lifting his arms up and down the fans copied and cheered so that fans and the player were as one. It was a great scene!

The Serbs and Croatians sometimes brought a slightly sinister undertone, though. Loudly supportive of their own they would also wear flags and banners that it was suggested contained unpleasant reference to racism. When a group of Serbs went to watch Ivo Karlovic, the giant Croatian, I radioed for security to keep a close eye on events. No trouble took place this time but in the past there have been clashes when these two elements have met each other on outside courts and the scheduling of matches needed to take account of where in the grounds they were playing and when.

Another appealing factor is the Aussie support for the underdog. Lars Burgsmüller, a relatively unknown and undemonstrative German, was the surprise recipient of a group of Aussies picking him out from the draw to support! They arrived in good time courtside dressed in T-shirts and bandanas proclaiming their undying love for Burgsmüller and proceeded to loudly support him throughout the match. Again it was totally positive and contained well-rehearsed songs at suitable moments. My favourite this time was a rendition of 'It's Got to Be Perfect' with lyrics 'some people take second best, but we won't take anything less, it's got to be, Larsie!!!' The more basic but very loud 'Larsie army' was a regular heard across the courts in Lars' charge all the way to the second round. These guys got TV coverage and admitted they wanted an outsider so that they didn't have to fork out for show-court seats and could watch the back-court action.

Less organised but equally funny were the fans who just loved to barrack while watching a game. Again they would be courtside but probably had a bet on the match and so got involved. Beneficiaries of this type of support were Tomas Zib of the Czech Republic who must have been surprised when chants of 'Let's go Zibby, let's go' broke out and also Nikolay Davydenko who drew cries of 'Come on, Davo' in broad Aussie accents. As these are players who show little emotion on court they rarely attract support like this outside of their own families let alone the other side of the world!

Good on youse, Aussie fans! They help to make the Australian Open the great event it is.

Aussie Open 2007

The organised Aussie 'herd'/Fanatics were there courtside waiting for the start of Molik v Kanepi. In the previous match they'd decided to support Kudryavska against Hingis because 'We love you, cos you're in yellow'. Hingis had looked a bit put out but won anyway. Then came a bit of home-brewed fun between matches: 'We're all pointing at the cameraman' complete with big floppy hands picking out the bloke quietly going about his job courtside. Then came the *Where's Wally* character in the middle of the group dressed in his costume and carrying a sign with 'Wally's here' and an arrow pointing down. And naturally, a 'convict' was also there dressed in arrows and carrying a swag bag.

Then a guy in a yellow and green cape with a large A on his chest raced down the steps around the others and settled himself in front of the herd – 'Allow me to introduce myself. I'm Captain Australia and I'm here to make sure you're all right'. Came the orchestrated response, 'He's Captain Australia and he's all right'. During the match they spotted a local radio DJ in the crowd. 'Hughesy, give us a wave' – he did and they cheered. Then they followed up with, 'What do you think of Hughesy? He's all right. What do you think of Molik? She's all right. What do you think of the other one? She's all right!' The small group of Estonian fans supporting Kanepi loved that and cheered back!

Later on the same court Andy Murray went two sets, 2-0 up after more than two long and brutally tough hours of top-class tennis and Fernando Verdasco served a double fault to go 0-30 down. His shoulders slumped and suddenly he looked very tired. A big, Aussie male voice that was clearly an ABBA fan boomed out of the crowd, 'I can hear the drums Fernando!' In the same match and when Murray looked typically miserable some guys in the crowd started whistling, 'Always look on the bright side of life!'

Back on the outside courts and one player's fan club was calling out, 'Let's go Alex, come on Alex, way to go Alex', etc. It died down and with perfect timing a solitary voice from behind the back netting who just happened to be walking past and wasn't even watching the match called out, 'Let's go the other one!'

Davydenko was playing Muller on Vodafone and when two very squawky seagulls flew overhead Gilles Muller looked up and went 'Shush'. A minute later 50 seagulls came over and dumped all over his end of the court in a very impressive air raid. Play had to stop and the ballkids cleared up the mess with towels. Don't mess with seagulls or they might mess with you!

The Aussie tennis Fanatics have a long history. Here's one from a Davis Cup tie with GB in 2003 in Sydney. The tie itself was not interesting as it was so one-sided so the competition was off court. The Fanatics stood as one singing, 'God Save the Queen' as the 'Queen' came in to join them. He was wearing robes, carried a face mask and walked regally down the steps giving the royal wave. When he arrived at his seat he gestured for them all to sit. He then reached down, took out a beer and chugged it in front of them all with an extravagant gesture to huge cheers. And the match hadn't even started!

Aussie Open 2009

Rafael Nadal was playing in an early round and while he was playing brilliant tennis it was also a little dull because the result was never in doubt. Now Rafa has a well-known, set ritual before serving that includes a pull of his shorts to get everything in the correct place before he starts the service action. Just before one serve a loud Aussie voice called out, 'Rafa, if you can hear me pick out your wedgie!' The timing was impeccable because Rafa immediately then reached behind, picked out his wedgie and the same voice cried out, 'Yeahhhhh!' The crowd all laughed and giggles could be heard for several points afterwards every time he served! Rafa was looking around vainly trying to work out what the disturbance was all about.

Out on the Margaret Court Arena Stanislas Wawrinka played an excellent match with Tomas Berdych. Berdych was cheered on by a loud and boisterous group in special T-shirts and national colours complete with little ditties and songs that really added to the atmosphere. Berdych is about 6 foot 4 inches so, as is the Aussie way, had a nickname – he was 'Big Bird'! At the other end pronouncing Wawrinka was causing the crowd problems until the middle of the second set when one guy yelled out, 'Come on, Wozza!' This quickly caught on and soon there were plenty such calls to counter the Big Bird Army who were armed with plenty of musical contributions such as 'Glory glory Tomas Berdych, Glory glory Tomas Berdych, Glory glory Tomas Berdych, And the Bird goes marching on on ON!'

Back on Rod Laver Arena Rafa met another joker. It was a changeover and a sweaty Rafa was lifting his shirt. Three good-looking girls in the front row with tight T-shirts were watching intently and one of these shouted out, 'Take it off, Rafa!' Back came a reply in a deep voice from the other side of the court, 'He'll take his off when you take yours off first!' She didn't oblige!

Dudi Sela from Israel had a wonderful run, defying a nasty-looking injury before qualies to first qualify and then reach the third round of the main draw. He then was promoted to Centre Court where a small but loud group of Israelis were backing him in Hebrew. They chanted something that only Sela could have understood but a helpful solo Aussie then translated by responding to the same tune 'Happy Birthday'. Every time they sang it he replied from the other side and the crowd laughed along. He was dressed in a wig of bushy hair and a loud red bandana around his head so was very visible, especially as he sat in the front row. Two/three times later he changed it to 'It's my birthday' and the crowd cheered him to which he stood and waved his thank you to more cheers! Somehow the slightly aggressive chanting in Hebrew now just seemed funny!

Not so amusing but still adding to the colour was a magnificent match out on Court 13 where Amer Delic staged a stirring comeback against Paul-Henri Mathieu. Two sets down Delic slowly clawed his way back to the delight of a small army of very loud but rather aggressive Bosnia Hertzogovenians who didn't mind at all that Delic was American and only had Bosnian heritage. The French supporters tried to raise their man but Delic looked the more likely going deep into the fifth set. Midway through that fifth it didn't help that Janko Tipsarevic of Serbia finished his match on Court Two and his own group of fans moved menacingly towards the Bosnians. Now Balkan wars sometimes lead to world wars so need to be taken seriously so this wandering band were fortunately closely monitored by security as they crossed the grounds. Finding the Bosnians they started a series of chants. I had called for security that spoke Balkan languages and when it was discovered that the Serbs were rather unhelpfully singing that Srebrenica (where the terrible massacre took place in the Balkan war of the 90s) was actually Serbian it was time to move them on to a less explosive area! Delic won the match and afterwards appealed for calm from his supporters. The appeal fell on deaf ears and after he lost to the Serb Novak Djokovic a skirmish took place during which some chairs were thrown and a girl was knocked unconscious. Now that's not nice boys!

Aussie Open 2013

The herd hit on the idea of providing entertainment in the time it took players to change ends after the first game when there were no adverts played on the big screen and they had the crowd's attention. As the players walked towards the chairs in a fairly routine early-round match one guy stood up and shouted, 'Has anyone seen the cookie thief?' Two others then jumped up and pointed across the stadium shouting, 'There's the cookie thief!' Of course, all eyes followed their pointing where there was a man dressed in prison garb complete with arrows crouching down and looking around him furtively. Around his middle was a huge round cookie! At this the first man shouted, 'Send for the cookie police' and a couple of guys dressed up as Keystone Cops then leapt up and charged around the stadium in hot pursuit of the cookie thief for the rest of the time it took the players to change ends!

Another first-game end change was filled with initially a guy pretending to be a mobile phone by going 'Brrr Brrr' very loudly. Across the stadium another guy stood up and 'answered' with an enormous mobile up at his ear and a loud 'Hello'. Then followed a 'conversation' with the first guy who had his own phone to his ear as well. This continued up to the time when the players approached the far end. Steve Ulrich, the vastly experienced and amusing American chair umpire, then leaned into his microphone and said, 'Just a reminder to all spectators to keep their mobiles turned off' to huge laughter and applause from the crowd.

Aussie Open 2017

This time I was walking my patch of courts on the city side of Melbourne Park and noticed a large group of Israelis gathering together in readiness for a Dudi Sela match that was due on that court. Knowing they could get noisy and boisterous I reported in to the control centre and suggested they had some visible security around the court just in case it got out of hand.

I kept an eye on it and when Dudi and his Slovenian opponent came to court it was indeed packed out and the opponent also had a small fan club, which would add to the atmosphere. Some of these groups of fans rehearse and know the routines they're going to use and this was a good case in point. Mostly, it was fairly standard stuff but then came the ripper. To the tune of 'Pretty Baby' the Israelis serenaded Dudi with 'Oh Dudi Sela you're the love of my life, Oh Dudi Sela I'd let you shag my wife!' Everyone found it funny and had a good laugh but it did set me wondering how it would go down if they came to Wimbledon and I scheduled Dudi under the members' balcony on Court Six!

Aussie Open 2019

I was on the late shift on the Margaret Court Arena covering Benoît Paire and Dominic Thiem in a match destined to finish at 2.15am. Few were still left at Melbourne but a few hardy souls stuck it out to the end. I was next to the court in the regular supervisor's seat when a seagull flew overhead catching me with part of its bombload. I made a mental note in case I saw the same bird again one day but also had to agree that if I was a seagull I'd have such fun doing exactly the same thing! Back to the tennis and the steadily dwindling crowd decided that Benoît and Dominic were far too difficult to say so fervent support was offered to both players now nicknamed 'Benno' and 'Dommo'!

Aussie crowds are great but New York has fun too!

US Open

The US Open works very hard to improve the fan experience. The event is 'improved' by adding more and more of everything to the point where the tennis can seem a mere backdrop. It always involves a lot of noise and so announcers shout hysterically at the punters to wave, scream and shout and in return they may be rewarded with a signed tennis ball, a seat upgrade (from our sponsors, of course) or possibly even the best dream of all – the chance to be seen on the big video screen that goes out to all across the main Ashe Stadium. For this people will gyrate wildly to the loud music played at the changeovers, be caught unawares and then react on camera when they realise they've been seen or occasionally be seen smooching with their companion to big cheers from the crowd. To ensure that standards of wiggling remain competitive the Open gives free tickets to Superfan who is basically employed to get up at a set break and go nuts at the front of the upper tier (all on camera and stage-managed, of course). He leaps around like a demented rock star showing off all sorts of dad dancing moves to the loud rock music and the crowd love it while the two players and chair umpire look up at the screens in total disbelief! Some love it and some hate it and that's fine but the danger is that the real reason people come (the tennis) gets devalued in the process.

One innovation that was brought in a few years ago was the practice of allowing the fans to keep any stray ball that flew into the crowd. This means that the officials have to keep a very large number of spare balls handy to replace those lost and also ensure they're of the same level of wear as those that get lost. It's another largely unseen demand on the officials but an important one. Memorably, this practice did bring a moment of pure comedy during one night match when the crowd was rocking and had been well oiled with alcohol through the evening. The local New York Mets baseball team had been having a terrible time and had lost six straight games to the disgust and scorn of the local media. Everyone was on their case and their problems were getting enormous airtime on TV as everyone bemoaned their ability to run, bat or catch at all. In one of the sponsor boxes at the Open that night was a group of six young men who were on a jolly and having a good time. A ball flew high up into the night sky and was starting its descent right in the middle of this box. Twelve arms reached skyward as the six guys got competitive in an attempt to catch the ball. The crowd looked on with anticipation to see who would win. The lads' jostling caused the ball to first bounce back up off a hand and for a second time they reached out, once again a mutual fumble causing the ball to drop this time on to a railing and then down some steps out of sight. A big groan of disappointment went around the stadium with a few boos and derisive comments. Then with perfect comic timing came the killer line from somewhere high up in the crowd but heard by all, 'Are you all Mets?' It was the most public humiliation!

And finally, here's one involving fans from Centre Court, Wimbledon.

Wimbledon Ladies' semi-final 2008

The physically superior Serena Williams was about to play the diminutive Chinese girl Zheng Jie and I'd just put the match on to court. The players were walking away from me towards the umpire's chair when I overheard two young guys talking behind me. Said one to the other, 'If this were a boxing match they wouldn't allow it!'

Chapter 32

The Sporting Passion

It's often said that fans make the sport. This is true of tennis, of course, and I have plenty more tales that didn't make it into the previous chapter to prove that over and over!

While I've had a professional relationship with tennis I've long been a fan of other sports but particularly football. I love the community-based shared cultural experience it brings. It's a world that has given me so much joy, despair, pride, shame, pleasure and frustration. Those who 'get it' may recognise some of the chronic symptoms.

It's been with me all my life, a passion for sport that has bordered on obsessional. The little boy inventing games in the garden on his own had to find a way to emulate his heroes (of all sports). The problem of playing for both players/teams simultaneously was solved with the use of walls and a vivid imagination. Books, newspapers and magazines were devoured for further knowledge and the desire to be in every team for every sport led me to compete at an early age in football, cricket, tennis and rugby plus a few sports that don't really count like table tennis, etc.

The power of sport to move, inspire and excite is like a drug. The Jonny Wilkinson moment in the Rugby World Cup 2003, the taking of the key wicket in an important cricket Test match, the vital break of serve in the final set of a tie-deciding tennis match or the ultimate – when your team scores a last-minute winner against your hated local football rival. You just can't beat it. Everything else in life becomes a mere sideshow when you've got the bug. Work, play, school, mealtimes and even sleep are just a waste of time compared with the anticipation, the enjoyment and then the memory of the moments that you live for as a sporting obsessive. Nothing even comes close.

There's no question my obsession gets in the way at times. One of the first things that goes into a new diary are the Derby County fixtures and everything else is booked in while bearing them in mind. A very good friend got married on the day Derby played Forest at home. Bad mistake! Four of us went to the church service and down the reception line at the subsequent party held at a local hotel afterwards, then slipped out the back door, went to the game and returned for the end of the wedding reception later. Well, you can't miss a game like that, can you? I've also skipped school, rearranged meetings, raced off early and even tanked tennis matches just to make sure I was there at the ground for the next 'unmissable' match. Was it wrong? Of course it was. Very. But when you're hooked … it's an addiction.

It all manifests itself with what goes on inside the head. You find yourself picking Saturday's team, worrying about so-and-so's injury and whether he will be fit, singing the songs from the terraces and seeing all your workmates in terms of which team they support. It can live alongside all other activities and just becomes an accepted part of your life. Don't try to analyse it because it really makes little sense. But it does provide an enormous amount of fun and good banter and I pity those who just don't understand it. As I get older I miss the good old days. I miss the standing on the terraces, the dreadful conditions we all endured in terrible weather up and down the country, the tribal violence that meant you couldn't guarantee you wouldn't run into a group of opposing fans and have to run for it, the occasional heavy loss and the inquests that followed, the booing of the away team when they ran out separately from your own men to let them know they were unwelcome visitors (now they hold hands with small boys and girls in replica kit and that looks very dodgy to me in the current climate of political correctness!), the crunching tackles and so much more. But that moment when you see the opposing keeper's desperate dive, the bulge in the back of the net and your own centre-forward wheeling away to start the celebration is like nothing else. It is pure joy and that hasn't changed.

There's so much to get grumpy about in football these days but the passion still survives somehow. Money has taken over completely, TV reigns supreme and the talking heads that fill our screens only seem to promote the Premier League and European football. Many sports have gone a similar way and not for the better. I prefer the lower levels where the locusts don't focus and that can mean conflicting interests. I walked away from Wembley saddened after Derby's totally unjustified 0-1 loss to QPR in the Championship play-offs a few years back but consoled myself with the thought that at least I'd be able to enjoy the following season much more having failed to get promotion to the Premier League. It's frequently said that the journey is often more enjoyable than the arrival and I can relate to that.

The sporting passion does extend. It might be getting up early to make sure that I'm in my seat to see the first ball hit at 6.20am at the start of the Open Championship golf at Muirfield or perhaps driving down to the Gabba in Brisbane at the crack of dawn from the Sunshine Coast in Queensland to witness the first ball of the Ashes series cricket between Australia and England. The roar of the crowd as the Aussie quick came running in to bowl to the opening Pommie batsman was pure hair-raising excitement. I can't miss any of the action and love seeing the preliminaries with the practice and the coin toss or perhaps the ceremonial side of things. It's all part of the spectacle and builds the anticipation of the moment when it all starts.

But high finance increases corruption in sport. There have always been cheats even without the possibility of making money too. The desire to win is strong and they will use fair means or foul. There will be tennis players who deliberately make bad calls, footballers who dive to win a penalty, golfers who replace their ball closer to the hole and all the thousands of other ways in all the sports that low life can try to steal an advantage. It's life because it's no different to those in business who cheat in order to steal a dollar from the customer, the burglar who robs a house or perhaps the people at Nottingham Forest who charge admission fees to those going to watch them!

Sport has to be played on a level playing field. It has to be fair. That's why I can never watch sports like athletics, wrestling, weightlifting or cycling. They've been too corrupted in the past and I can't believe them ever again. It's why it's so important to have zero tolerance for any kind of cheating. The rewards are too great, too tempting for the cheaters. If you offer a group of kids gold medals, Grand Slams, major golf titles, World Cups in any variety of sports (together with the vast fortunes that go with them) in exchange for taking performance-enhancing drugs there's a grave danger that many will say, 'Yes please!' Our sporting heroes have been elevated to god-like status and it's so wrong. The losers are treated with derision and scorn and that's equally wrong. Keep a sense of perspective. They are human beings with all the same doubts, fears and insecurities as the rest of the population. But the power of the dollar is great and managers, agents, advisors and general hangers-on descend on the talented to push them ever further onwards with dangerous results.

Drugs in sport have become an industry of their own. An aspirin will be performance-enhancing to the player who has a headache. That's apparently OK. The steroids to build muscle with potentially life-threatening side effects is also performance-enhancing. That's apparently not OK. In between these two extreme examples are all the other possibilities that need to be deemed acceptable or not. It's become a battle between the good scientists and the bad scientists. Most people don't understand it so very expensive legal battles must be fought with lawyers doing their best to bump up their fees while not necessarily having the best interests of the sport in mind.

Gambling is the other big evil. 'Businessmen' will try to fix the results of sport and profit heavily from it. They may also not need to 'buy' results since in-play betting allows them to make money on things like 'no-balls' in cricket, first throw-ins in football, double faults in tennis, etc. as well as simply who will win a particular match. Shady business connected with sport has the potential to kill interest in a sport. Why should I pay to watch something where the result has been predetermined? If I want to do that I'll go to the cinema to watch a Hollywood blockbuster featuring an American superhero against whoever is unwise enough to take him on.

I hate cheating and corruption so a curse on all that would damage my sport and all of our sports. Go and crawl back under your stones. Maybe it's partly why I was a tennis referee. I was impartial and wanted to protect my sport against those who would hurt it for personal gain. I know the dangers that great commitment can bring to a sense of fair play. But I'm also something of a romantic when it comes to sport. Good should triumph over evil and so by supporting the good and confronting the evil you find a purpose on the playing fields of the world. Nowhere is it more dramatically played out than on the partisan football fields of English football.

One of the great glories of being 'just a fan' is that you can be completely one-eyed and irrational. I love it! Once your personal colours are nailed to the mast there's no changing. As is often said you can change your religion, your nationality and even your spouse (sorry, Dannie!) ... but never, ever, your football team.

Part Five
The Final Set

Chapter 33

Tennis at a Crossroads?

Since the start of Open tennis in 1968 the many amateur organisations that run the sport have been forced into trying to become more professional. Vast amounts of money have been attracted in terms of sponsorship and television. That in turn has brought in armies of extras to feed off the proceeds. The various governing bodies have also had to adapt to the demands of new legislation across the world. Political correctness has taken its toll and basic common-sense decisions now have to be backed by lawyers and standards enforcement officers to ensure that all the employment and discrimination laws are adhered to.

Simply running the sport has become very expensive. On the positive side, though, the facilities being offered around the world have taken a quantum leap forward. For example, the players can now get cross about the brightness of the electronic scoreboard as the evening approaches rather than getting mad because letters from their name dropped off the scoreboard when a ballboy happened to brush against it. Training methods and equipment have produced players that drive their bodies longer and harder, producing ever higher standards. I've been lucky to see it all evolve over the decades.

Many sports have muddled administration and tennis is certainly one of those that could do with greater clarity. Several organisations in tennis think they run the sport and they often get in the way of each other while vigorously protecting their own patch against the others. The International Tennis Federation (ITF) are supposedly the sport's governing body made up of all the national associations (NAs) around the world. Naturally, these NAs (such as the USTA, Tennis Australia, LTA and many others around the world) are their own empires and often pay only lip service to the ITF. They're frequently run by unpaid officials who have a passion for the game but perhaps little knowledge or experience of top-class tennis. Then there are the regional associations such as the ETA (European Tennis Association), ATF (Asian Tennis Federation) and COSAT (the Latin American version), all of whom have important people that I've never heard of running them. They all plead poverty but manage to send their representatives around the world to conferences and meetings that only rubber stamp decisions that could be made electronically. Maybe the world pandemic will work as a positive force if it can help to eliminate these practices.

Then there's the professional game. Long ago the Association of Tennis Professionals (ATP) and the Women's Tennis Association (WTA) came into existence principally because the players got fed up with the amateur attempts to run the sport through the various national associations. It was no surprise that the players wished to take their destiny into their own hands. It was a painful birth as the NAs saw their control being taken away but enough negotiation took place to allow all a share of the growing tennis pie. Since then an uneasy truce has existed interspersed by the occasional outbreak of hostility.

One of the major battles that takes place concerns the tennis calendar and 'ownership' of the different weeks in the year. Most of the calendar is dominated by the main Tour events for the ATP and WTA but the ITF has retained some weeks for the Davis Cup and Fed Cup (now renamed), which they continue to organise as their showpiece events. In addition to this are the Grand Slams who in theory speak with one voice but who are increasingly seeing a different future for the sport. Has international tennis governance ever been more divided? The US Open and Australian Open vie with each other to see who can be the most innovative or progressive of the Slams while Wimbledon and the French Open prefer a more traditional approach.

All of these events have their own boards and spokesmen who frequently get frustrated with the others' approach and they are the ones supposedly on the same side with or against the ITF and the Tours. These entities come together and do work alongside each other at the Slams but the tensions are never far from the surface. The leaders of the various organisations making these decisions may have played to some level but many are inexperienced when it comes to tennis at the highest international standard. Then suddenly they have a voice affecting the top of the sport and are making decisions affecting the professionals. It quickly gets unnecessarily complicated. For example, common matters such as the basic rules of the sport have alarming differences. The WTA decided that on-court coaching was a good idea. The ATP disagreed. So the women have coaches trotting on court regularly to offer their pearls of wisdom while the men don't. The Slams have become split on the issue and so it's become one rule for one and another for another. Logo sizes on clothing is another battleground. Here the Tours are subservient to their masters, the players, and they in turn are prodded with a big stick by their agents to get themselves logoed up to maximum commercial advantage. The Slams on the other hand find this all a bit tacky and so don't agree. This results in players having to pack tennis clothing with different-size logos if they are playing Tour events and Grand Slams on the same trip.

Shot clocks were trialled and then introduced at the innovative US Open. Others followed suit intending to reduce the time taken between points. But while it may have quickened up a small handful of slow players it has also slowed down others that now realise they have extra seconds to prepare for points. Net result: the game has arguably slowed down further according to one respected journalist who did the research. It's a lesson in unintended consequences. Players needing extra time will either initiate a conversation with the chair umpire thereby stopping the clock or throw the ball up 'wrong' with the same effect. And, as we know, the shot clock rarely starts when the previous point actually finishes. I wonder if we'll now be introducing no lets on serve to try to claim back the lost time.

At the start of 2019 came the realisation that the four Grand Slams, supposedly speaking with one voice when debating tennis issues with the others, managed to come up with four different versions of how to play out a final set. The Australian Open went with a ten-point tiebreak played at 6-6, the French Open stayed with an advantage final set, Wimbledon decided on a seven-point tiebreak played at 12-12 while the US Open agreed with the seven-point tiebreak but instead felt that 6-6 was the time to play it. Each Slam justified its own version by claiming that consultation with the players took place before any change was made. If that was true how did we end up with such variance between them? At least that ludicrous bit of idiocy has been standardised now. Players will often feel that change is needed but rarely agree on what that should be. Generally, younger players are more open to radical new ideas while the older ones want to retain the traditional values. That merely reflects life generally. So consensus is nearly impossible.

Naturally, money is at the heart of all issues and that means that the big companies such as Nike and Adidas together with the agents are never far away from the discussions. This has led to the ITF selling off the family jewels by way of the sale of the Davis Cup as we know it to create another competition (handily named the Davis Cup) that bears little resemblance to the famous old competition that used to mean so much. Apparently, it had to be done or the ITF would have risked bankruptcy or so we were told. Tempting as it was to take the view that this was another good reason to keep it going the decision has disappointed traditionalists in the sport.

The Tours raced to fill the gaps left in the calendar by Davis Cup's demise and to provide a new competitor to Davis Cup just prior to the Australian Open. The ATP Cup was created and it was a nice little earner for the players as it was nearly an exhibition event. The women are now part of the discussions as well with a joint team event planned that will guard against sexist complaints. Whatever the format it's an attractive vehicle for the leading players as they practise and acclimatise for the upcoming Grand Slam.

Oh, and don't forget China! They have taken to tennis in a big way ever since the Beijing Olympics and, backed by the government, they have almost limitless funds to throw at the sport. They would dearly love to have a Grand Slam in China together with more of the top-level Masters and Tier 1 events. The existing status quo in tennis could be bought and a very different tennis world would emerge on the other side of the changes that this would bring. Would this be beneficial for the sport? Let's see what the Grand Slams, the national associations, the ITF, the Tours, the regional associations, the media and the man in the street think about it all and report back! In the meantime some sponsors, an ambitious agent and Roger Federer might simply set up something called the Laver Cup and it will simply happen anyway. Just a minute, it's already happened!

The world of golf has been wrestling with the advent of LIV Golf and the defection of players from the PGA Tour. What's to stop something similar happening in tennis? The ATP and WTA Tours could be under threat from a financially backed Saudi challenge that would change tennis as we know it. Regional associations have in the past explored the possibility of setting up tours in their jurisdictions and Novak Djokovic has long been keen on a figurehead position in a rival tour. With the Tours electing to remove ranking points from Wimbledon following their decision to ban Russian and Belarussian players in the wake of Russia's invasion of Ukraine it's easy to imagine the following scenario: an exhibition event set up in the same two-week period as a non-point-carrying Wimbledon offering three/four/five times the prize money (you pick the number). How many players would choose to miss Wimbledon to play for the riches on offer? Answer: a lot!

There will always be change. Tennis in 2020, like the whole world, faced the enormous upheaval caused by the coronavirus pandemic. Wimbledon and many of the year's major events were cancelled and those that remained were forced to operate inside health bubbles and with few, if any, crowds. While the focus was on the leading events and players the damage done to the lesser events and middle-ranking players was terrible. Those living on or close to the breadline had nowhere to play or earn a living. So even greater change may well result off the back of the forced circumstances that 2020 brought. The whole world has changed as a result of the pandemic and tennis is no different.

The race to reduce the formats to something that suits television, with the advertising breaks they crave in their coverage, will continue. I've watched many excellent three-set matches but the truly great matches have all been played over the best of five sets so shortened formats come at a price. It's likely that the Grand Slams will be forced to accept three-set matches in the future. Meanwhile, the drive for equality between the sexes will continue. This means that whatever miserable demise the Davis Cup eventually faces will be mirrored in some way by the unloved Fed Cup, which has to follow in its wake so as not to be sexist. The Grand Slams will continue to defend their position of pre-eminence in the sport while fending off the jealous competition. And the players, egged on by their agents, will continue to demand more of what they see as their rightful share of the pot.

Thank goodness for Wimbledon, though. Of all the major events it is the one that always considers the well-being of the sport. The exciting and ambitious development plans there mean that its position as the leading event in the world will likely be secured into the middle of the century, provided the players continue to support it. That type of stability is going to be important with so many conflicting influences in tennis. If British tennis can also be strong the next few years at SW19 can be ones to be savoured. The incredible emergence of Emma Raducanu at the 2021 US Open shows what can be achieved. With the influence of Andy Murray still around other young players like Jack Draper can also push through to lead the way for the next generation of home players.

Some things may not change, though. I expect that the US Open will continue to encourage its patrons to 'Make some noise!' while Wimbledon will urge theirs, 'Quiet, please!' So as tennis debates these mighty issues there will continue to be much merriment and disagreement on its future. Evolvement never stops and each organisation strives to maintain and increase its market share. Its diverse leadership prevents tennis speaking with a unified voice when it comes to sport-wide issues. Growing interest in fringe sports like padel tennis and pickleball can become more than a pastime. In the meantime the power struggles continue!

Chapter 34

The Final Months in Officiating

My last few years in officiating saw my commitment to other events reduce steadily. Dannie and I spent more time travelling for ourselves as well as loving time in Panama and Australia. Luckily, after many years of marriage, she still tolerated me (most of the time, anyway!) and we still wanted to make the most of our lives while we still had a little energy left. Tennis officiating was no longer the same motivating force it had once been for me and I felt I couldn't just stay on at Wimbledon if I wasn't able to give it the total commitment it required and deserved.

I first raised the possibility of retiring from Wimbledon three years before it happened but was persuaded to stay on to see the opening of the Court One roof and to allow greater time to help with succession planning. It wasn't ideal for me personally but the last thing I wanted was to leave Wimbledon in a difficult position. So I stayed on but steadily reduced my commitments elsewhere. I was also keen to help plan for the succession process in the Referee's Office that would be required.

For several years I'd worked at the China Open in Beijing in October and then gone on to Australia to enjoy the many delights of the Aussie summer before acting as a Grand Slam supervisor in Melbourne in January. It was a long trip but it had the advantage of missing the worst of the northern hemisphere winter. Australia has always been kind to me and I loved my time in this beautiful country. Whether playing, coaching or officiating it always seemed like home and I felt more familiar there than I'd ever felt in London. Back in the 1970s and 80s some of the players had looked at buying a plot of land in Sydney's northern suburbs. Maybe if I'd done that life may have turned out quite differently. Such are the consequences of decisions made in the passage of time!

My final Beijing was completed with minimal fuss. As referee there my role was to support the ATP Tour supervisor and to work alongside Pam Whytcross, the WTA referee. Pam and I had played at the same time many years previously and it was always such a pleasure to spend time with her. What an incredible servant to the sport she has been. Hard-working, dedicated and totally supportive of women's tennis for decades Pam doesn't seek the limelight but simply gets the job done. Everyone knows her and I was lucky to have her working with me at Wimbledon in a Grand Slam supervisor role. In Beijing we called the matches, got the players on court and generally liaised with the tournament staff to ensure that the courts, officials and ballkids were prepared and ready to go when needed. I was happy when it was over though because it meant I was off to Oz once again.

The second-best Grand Slam, the Australian Open, was a suitable place for me to work my final Slam away from SW19. Dannie and I enjoyed our three months each year down under and it was a short flight away from our temporary 'home' on the Sunshine Coast to go to Melbourne for the first week of the Aussie Open. The Victorian government has spent a lot of money in developing Melbourne Park and it was interesting to see the new improvements. The larger player facilities building was much admired and it's a new standard in the continuing arms race of upgrades seen at all the Grand Slams. Indeed, it was so big that one player complained he couldn't find his coach as there were too many places where they could lose each other!

The start of every Grand Slam always involves reunions. There are so many people to see and you have the same conversation as you rush around the corridors. It goes, 'Hi, nice to see you. How are you?' 'Good, thanks. Where've you been?' And then you move on to the next again, and again. The officials' meetings followed a similar format to all those we've all attended over many years except this time the new innovations of the shot clock, coaching in qualifying and the new Aussie heat rule were explained. Then finally the tennis started.

I patrolled the patch I'd been given for 14 hours in the hot sun the first day, 17 hours on the second day and then 13 and a half hours on the third day. Apparently, I didn't drink enough because on the fourth morning I felt distinctly unwell, went to the medical centre to be seen by the Aussie Open's excellent health team and an hour or so later found myself in hospital on a rehydrating drip having tests for what they suspected might have been a TIA or minor stroke. It was all a little bit scary but Dannie provided some light relief when she joined me in the A & E department and immediately spotted the problem – I had a hole in my sock! Wives, bless 'em!

The whole incident was something of a wake-up call, though. At one point they'd been asking me basic questions like, 'What day is it?' and 'What did you have for breakfast?' The answers were coming out too slowly and then I realised the staff there were keeping me under close watch in case something worse happened. One of them wouldn't leave my side until another took their place. That was scarier than anything else and I suddenly felt vulnerable and realised how precious good health is. At an age when bad things are more likely to happen than they were 30 years ago there's no time to wait. Dannie and I must make good use of every day we have.

Because I'd worked in Australia I had a work visa while Dannie was on a tourist visa. This created a technicality in that my visa ran out and needed renewing while she was fine to stay. As common sense doesn't necessarily play a role in these things I was required to leave the country in order to reapply for a tourist visa to return. It wasn't possible to do the same application from within Australia. So where to go? New Zealand or Bali are the obvious destinations for most people on short breaks from Australia but the traveller in me saw an opportunity to visit somewhere new, Papua New Guinea (PNG).

Port Moresby in PNG is reckoned to be high on the list of dangerous places to visit according to various websites so I chose a hotel with decent security and booked myself a 48-hour visa run. It turned out to be most interesting and once I'd made my visa application I persuaded a friendly hotel driver to take me for a tour. He acted as guide, driver and security all rolled into one and was happy to tell the stories the guidebooks don't tell you. At one point he pointed to the local police station and told me how it had been attacked by a group of army guys from a different tribe. Apparently, PNG is split into many different tribes and their rivalries can often spill over into the violent, hence the security issues for PNG.

Then there was his story of how Port Moresby had hosted a South East Asian conference as a regional summit, bought 50 special limos to ferry around the dignitaries and then seen the whole lot suddenly disappear never to be seen again! The problems of corruption and misappropriated funds are devastating in developing nations and I was able to witness it at first hand for myself there. My travels over the decades in tennis provided many such examples from around the world and what a great life experience it has all been.

Back in Australia once a new visa had been secured I continued work electronically in helping to finalise the officials who would be involved at SW19 in just a few months' time. The amount of work that is done behind the scenes at all major events is extraordinary and is unseen by the public. My own part in this was relatively small but nonetheless very important. I gave it my total focus. Because there remained one final Wimbledon for me and I wanted it to be a great one.

Chapter 35

My Wimbledon Final in 2019

very Championships writes another chapter in the continuing Wimbledon story. Each one provides its own stand-alone drama but then the focus is on to the next. 2019 was the final chapter for me, though, and I was keen and slightly apprehensive that it would go well. I didn't want a major incident to be the one thing people remembered from my 14 years as Referee.

Over the years I've been asked many times which is the best Grand Slam. I was always very diplomatic saying I was too close to Wimbledon to fairly judge. But now I can reveal that having given it great consideration I can rank all four very easily: first, Wimbledon; second, Wimbledon; third, Wimbledon; fourth, Wimbledon.

The other three? You must be joking! Why is Wimbledon the best? I wish I could tell you. I have many wonderful anecdotes and reasons about the club and the outstanding people I worked with there to back up my view but, out of respect to the club (and also the confidentiality clause in the employment contracts for those who work there), they must stay in my long list of outtakes that don't make this version of events.

In the preceding weeks to Wimbledon the weather was dreadful.

I went to Nottingham for one of the pre-Wimbledon events but never saw a ball hit. I blamed whoever was responsible for the giant banner that was flapping in the ferocious wind and rain that proclaimed, 'Welcome to Summer!' You don't provoke the weather gods like that now, do you?! Another damp, cold and miserable warm-up event I visited was Surbiton where the courts were not up to their normal standard. Apparently, they'd lost their head groundsman and were paying the price. Wimbledon had sent staff to help out but playing conditions there were difficult. Queen's was also wet and I was starting to fear the worst for Wimbledon when the sun finally came out over England. Unbelievably, there it would stay for the rest of the event all the way through to the end. My prayers were to be answered as we had a totally rain-free event, a real rarity.

Back at SW19 the preparations for The Championships continued with the usual wild card decisions and then the seedings all being settled. Deciding wild cards can be contentious and that's the same at every event the world over. Whenever subjective judgment is involved there will be different opinions. Inviting a major drawcard that doesn't qualify on ranking to play may seem obvious but deciding the relative merits of supporting local younger talent against others who have been affected by injury or other reasons can be tricky. Different Grand Slams have different attitudes regarding this so there's only one way to ensure you're included in the draw: get a ranking good enough to get in as a direct acceptance then you don't need to worry!

The Wimbledon seedings used to have two different systems, one for the men and one for the women (though this has now changed). A mathematical grass-court formula was used that took a player's grass-court performance into account over the previous two years and then rearranged the top 32 players accordingly. The ATP bought into this process in 2004 and it promoted good grass-court players and relegated those with indifferent past performance. You know what? It worked pretty well and the ladies would have benefitted too if they'd followed suit. But it provided some controversy and perhaps this influenced the change to simply following the Tour rankings as now happens. Surface-based seedings do make sense, particularly on specialist surfaces like clay or grass. But if it's not accepted and used widely elsewhere it becomes easier to simply go with the majority view no matter how well intentioned and effective it is.

Why is seeding position so crucial? Well, it's done in groups so it doesn't matter where a player is within a particular group because their position in the draw will be decided by chance. But if they're out of their natural group that's where there may be advantage or disadvantage depending on if it's promotion or relegation. The important numbers are to be in the top two, four, eight, 12, 16 or 24 as this means you get increasing protection by not having to face the higher-seeded players until later in the tournament.

It's well known that Wimbledon has grass courts in the best possible condition. If you don't believe it go and inspect them before the players have been on to mark them. In the sunshine on a warm day they look perfect and it's the one surface that even today makes me want to hit a few balls. It's the ultimate surface to play tennis on. But it's precious. It's a living surface and it needs to be respected and protected. Rackets can leave damage on grass that can't be repaired until the end of the summer when it can be resewn and lovingly brought back to perfection. Until then every other player that plays on that court will have to suffer the consequences of possible bad bounces. This is why Wimbledon and all grass-court events need to do whatever they can to discourage damage.

Court damage caused by racket throwing in practice is not so easily managed. When it happens in a match it's fined under 'racket abuse' but what should happen if it's in practice? The possibilities are to fine as an on-site offence, to restrict practice to non-match courts or to treat it in a different way entirely. The ground staff put so much love, care and attention into their work that they deserve as much support as possible.

I'd thought about it many times over the years as protecting the courts was a passion of mine. One early morning in the solitary time I sometimes enjoyed up on Wimbledon Common I was playing golf at dawn instead of just lying awake in bed. Even during The Championships I took the opportunity to get some fresh air away from the crowds as a way of relaxing. I don't sleep much anyway but during the event the pressures reduced this to about four hours a night so there was time enough to play a few holes!

I'd just putted out at one of the holes and suddenly thought that if I was a golf club member who hammered his club into the green causing damage I would expect to be thrown out of the club. Why should it be any different for a tennis club? A threat to suspend their membership would be a better deterrent than a fine. It would be a membership issue and the message would get across to the dressing room that the match courts were worth protecting and it didn't matter who you were. If the player were not a club member then in reality the best response could only lie in fining heavily and a restriction on match court practice. The courts are fragile and precious and need to be protected. And the locker room expects that no favours are given.

With the final entry lists confirmed the draws were made and suddenly the tournament was underway. All the preparations mean that the excitement of the anticipation is replaced by the reality of each day. Managing the matches on to court, dealing with the myriad of ongoing issues and queries every waking hour, trying to second guess what might lie ahead all the time and reacting to problems came all in a rush as always. Fortunately, the sun kept shining so the stories were mostly about the tennis. The appearance of Andy Murray in the men's and mixed doubles with Pierre-Hugues Herbert and Serena Williams respectively caused some scheduling issues. It's funny how a celebrity pairing can suddenly be seen as more important than the best singles matches on offer that day. Are we now so obsessed with celebrity that nothing else matters? Yes, it would seem. Hollywood stars in the crowd don't affect the scheduling but Andy and Serena together needed much more careful thought!

Meanwhile, back in the singles events tennis royalty in the forms of Novak, Roger and Rafa made their way to the semis of the men's while Serena built up momentum to reach the ladies' final where she was beaten by an inspired Simona Halep. Roger beat Rafa (scoring a win for the grass-court formula in the process) in the semis and then held two match points in the final on his own serve against Novak before falling at the final hurdle.

Having introduced the final-set tiebreak at 12-12 it hadn't been needed at all through the qualifying (though we did reach a 13-11 once when crowds gathered ready to see history made only to immediately see a break of serve!). Then in the main draw there had been a men's doubles and a mixed doubles that went the full distance but no singles – until the final. I sat in my seat courtside as the scoreboard ticked over to 12-12 with Novak about to serve at the start of the first tiebreak to ever decide the men's champion.

In a way it was the perfect way for me to finish at Wimbledon and I couldn't have written a better script. Novak, Roger, Rafa and Serena had all been there throughout my time and all made it to the semis or better in 2019. Funny how these players become known by their first names, isn't it? In golf it's Tiger, Phil, Rory and others but tennis has its own royal family too. They are treated very well, royally even, and the pretenders aspire to their thrones and some will achieve royal status soon. But for now some of the princes are known as Alcaraz, Medvedev, Zverev, Sinner, Kyrgios, Thiem, Ruud, Tsitsipas, Auger-Aliassime, Fritz, Rublev, Rune and Norrie, while the princesses include Świątek, Halep, Gauff, Jabeur, Osaka, Sabalenka, Pegula, Garcia, Sakkari, Rybakina and Kasatkina amongst many others! Off court I briefly left the north side of Centre Court to meet and chat to William and Kate (first names so full royalty here I'll have you know!). This was all on the men's finals day with Roger and Novak so all in all I suppose I could say that my last day as Referee had a bit of a royal send-off!

In terms of official send-off there was my farewell party on the final Saturday night after the ladies' final. It was a party usually held as a way of thanking all the staff in the Referees' Office but it served a dual purpose this time. Some went to great efforts to personalise it for me. Richard Lewis, the CEO, reminisced about a past low point we'd shared when we used to play, Mandy in the office had arranged a decoration of a ferret (my former playing nickname) on a cake and Denise, Sandra and Sally had worked on a beautiful 'book of remembrance' containing all sorts of photos from my 14 years.

I was relieved that it had been done in the relatively low-key way that I always prefer. It was good because they were trusted working colleagues, some of whom had become friends. I didn't want anybody there who felt they should be there because it was obligatory. No fuss, no bother, no la-di-da. Get it done right and do it with sincerity and above all a sense of humour. Please, no BS! Because that's just the way I like it.

Chapter 36

The Players Are People as Well

I'm often asked about the players and what they're really like. The answer is that they're human beings just like the rest of the population, no better, no worse. There are so many wide variations of character so it's impossible to generalise. Some are a delight, others a pain in the arse; some warm and friendly and some surly and rude. And as with most of us we can be all of those depending on the situation. With most you can enjoy a few minutes to chat and have fun while with others you merely deal professionally with them as they don't want anything more from you. You are after all only an official.

It's totally understandable that players are suspicious of outsiders. They have to deal with BS demands on their time and so many retreat into the safety of their own support groups. I had pretty simple dealings with nearly all of them in the course of working various events and I never sought to extend these dealings in any way. I wasn't their friend. I worked with the players, and their sometimes extensive entourages, on all the practical issues of getting them in the right place at the right time to play their matches and fulfil their obligations to the sport. That was done in as friendly and approachable a way as I possibly could but the bottom line is it had to be done for the successful running of any event.

I was also very careful about such things as social media. I didn't use Facebook or Twitter, for example. I never saw the point anyway. There was the telephone, email and text to have any communication I wished to make so why offer (or read!) endless meaningless and usually worthless comments on everything. So with my dinosaur credentials well and truly established here are a few very tongue-in-cheek and rather random recollections of just some of the players.

Victoria Azarenka (also Maria Sharapova and many others)

Why do they make those dreadful shrieking noises? People don't want to listen to it; I know because they wrote to me to tell me they didn't! And I agreed with them because I didn't either. But why do some players make noise only some of the time? Why shriek at some points (gloriously, even when making a delicate drop shot) and not others. Could it be they are just faking it? Quiet please!

Elena Baltacha

You beautiful, beautiful girl in every respect. How can the unthinkable happen to take you away so cruelly? You gave to everyone and then were taken yourself. Things happen regularly to remind us all that tennis isn't everything in life and here was the perfect example. RIP you angel.

Marion Bartoli

Both quirky and delightful Marion won Wimbledon in 2013. That same year she supported a young American player called Jack Sock, trying to get him a wild card into the main draw. I couldn't work out why she was batting on his behalf and I never heard from Sock at all. What was this really all about?

Ashleigh Barty

She's the real deal. Her wonderful array of talent on a tennis court is only superseded by the warmth of her humanity off it. A most popular champion the world over she is a perfect ambassador for the sport. She retired for a second time at the age of 25 as the world number one. The tennis world hopes she might retire a third time one day!

Nikoloz Basilashvili

A nice guy with a name that rolls beautifully off the tongue when you're announcing a draw. He was happy to tell me about Tbilisi in Georgia where he lives. After winning the China Open in Beijing in 2018 he was asked to take off his headband for the presentation ceremony. He politely informed the supervisor that no, he wouldn't, because the fine of $1,000 was well worth it compared with the value of the winner's photographs to his sponsors. It says a lot about the level of fines compared with a player's income these days.

The Bryans (Bob and Mike) – because they come as a pair!

Identical twins and a brilliant doubles team the brothers once had a problem at the Australian Open when Bob got mad with Mike, cuffed him after he'd missed a shot and Mike was knocked over and felt woozy enough to call the trainer. In true overreaction the trainer called the doctor and by the time they'd waited several minutes they decided they didn't need him now anyway and just carried on. What a pantomime! The chair umpire wasn't very impressed and wondered whether it would have been fun to give Bob a code violation for physical abuse!

Marco Chiudinelli

It's been noticed that whenever he loses a first set he goes to the toilet. Whenever he wins a first set he doesn't. Does that mean he needs to consult a urologist to sort out his peeing problem, a psychologist to sort out his head problem or does the sport need to address gamesmanship better?

Marin Cilic

Quiet, understated and not seeking attention Marin was walking alone in Manhattan as the reigning US Open champion. He wore a baseball cap and sunglasses but nobody else recognised him as we passed in the street. A brief nod to acknowledge the other was all that was needed. He doesn't need to make a fuss!

Kim Clijsters

Popular the world over Kim has always been a delight on and off the court. She's made a few comebacks now and there wouldn't be anyone who wouldn't want her to stay around the sport forever.

Gabriela Dabrowski

In 2018 this girl earned more in one week for reaching the final of the ladies' doubles in China than I did in my entire career earnings on court. That says a couple of things: first I wasn't very good and second there are some very average players now earning very good livings. I didn't even know what she looked like until she walked on court in front of me for the final and I doubt if I would recognise her now!

Nikolay Davydenko

His mates call him 'Davo'. (PS Apparently not many call him 'Davo'!)

Juan Martín del Potro

He was badly injured as he fell and twisted a knee in the first game of winning a quarter-final v Ferrer in 2013. We wondered whether he would be fit enough to even start his semi against Djokovic and made enquiries in case we needed to bear it in mind for the scheduling. The word came back that the doctor had recommended he get a scan to establish how bad the injury was before deciding. Delpo had replied that he didn't want the scan as he didn't need to know how bad the injury was until the end of the tournament. As far as he was concerned he was in the Wimbledon semi-final and the doctor's only job was to take away as much pain as possible. If he was going to make it worse by playing it would only be excess mental baggage and he was playing anyway. Total respect!

Novak Djokovic

As one of the most significant leaders of world tennis in his era I had many dealings with Novak. Perhaps my favourite ones were of several Davis Cup ties in the early years when he was proudly leading his band of pals as they rose to prominence together. Strongly supportive of each other they were destined to win it together in 2010 and I bet that, despite his many titles, this is one of his favourite memories.

Ivan Dodig

He may not be all that well known but if I was coaching young players he'd be one I'd urge them to watch as he went about his business. Hard-working, tough and competitive from first point to last nothing would stand in his way as he gave everything to the cause. He's carved out a great career and has been an excellent tennis professional.

Dan Evans

He's had his well-documented problems in the past but I've always enjoyed him. In Australia he saw me on court at 6-5, while his opponent was having treatment, and started to complain (with his cheeky grin) that the chair umpire wouldn't allow him to go to the toilet. I congratulated him on even needing to go since it was so hot and shortly afterwards play continued. A few minutes later at the set break Dan was then trying to organise his coach to get a racket for him and so I asked him if he still needed to go to the toilet because he seemed to have forgotten. More laughter as he left the court so clearly it wasn't that urgent! A few games later he called for the doctor for two paracetamol tablets for a headache. What a loveable clown; he'd shaved his head, didn't wear a hat in the Australian summer heat and then wondered why he'd got a headache!

Chris Evert

A wonderful player. She first married English tennis player John Lloyd, then later American Olympic skier Andy Mill and then Aussie golfer Greg Norman. I just hope she can marry a Frenchman one day and, if she does, will she be the first to complete a marital Grand Slam?

Roger Federer

He played probably the most beautiful tennis to watch of all time, all seemingly effortless with a bit of brilliance in reserve. He then went into press conferences, looked immaculate and was perfect in everything he said and did using three different languages. Apparently, he was also the role model for the modern father including changing nappies. I do hope he swatted a fly at least once in his life because otherwise he'd be perfect!

Fabio Fognini

Poor Fabio. He just can't help himself sometimes. Despite his frequent indiscretions I love to watch him play. He's fluent in Italian hand signals and his moody looks and genius ability with his racket (when he can keep it in his hand long enough) make him pure box office. When he got thrown out of the US Open doubles for being very rude to a female chair umpire I wonder what he said to his wife, former US Open-winning pro Flavia Pennetta, when he got back that evening and she asked, 'How was your day, tesoro?' I suspect that poor Fabio may have got an earful when she found out!

Camila Giorgi

She's the tiny Italian who has a father with wild hair that makes him look like a professor out of a science laboratory. They make a colourful combination together and I always enjoyed dealing with them. He fidgets on the side of the court from where he can't help himself from coaching a bit, not necessarily with her approval. At

Birmingham one day he offered advice on her ball toss mid-match. Camila got mad with him, served a deliberate double fault and then glared back at him. The little minx! Never assume all is hunky-dory in the cosy little world of player and father/coach.

Sam Groth

He's big, very big! So he towered over me when Gerry Armstrong and I had a chat with him about a report that he'd verbally abused a ballgirl one year. Being the friendly, affable Aussie that he is he listened to the charge and then said, 'Well, I'm no saint out there sometimes but I don't do stuff like that'. We believed him too. He'd been playing Jack Sock and it was just possible it might have been a case of mistaken identity. We did a deal. Sam went to see the ballgirl, gave her a towel, did a selfie with her and gave her an apology and we forgot all about it. Everyone, including the ballgirl, was delighted with the arrangement and Sam played his part to perfection. Sometimes you can't get to the bottom of every problem but this seemed like a practical solution.

Victor Hanescu

The brooding Romanian looks every bit the strong, silent type. He says nothing on court and just gets on with it. So I was suprised one day when he lost his rag with a spectator who was getting into him. So much so that he stood on the baseline to serve and deliberately foot-faulted himself out of the match. I fined him for 'Best Efforts', a rarely used section of the code, and he apologised later. Like us all occasionally he'd reached his breaking point but it wasn't the best time to do it.

Tim Henman

His outstanding career was occasionally criticised and he was even lampooned in Britain for going deep in events but not landing an elusive Grand Slam. I just wish I could have been as 'unsuccessful' in my playing career as he supposedly was in his! Less well known is that he's a very handy golfer. One morning he fitted in a round before playing at the Centre Court roof test event in the afternoon. I could imagine Lucy, his wife, when he came home for his tea that night: 'Hello, dear. Did you have a good day at work?' 'Yes, sweetheart,' Tim could have replied. 'I went two under par at Sunningdale this morning and then played Andre Agassi on Centre Court with a capacity crowd.' Now that's not a bad day at the office!

Jelena Jankovic

She was scheduled on an outside court one year and protested long and loud, even referring to needing a helicopter to even reach it! I rather liked that line but stopped short of arranging a landing zone when she was next scheduled there!

Ivo Karlovic

The giant Croatian, all 6 foot 11 inches of him, has the biggest shoes I've ever seen! No wonder he had to have them specially made. I wondered what he would do if he ever lost his tennis shoes? He couldn't just pop down to the shops to get another pair, could he?!

Paul Kilderry

Perhaps not the greatest tennis player ever but he did produce one of the funniest off-court moments during the final minutes of the mixed doubles sign-in one year, a time when a bit of last-minute negotiation can get you a place in the draw … or not. The rankings of both members of a doubles pair are added together to form a team ranking. 'Killer' had done his maths carefully and knew the cut-off number required. It called for a radical approach. He jumped up on a table above the 30 odd other players crowding the room to make his announcement. 'Hello, everyone, I'm Paul Kilderry from Australia and not a bad looking guy as you can see. I'm looking for a mixed partner ranked in the top 20. Any takers out there?' Amongst the players there, all smiling at this unusual approach, was

Sandrine Testud, a lovely French girl who happened to be ranked 11 in the world, and she accepted! Delighted with his success Kilderry jumped down, signed them both in but then returned to his table platform. 'OK, now,' he announced, 'anyone in the top ten?!'

Petra Kvitova

What a delightful human being she is (and this double Wimbledon champion's not bad at tennis as well). Everyone wishes her well. And how brave she's been to return to the top level again after being attacked by a madman in her own home. It's another story that keeps tennis in perspective.

Nick Kygrios

He was being treated away from prying eyes on an off-court medical timeout at the US Open when he turned to the supervisor and said, 'What's the score, mate?' 'You're a set up and leading 4–3 in the second,' came the reply. 'Is that with a break or not?' Nick continued. 'With,' the sup replied. 'Sorry mate, I'm not really into this match' just about summed up Nick's love–hate relationship with the sport. I would definitely cross the road to watch him play his genius brand of tennis, though. He's our sport's greatest entertainer and pure box office. He's just trying to work out how to fit tennis into his life. I could relate to that more than a bit.

Ivan Lendl

Quite why his image to the public has remained so austere and humourless is a mystery to me. This warm and generous man off court has a keen sense of fun and humour but if you only see him on and around the tennis court then you see him in his office mode. When he's in his office he is the ultimate in single-minded determination and he changed tennis with his ruthless dedication to being the best. He played better tennis than me and I've heard he's much better than me at golf as well. I think I should dislike him more than I do!

Feliciano Lopez

Sometimes it's tough getting players on court at the right time; they can be a little slow. Best way to get Feliciano out of the locker room on time would be to remove all the mirrors in there.

Paolo Lorenzi

A lovely Italian with a sense of humour. He was playing big-serving South African Kevin Anderson one day at the US Open when he noticed me sitting at the side of the court. 'This court's faster than the others here,' he complained. I gave him a sympathetic look and a shrug as you don't need to get involved in conversations like this. 'But maybe it's because I'm playing Anderson,' he continued before concluding with a final thought, 'or maybe it's because I'm getting old'! I couldn't help but smile at and laugh with the 35-year-old.

Daniil Medvedev

He seemed to rather enjoy playing the pantomime villain when crowds went against him in New York. I wonder if he's a secret Millwall fan embracing their anthem 'No one likes us, we don't care!'? As time goes by most fans start to develop a sneaky regard for Millwall and Daniil is learning how to better play the crowd.

Andy Murray

He likes the occasional grumble but don't we all? He has almost single-handedly made the LTA recognise there's life outside London. It may be one of his finest achievements. To recognise this perhaps they should name Scotland's famous rugby ground after him. Something like Murrayfield perhaps? His inner circle knows he's a good bloke but too many outside that group don't get the opportunity to see that side of him.

Rafael Nadal

Over many years in several different countries it's been a pleasure dealing with Rafa. He's always been a great ambassador for the sport. What a mighty warrior and so professional. I can laugh now about the efforts I sometimes had to make to get him to court (nearly) on time and I got used to him suddenly stopping just when I thought he was finally walking on to court to tie his shoelaces. All those quirky rituals but also that smile.

David Nalbandian

He asked to play his match at Wimbledon at a different time to Argentina in the World Cup. I told him it might mean him playing on a lesser court than he would expect. Back came the reply, 'I'll play at Aorangi Park (the practice venue) if it means being able to see it'. As I'm a football fan I completely understood and granted the request. Also, as a football fan I felt his pain as he lost both the tennis match and then watched his team lose later on the telly! A tough day.

Alison Riske-Amritraj

We gave her a wild card into Wimbledon one year and she made a point of coming to see me to say thank you. She meant it too; it wasn't one of those quick thanks and move on. She also followed it up with a card to the committee expressing how much it meant to her. And since then she has always stopped for a friendly chat every time we see each other. She's a delight and a wonderful human being. Anyone else who ever comes into contact with her says the same.

Andy Roddick

A wonderful player and hugely popular in America but the officiating world didn't cry when he retired!

Anastasia Rodionova

For some reason problems seemed to follow her matches and if you got called to a court where she was playing you could assume she was going to be involved. I never minded my occasional dealings with her in a perverse sort of way. It was very easy to say no to any player if they were in the wrong.

Andrey Rublev

An outstanding talent who could do a wonderful impression of a stroppy teenager. Wait a minute … Oh yes, I forgot!

Dudi Sela

An Israeli warrior. Relatively small in size compared with the current basketball-type physique of professional tennis but he makes up for this lack of stature with a battling heart as big as a house. Lovely bloke and good to see guys like this still have a place in the sport.

Sergiy Stakhovsky

He once beat Roger Federer at Wimbledon but I always knew him as the player most likely to come and sit on my desk at events I refereed just because he wanted to have a chat! A few years later he went to defend his country following the Russian invasion of 2022. What a proud and brave Ukrainian.

Bernard Tomic

He manages to find a way of upsetting people a lot of the time but I don't think he cares. He once finished a match and went into his obligatory press conference and said he'd been too bored to play properly out there. Later on his agent was chasing about his prize money. It was suggested that the event was too bored to pay it.

Dmitri Tursunov

Seemingly angry at little provocation he's not an obvious choice for a global world ambassador. He did, though, have the 'nous' to be able to successfully milk the system to get multiple entries to Grand Slam events on a protected ranking. He's now leapt into the coaching world so will presumably be working on his diplomatic skills more now.

Coco Vanderweghe

She's no clown despite the name. This big-hitting player isn't slow to offer an opinion and has been known to get a bit loud and aggressive if she's not on her best behaviour. I bet her post-match analysis chats with her straight-talking coach Pat Cash would've been worth listening to.

Stan Wawrinka

What a career he's had but it's gone just a little unnoticed because others always seemed to take the limelight. He was seen as the Swiss number two after Roger Federer but this man won three Grand Slams, the same as Andy Murray. More credit is due to him I think.

Serena Williams

She has earned respect for the wonderful tennis player she was but wasn't seemingly adored by many of her peers. The press and media fawned over her and no one dared to say anything negative. She gushed to the cameras and microphones but otherwise it was cold and aloof that was often projected rather than warm and friendly. Has she set a record for withdrawing more times before or during events than any other player?

Venus Williams

Poor Venus! I feel a bit sorry for someone who has won so many titles around the world but isn't even the best player in her own family.

Caroline Wozniacki

The sweet and pleasant young Caroline first came on the scene and appeared as a youngster at a Hong Kong exhibition event I used to referee. As the years went by she climbed to number one in the world, became a leading star and then only wanted to play on the major courts. But she would always tell me with a smile!

And just one more. Who was it? (Shush, don't tell anyone!)

The almost entirely white dress code at Wimbledon is well known and players and staff work together on this. As an example, a male player came into the office to ask for some white underwear to comply with the rules. None could be found in his size so he was given a pair of Bridget Jones-type ladies' instead. He went away to try them on and came back saying, 'Yes, they're fine'. The next day he was scheduled on Centre Court. Is he the only man to wear women's underwear on Centre Court? I don't know! But I do know he may be the only player on the Tour who didn't realise as the story went around very quickly. I do hope no one told him!

Tennis players are popular figures. They're usually surrounded by others who want to be with them, sometimes for good reason but other times just because of who they are. Funnily enough, the top players seem to attract more 'friends' than lowly ranked players and so it's no surprise that many become suspicious of those outside their inner circle. It's not easy for young, highly paid men and women to deal with this and understandably many put barriers up as a protection against the hype.

Players are, after all, simply people who have particular skills. 95 per cent are absolutely fine for 95 per cent of the time. But even the most mild-mannered can have the occasional lapse and then officials have to deal with it. It's just part of the job. You have to stay aware and try to understand the reasons. Are there bad guys out there? Well, there may be but they're few and far between. After all, champions are just human too!

And Finally...

Much is written by the famous at the top of the world game and I was never one of those. But I did share a court with some of them as I either played against, coached or officiated them at close quarters. Tennis is wonderful and it reflects life. There are the good bits, the bad bits, the boring bits but also some outrageously funny bits. You've got to enjoy and embrace it all.

I think there's a part of me that remains the small boy I was when I saw Rod Laver and Tony Roche play in that 1968 Wimbledon final, watching them compete hard before shaking hands with a smile at the net. They oozed respect for themselves, each other and the sport. The example they set was an inspiration and made me want to emulate them one day.

As the names of the leading players inevitably change with the passage of time the great traditions of the sport must endure. In 2019 I watched on from my seat at the back of Centre Court as other youngsters were inspired by Roger Federer and Novak Djokovic. It's exciting to think that some of these will play their own part in the world of tennis in the future.

Acknowledgements

To my daughter, Jasmine (Jazz) – You were the motivation for writing this. I hope it sheds some light on what I got up to before your birth changed everything for the better, forever.

To my wife, Dannie – Love at first sight was a ridiculous concept until I met you. We share everything with our joys doubled and problems halved.

To my parents, Len and Joy, and brothers, Roger and Clive – I wish we could have shared this world together longer than we did. It always reminds me to cherish every moment spent with our loved ones.

To Julian, Olly, Rob and Raynette – Thank you for all the massive encouragement. Your support and belief were the difference between having the idea and making the project happen.

To Angie, Sally, Roger, Mark T, Beccy, Mike, Alistair, Rodrigo, Mark C, Amanda, Alvin, Noel, Andy, Dennis, John and Keith – For reading and sharing your honest opinion that helped so much in shaping the final version.

To Tim – For your support to me at Wimbledon and for writing the foreword to this book. Good luck in all your future ventures.

To David – Your detailed research is incredible and proved better than my memory.

To all my amazing team in the Referee's Office at Wimbledon – it was a pleasure and a privilege to work with you all. Together we always managed to bring it through to a successful conclusion.

To Dennis, Jonathan, Chris, David, Colin, John(s), Richard, Buster, Robin and all my other doubles partners down the years – Thanks for putting up with me and giving me so many memories. And yes, I was trying even though you could be forgiven if you doubted it at the time!

Made in the USA
Columbia, SC
27 June 2023